# The Civil War in Popular Culture

# The Civil War in Popular Culture

## Memory and Meaning

Edited by
Lawrence A. Kreiser Jr.
and
Randal Allred

UNIVERSITY PRESS OF KENTUCKY

Scholarly publisher for the Commonwealth,
serving Bellarmine University, Berea College, Centre College of Kentucky, Eastern
Kentucky University, The Filson Historical Society, Georgetown College, Kentucky
Historical Society, Kentucky State University, Morehead State University, Murray
State University, Northern Kentucky University, Transylvania University, University
of Kentucky, University of Louisville, and Western Kentucky University.
All rights reserved.

*Editorial and Sales Offices:* The University Press of Kentucky
663 South Limestone Street, Lexington, Kentucky 40508-4008
www.kentuckypress.com

18  17  16  15  14      5  4  3  2  1

Library of Congress Cataloging-in-Publication Data

The Civil War in popular culture : memory and meaning / edited by Lawrence A.
Kreiser Jr. and Randal Allred.
     pages cm
  Includes bibliographical references and index.
  ISBN 978-0-8131-4307-1 (hardcover : alk. paper) — ISBN 978-0-8131-4322-4 (pdf)
  — ISBN 978-0-8131-4321-7 (epub)
  1. United States—History—Civil War, 1861-1865. 2. United States—History–
Civil War, 1861-1865—Battlefields. 3. United States—History—Civil War, 1861-
1865—Literature and the war. 4. United States—History—Civil War, 1861-
1865—Motion pictures and the war. 5. Collective memory—United States.
6. Popular culture—United States. I. Kreiser, Lawrence A., 1969-  editor of
compilation. II. Allred, Randal, 1956-  editor of compilation.
  E468.9.C4746 2014
  973.7—dc23                                    2013033128

This book is printed on acid-free paper meeting the requirements of the American
National Standard for Permanence in Paper for Printed Library Materials.
♾

Manufactured in the United States of America.

Member of the Association of
American University Presses

# Contents

## Section IV. The Civil War in Fiction and Film

## Section V. The Civil War as Entertainment

# Introduction

*Lawrence A. Kreiser Jr. and Randal Allred*

Perhaps no other event has captured the national imagination to the extent the Civil War has. Portrayals of the war in songs, books, and movies, among other cultural and media outlets, continue to draw widespread attention. *Gone with the Wind*, the 1939 epic that follows Scarlett O'Hara through the tragedies and triumphs of the Civil War era, remains one of the top-grossing and most influential films of all time.[1] More books have been written about Abraham Lincoln than any other figure in world history, with the exception of Jesus Christ. In 2012 historians constructed a tower consisting of books on Lincoln; it rose three and a half stories tall and contained fewer than half the published titles on the sixteenth president.[2] Type "Civil War" into an Internet search engine, and nearly 24 million results are returned—nearly double the results from the nation's three other major nineteenth-century conflicts combined.[3] In a "meditation" published in 2002, Kent Gramm, a nationally recognized novelist with a focus on Abraham Lincoln, offers a frank but not surprising confession on behalf of all who are absorbed by the Civil War: "Presumably we are not sociopathic maniacs. Many of us—probably most of us—abhor war. Yet we love this one. And 'love' is not too strong of a word. We pretty much give ourselves to this war. We spend not only our leisure on it, but also all our spare change. And we think about it all the time, even when we are with someone else. You might even say that the Civil War itself is somebody's darling: ours."[4]

Attention has increased all the more during the sesquicentennial celebration. Two reenactments during the spring of 2012 marked the fighting at Shiloh, Tennessee, and the commemoration at Gettysburg, Pennsylvania, in 2013 is expected to draw record crowds. Not all the highlighted events are connected to the battlefield. A ball held in Charleston in late 2010 celebrated the secession of South Carolina, while a series of operas commemorated the 1862 Emancipation Proclamation. As reenactors and musicians memorialize

1

the past, the *New York Times* hosts a website with firsthand accounts and modern-day analyses of "the Civil War as it unfolded." Readers of the Disunion blog can access a treasure trove of articles covering soldiers' motivations and experiences to life on the home front. Historical societies and professional organizations are keeping pace, with lectures and conferences abounding. Some of these meetings are televised (and posted to the Internet), with American History TV on C-Span devoting several hours each week to the Civil War.[5]

Despite the considerable attention, the memory of the Civil War remains a disputed landscape. Virginia governor Robert McDonnell created a furor in 2010 when he declared April "Confederate Heritage Month," encouraging Virginians to honor the "sacrifices of the Confederate leaders, soldiers and citizens" who had defended the state. He made no move to honor the slaves, who numbered as many as 500,000 people in 1860, noting that the institution of slavery was not "significant" to Virginia. Critics countered that McDonnell's view of the past was "offensive" and "mind-boggling" and claimed this narrow perspective reduced "slaves and their descendents to invisibility once again."[6]

Another controversy involves the ongoing dispute in Selma, Alabama, over whether to construct a monument to Confederate general Nathan Bedford Forrest in a city park. Forrest led the unsuccessful Confederate defense of the city in the spring of 1865. Supporters of the statue claim they simply want to honor an important figure in Selma's history. Critics counter that a monument to the postwar founder of the Ku Klux Klan in a city so strongly associated with the civil rights movement would be needlessly provocative. Regardless of whether the statue is ever constructed, many residents bemoan the seeming lack of progress since Forrest surrendered the city. "Here we are on the 150th anniversary of the Civil War," one frustrated onlooker declared, "and we're still having the same fights."[7]

Clearly, the memory of the Civil War stirs many different responses among the public, making it all the more surprising that, until recently, scholars have neglected the field of popular culture. Several titles on the Civil War in the larger culture have appeared in recent years—two by nationally known scholars: Gary Gallagher's *Causes Won, Lost, and Forgotten: How Hollywood and Popular Art Shape What We Know about the Civil War* (2008) and Alice Fahs and Joan Waugh's *The Memory of the Civil War in American Culture* (2004) build on Jim Cullen's influential *The Civil War in Popular Culture: A*

*Reusable Past* (1995). Yet works on the Civil War and popular culture are still the exception in a field crowded by studies of battles and leaders. The peril is that, as indicated by events in Virginia and Alabama, scholars will cede the shaping of popular attitudes toward the past to, among others, politicians, novelists, film directors, and, increasingly, bloggers.[8]

There is much to remember about the Civil War because of the scale, the costs, and the results of the fighting. A greater percentage of the American population served under arms during the Civil War than in any conflict since the Revolutionary War.[9] Nearly every family had a father, husband, son, or brother in the ranks. "The Civil War," historian T. Harry Williams reminds readers, "was the first big American undertaking of any kind."[10] The mass armies inflicted and endured almost overwhelming battlefield carnage, making the Civil War the bloodiest in the nation's history. Between 1861 and 1865, more than 1.2 million Americans were killed, wounded, and declared missing—nearly 3 percent of the 1860 population. A similar level of bloodshed, if carried out today, would result in an almost unimaginable 10 million American casualties.[11]

The results of the Union triumph were as stupendous as the effort and cost to achieve them. The United States and its republican form of government survived—not a foregone conclusion among many domestic and foreign observers in the mid-nineteenth century. Recognizing the perpetual nature of their nation, Americans since 1865 have referred to "the United States" rather than "these United States." The Union victory freed 4 million slaves, now referred to as "freedmen," and African Americans took their place as citizens in the reborn nation. Yet the transition from slavery to freedom was difficult, and the process of securing a place in the fabric of American society would continue through the mid- and late twentieth century.[12]

The essays that follow analyze the varied ways Americans have used memory and popular culture to remember the largest war ever fought in North America. *Public memory* can be defined as any event that transcends time for large segments of the population. For example, the bombing of Pearl Harbor and the assassination of President John F. Kennedy are episodes seared into the public mind, even though many Americans have no living memory of them. For much of the nation, the terrorist attacks of September 11 are as vivid today as when they happened in 2001. As historian Carol Reardon has argued, such events "possess the ability to bridge past and present. In ever changing and often contentious ways, these episodes touch on basic values, honored traditions, deep-seated fears, unfulfilled hopes, and unrighted wrongs."[13] This is not to say that public memory consists of an agreed on or even a correct narrative. As the authors in this volume demonstrate, the public memory of the Civil War varies widely. That Americans still care enough to argue the point—as demonstrated by the controversies in Virginia and Alabama—reflects the Civil War's enduring effect on our sense of ourselves as a people and as a nation.

Even more than public memory, *popular culture* is a notoriously tricky term to define. Popular culture can mean anything from what people eat for dinner to which television shows they watch. The innovative nature of the study of popular culture stems from such elasticity. In this volume, popular culture is defined as any widely consumed public event that influences the perception of the Civil War. Thus, the essay on William T. Sherman focuses not on the Union general's leadership but on white southerners' reaction, then and later, to his March to the Sea in 1864. The essay on Gettysburg focuses on the many ways the National Park Service has commemorated this decisive clash between the Confederate Army of Northern Virginia and the Union Army of the Potomac, rather than on battlefield tactics. Source materials also vary widely. Letters and diaries figure prominently in some essays, while movies, novels, and even instructions from military board games form the analytical foundation for others.

This volume is organized around five themes that reflect some of the most significant directions in the scholarship of both the Civil War and popular culture. The aftermath of battle is the first theme. As injured American soldiers have returned from Afghanistan and Iraq, scholars have paid more attention to the mental and physical scars of war, and the Civil War provides some insight. Michael Schaefer reminds readers that the violence of combat does not stop when the shooting stops, and he explores how Civil War soldiers grappled with the knowledge that they might have killed other human beings. Many men displayed signs of "unresolved distress" that rippled into their postwar lives. Next, Brian Miller analyzes how southern amputees reconciled their disfigurement with their sense of manhood. The challenge was particularly acute for these veterans because, unlike their Union counterparts, they lacked the balm of a war ultimately won.

Many veterans revisited the scenes of carnage from their youth, and these reunions, along with efforts at battlefield preservation, constitute the second theme of this volume. Although former Confederate and Union soldiers met separately soon after the fighting ended, they began to meet jointly at the Chickamauga battlefield during the late 1880s. Daryl Black analyzes how survivors of the second-bloodiest battle of the war found common ground, even going so far as to praise their erstwhile opponents' wartime "devotion and gallantry." Gettysburg was the scene of the bloodiest battle, and it was here, in late 1863, that Abraham Lincoln most memorably articulated why the Union was fighting. But as Robert Weir argues, until recently, visitors to the National Military Park were hard-pressed to find any official explanation of why soldiers had fought and died. Military minutiae had trumped the war's larger issues. Visitors to Gettysburg left the battlefield and cemetery little the wiser in terms of why the Civil War started, why soldiers fought, and what role civilians played in the three-day battle and its aftermath. Moving beyond reunions and interpretations, Susan Hall explores the relationship between battlefield preservation and popular culture. Although preservationists once dismissed new and popular technologies as too trivial to honor the memory of the Civil War dead, they are now leading practitioners in the use of texting, cell phone applications, and social media to help preserve the nation's shared past.

Remembrance of the war over time is the next theme. The march of Sherman's Army of the Tennessee from Atlanta to Savannah is one of the most enduring episodes of the war. Jacqueline Campbell analyzes how white southern women responded to the campaign, both as it was happening and long after the last guns fell silent. Although the March to the Sea evoked a variety of responses, many women willingly accepted their transition in the public imagination from willful defenders to helpless victims to maintain the strict gender and racial boundaries of the late nineteenth century. Once they captured the port of Savannah, Sherman and his army required resupply by sea, a critical but lesser known aspect of the campaign. Matthew Eng finds such neglect of the Union navy all too common. This lack of attention to "Uncle Sam's web-feet," a term first employed by Lincoln in 1863, in both the scholarship and the public memory distorts reality, since naval might played a crucial role in the Union's ultimate triumph.

The March to the Sea, the Union naval blockade, and other aspects and personalities of the war receive wide circulation if picked up by novelists and movie producers, and the Civil War in fiction and film is the volume's fourth theme. Daniel Stowell explores how popular presentations from the late nineteenth and early twentieth centuries utilized Lincoln's role as the defense attorney in an 1858 murder trial to cement the president's reputation for resourcefulness and quick thinking. Until recently, many scholars have turned up their noses at these depictions, but in doing so, they have ceded much of Lincoln's popular image to story and myth. Paul Haspel takes up a similar theme in his essay analyzing the depiction of Civil War combat in the 1989 blockbuster *Glory*. The movie reached a wide audience, and for many Americans, Matthew Broderick and Denzel Washington became the "face" of the Civil War. Although some scholars fretted about the film's inaccuracies, Haspel explains why *Glory* largely succeeds in presenting the past "in a responsible manner."

The Civil War as a modern-day hobby is the last theme explored in the volume. The commercialization of the war offends many social commentators, but the opportunity to cast the blue and the gray as a form of recreational play is ever present. Alfred Wallace details the popularity of the Civil War in board games. At their height, military-themed board games sold more than 100,000 copies annually—numbers only recently eclipsed by computer games. Wallace argues that because board games focus almost entirely on the war's military aspects, they fall victim to Lost Cause thinking. The Union's ultimate triumph was largely attributable to overwhelming numbers and material resources, rather than skilled political and military leadership. Christopher Bates takes the Civil War from paper and cardboard to real people, delving into the world of Civil War reenactors. These "living historians" most often don Rebel colors, and Bates explores why, whether deservedly or not, they are seen as Confederate sympathizers.

The essays in this volume are intended to point toward new avenues of research on the Civil War in popular culture, not to be a final word on the topic. The authors' varied academic backgrounds—from up-and-coming graduate students to tenured professors; from history, English, and art faculty members to museum professionals—indicate the dynamic nature of the field. An afterword by David Madden positions the study of the Civil War and popular culture as the nation moves beyond the sesquicentennial. Far from being overstudied, the Civil War and its role in American culture offer numerous opportunities for scholarly analysis. As more such studies are penned, perhaps the nation will move toward a greater understanding and synthesis rather than a rehashing of the "same old fights."

## Notes

1. "AFI's 100 Years . . . 100 Movies," http://www.afi.com/100Years/movies.aspx (2012). For a description of Americans' continuing fascination with the movie, see Molly Haskell, *Frankly, My Dear: Gone with the Wind Revisited* (New Haven, Conn.: Yale University Press, 2009). Some items from the movie are still highly prized by collectors; see Herb Bridges, *"Frankly My Dear . . .": Gone with the Wind Memorabilia* (Macon, Ga.: Mercer University Press, 1995).

2. "Forget Lincoln Logs: A Tower of Books to Honor Abe," February 20, 2012, http://www.npr.org/2012/02/20/147062501/forget-lincoln-logs-a-tower-of-books-to-honor-abe. Among the many books on Lincoln, a standard biography is David Herbert Donald, *Lincoln* (New York: Simon and Schuster, 1995).

3. On Google, the War of 1812 returns 6.9 million hits, the Mexican-American War 3.9 million, and the Spanish-American War 1.5 million. For an overview of interest in the Civil War between 1960 and the early 2000s, see Drew Gilpin Faust, "'We Should Grow Too Fond of It': Why We Love the Civil War," *Civil War History* 50 (December 2004): 368–83.

4. Kent Gramm, *Somebody's Darling: Essays on the Civil War* (Bloomington: Indiana University Press, 2002), xi–xii.

5. For the Disunion blog, go to http://opinionator.blogs.nytimes.com/category/disunion/. The Civil War programs on C-Span are listed at http://www.c-span.org/History/The-Civil-War/.

6. Anita Kumar and Rosalind S. Helderman, "McDonnell's Confederate History Month Proclamation Irks Civil Rights Leaders," *Washington Post*, April 7, 2010, http://www.washingtonpost.com/wp-dyn/content/article/2010/04/06/AR20100406044.html?sid=ST2010103105260 (1996–2012).

7. Robbie Brown, "Bust of Civil War General Stirs Anger in Alabama," *New York Times*, August 24, 2012, http://www.nytimes.com/2012/08/25/us/fight-rages-in-selma-ala-over-a-civil-war-monument.html?_r=0(2012).

8. Gary W. Gallagher, *Causes Won, Lost, and Forgotten: How Hollywood and Popular Art Shape What We Know about the Civil War* (Chapel Hill: University of North Carolina Press, 2008); Alice Fahs and Joan Waugh, eds., *The Memory of the Civil War in American Culture* (Chapel Hill: University of North Carolina Press, 2004); Jim Cullen, *The Civil War in Popular Culture: A Reusable Past* (Washington, D.C.: Smithsonian Institution Press, 1995).

9. For an overview, see Marvin A. Kreidberg and Merton G. Henry, *History of Military Mobilization in the United States Army, 1775–1945* (reprint; Westport, Conn.: Greenwood Press, 1975).

10. T. Harry Williams, *The History of American Wars: From 1775 to 1918* (New York: Knopf, 1981), 199.

11. J. David Hacker, "A Census-Based Count of the Civil War Dead," *Civil War History* 57, no. 4 (December 2011): 306–47.

12. The best single-volume work on the Civil War remains James M. McPherson, *Battle Cry of Freedom: The Civil War Era* (New York: Oxford University Press, 1988).

13. Carol Reardon, *Pickett's Charge in History and Memory* (Chapel Hill: University of North Carolina Press, 1997), 3.

# Section I

# The Aftermath of Battle

# 1

# "Really, Though, I'm Fine"

## *Civil War Veterans and the Psychological Aftereffects of Killing*

*Michael W. Schaefer*

Forty years after serving as an infantryman in the Confederate army, Texan George Gautier justified the title of his autobiography, *Harder than Death*, by explaining to his readers that killing other men, as he did during the Civil War, "will bring you to ruin and distress the balance of your life."[1] Although many historians argue that Gautier's guilt-ridden postwar life was anomalous among Civil War veterans, research into the experiences of veterans of more recent wars, coupled with an attentive reading of the memoirs of Gautier's peers, suggests that Gautier was an exception not in his haunted feelings but only in his willingness to state them so overtly.

It is common knowledge that a considerable number of soldiers who served in America's wars of the late twentieth and early twenty-first centuries—Vietnam, the 1991 Gulf War, Afghanistan, and Iraq—suffer from depression or posttraumatic stress disorder. The figure among Iraq veterans in 2003–2004 stood at 16 percent, according to a July 2004 report in the *New England Journal of Medicine*.[2] What is less well known is that a significant measure of veterans' distress, like Gautier's a century earlier, stems from guilt at having killed in combat, as Dan Baum points out in an essay in the *New Yorker*. This lack of awareness—and, in fact, much of the stress itself—is caused primarily by the army's reluctance to address the issue, which leaves veterans largely unequipped to confront their condition. The Army Medical

Corps' standard psychological manual on combat trauma, Baum notes, runs to 500 pages and provides a chart that "lists twenty 'Combat Stress Factors,' including 'fear of death,' 'disrupted circadian rhythms,' 'loss of a buddy,' and 'breakdown of Ur (narcissistic) defenses.'" However, the manual "makes no mention of killing, and offers no suggestions for ameliorating any psychological aftereffects," despite its admission that "casualties that the soldier inflicted himself on enemy soldiers were usually described as the most stressful events" of the combat experience. The manual goes on to acknowledge "the aversion most mammals have to killing conspecifics (members of their own species)" and notes that in war this is often overcome by "pseudospeciation, the ability of humans and some other primates to classify certain members of their own species as 'other,' [which] can neutralize the threshold of inhibition" as far as killing is concerned. However, this section continues, due to "phylogenetically strong inhibitions," soldiers are often "left with . . . psychological afterburn" in the wake of killing—the very condition for which the manual offers no treatment.[3]

As an illustration of this afterburn, Baum cites twenty-four-year-old Carl Cranston, whose self-assessment rejects Gautier's warning. A sergeant in a mechanized unit that saw a great deal of action during the initial phase of the Iraq War, Cranston admits "we killed a lot of people" but asserts that despite a lack of formal counseling, he has suffered no ill effects from the experience. However, Baum observes that Cranston, now back at Fort Benning, Georgia, obsessively and repetitively watches the realistically gory HBO series *Band of Brothers*, about American paratroopers in World War II—"'millions' of times," according to his mother-in-law. Cranston's wife describes an evening at Fort Benning's Afterhours Enlisted Club when Cranston, after several drinks, began shouting at the disk jockey, "I want to hear music about people blowing people's brains out, cutting people's throats! . . . I want to hear music about shit I've seen!" Cranston claims he has no memory of this event but admits that his wife is correct in saying that he suffers what she calls "flashbacks—like, he sits still and stares." Nevertheless, he reassures Baum, "Really, though, I'm fine." As he does so, his wife, sitting beside him, silently mouths, "Not fine. Not fine."[4]

A common view among Civil War historians is that veterans of that conflict really *were* fine. Despite an experience that Confederate soldier George Gibbs called a "dirty, bloody mess, unworthy of people who claim to be civilized" and that Union soldier Cyrus Boyd said "benumbs all the tender feelings of men and makes of them brutes,"[5] the vast majority did not suffer long-term trauma but rather "aged gracefully," according to James I. Robertson Jr. "Time healed most wounds and obliterated scars of body and mind."[6] Earl J. Hess similarly argues that Civil War veterans "were not victims [of] . . . but victors over the horrors of combat" and ascribes any interpretation to the contrary to "modern prejudices, ideological faddishness, and a desire for political correctness."[7] However, we may wonder whether this assessment is entirely correct.

It is undeniable that the consciousness of the Civil War soldier was constituted very differently from that of his modern counterpart with regard to manhood and death, as the work of Robertson, Hess, and others such as James McPherson and Mark S. Schantz demonstrates. Schantz, noting Edward Ayers's call for a "new revisionism" that places "more distance between nineteenth-century Americans and ourselves," argues strongly that, unlike modern American culture, antebellum culture enthusiastically embraced death, a stance that "made it easier to kill and be killed" for Civil War soldiers than for their modern counterparts.[8] Thus, drawing direct lines from twenty-first-century veterans back to those of the nineteenth century is problematic. Two historians who believe that war-related trauma was common among Civil War veterans, Eric T. Dean Jr. and Gerald F. Linderman, acknowledge these differences and admit there is relatively little direct, hard evidence for their own views. Surveying the extant records of nearly 300 veterans committed to the Indiana Hospital for the Insane, Dean says that "post-traumatic stress disorders in the Civil War veteran population . . . existed and do not appear to have been isolated," but he concedes that "the absence of modern diagnostic categories and the presence of a different set of cultural ideas in the nineteenth century concerning disease and suffering make it difficult to quantify" the extent of such disorders.[9] Linderman asserts that many veterans repeated the rubric that "time heals all wounds" not because they found it to be true but because they sought acceptance and advancement in a postwar society that had little interest in the reality of war and thus no patience for their ongoing psychological torment. Veterans who wrote autobiographies, Linderman says, "assumed that readers would be interested exclusively in their wartime adventures. They said little of their postwar experiences and opinions." Because "the groundsill evidence is less sturdy, conclusions regarding veteran attitudes . . . must remain more tentative than those regarding soldier attitudes."[10]

Hess uses this same silence in veterans' autobiographies to advance his argument for a lack of unresolved trauma. He reasons that if Civil War soldiers had suffered lasting torment over killing, they would have written about it. Yet he found few examples of writing on that subject in soldiers' memoirs—only three of the fifty-eight works analyzed in his book *The Union Soldier in Battle;* thus, he concludes that such psychological damage was anomalous.[11] Hess acknowledges, as does Robertson, that many soldier-memoirists stated quite frankly their unwillingness to fully disclose the horrors they had endured; some felt that only those who had undergone similar experiences would understand them, and others simply did not wish to confront those memories. But Hess imputes no dire motives to these demurrals. Such men, he contends, "were not trying to deny the reality of warfare" but rather "were engaged in a necessary process that every veteran had to undergo if he were to feel whole."[12]

Nevertheless, despite cultural differences and the extensive rhetoric of pseudospeciation carried on by both sides before and during the war, we might ask whether the phylogenetically strong inhibitions against killing members of one's own species could have been ameliorated as easily as Schantz and Hess maintain.[13] Consider the following: Georgia infantryman William Plane cuts off a description of the dead on a battlefield by saying, "None can realize the horrors of war, save those actually engaged"; Michigan cavalryman Borden Hicks declines to speak of killing "on account of the painful recollections, that it would recall to my memory"; Confederate cavalryman Charles Blackford tersely notes that "it is not agreeable even in war to see individual men killed in your presence."[14] Thus, we might question Hess's assumption that a simple refusal to deny reality is equivalent to a fully resolved response to reality and indicative of a recovery of wholeness. Indeed, closer attention to what such memoirs *do* say bolsters Linderman's and Dean's contention that George Gautier was not an outlier—that more than a few Civil War veterans suffered from the nineteenth-century equivalent of Carl Cranston's mental condition.

Many Civil War memoirists speak freely of killing, and they often ascribe their ability to overcome their aversion to taking a life to anger at seeing their comrades fall. Oliver Norton, who served with the Eighty-Third Pennsylvania at Gaines's Mill, says that when he saw two of his friends shot, "a kind of desperation seized me. . . . I jumped over dead men with as little feeling as I would over a log. The feeling that was uppermost in my mind was a desire to kill as many rebels as I could."[15] This feeling was reciprocated by Confederates: Texas officer Samuel Foster rejoiced at the memory of an engagement in which Yankees fell "like leaves in the fall of the year," saying, "Oh this is fun to lie here and shoot them down and we not get hurt"; Tennessean G. W. Waggoner fondly recalled a skirmish in which "I fired several rounds at the sons of bitches if I should say such a word. I cant say whether I hit one or not I tride like the devil."[16] Nevertheless, as Robertson notes, Rebels and Yankees were often hard put to regard the enemy as "other," even in the heat of battle (with the significant exception of white soldiers' response to African American troops). For example, Union private Warren Goss recalled that the walking wounded from both sides worked together to save the more grievously injured from a forest fire at Chancellorsville, and Union private Arthur van Lisle, who was wounded at Chickamauga, told of his enemy's compassion: "a Confederate soldier, standing over me, bravely fighting, seeing my bloody side and parched lips, stooped down and throwing the strap of his canteen over his head, put the nozzle to my mouth, saying as he did so, 'Drink, Yank. I reckon you're powerful dry.'"[17]

With these conflicting impulses in mind, along with the statement by a modern army company commander that "shooting people has [ultimately] been harder for most soldiers to come to grips with than the death of a friend," some readers might be inclined to see a greater or lesser degree of unresolved tension—of cognitive dissonance—in soldiers' memoirs, whereas others might see resolution.[18] Perhaps the mildest instances of dissonance are the implicit or explicit efforts of some memoirists to distinguish between legitimate killing and "murder" and to explain that they did not engage in the latter. Often, this distinction centers on the question of active aggression: if the enemy attacked, killing was warranted; if the armies were in stalemate, it was not. Sitting in front of Atlanta in August 1864, Illinois private Laforest Dunham and his fellow soldiers "maid a bargain with the rebs not to shoot at one another heare on the scourmish line unless one side or the other went to advance, so it makes it much pleasanter."[19] Similarly ensconced in front of Petersburg in September 1864, Maine private John Haley noted, "There is less firing [than previously]. This is as it should be, for to shoot men down, situated as we are, is nothing less than murder, and it amounts to nothing in settling this question." Some months later, only a few weeks prior to the collapse of the Confederate defenses around Richmond and General Robert E. Lee's surrender, Haley reported that while his unit was on picket "we could see the Johnnies plainly, as they made no attempt to cover themselves. It has become a policy with us to commit no more murder by shooting down pickets when they are on post and minding their own business. . . . Were we, or they, so disposed, we could make a fearful slaughter. Thank heaven, we are not so disposed."[20]

Although such distinctions provided a measure of comfort to some veterans, others seemed unable, for reasons of circumstance or temperament, to separate siege warfare from the heat of battle. Tennessee private Sam Watkins writes in his 1882 memoir that he only "tried to kill those that were trying to kill me," but when this justification falls short, he seems uncertain how to deal with that fact.[21] Recounting an 1864 skirmish in front of Atlanta, Watkins says that when Yankees ambushed his unit,

> I ran to a tree to my right, and just as I got to it, I saw [a] comrade sink to the ground, clutching at the air as he fell dead. I kept trying to see the Yankees, so that I might shoot. . . . In a few minutes I saw a young Yankee Lieutenant peering through the bushes. I would rather not have killed him, but I was afraid to fire and afraid to run, and yet I did not wish to kill him. He was as pretty as a woman, and somehow I thought I had met him before. Our eyes met. He stood like a statue. He gazed at me with a kind of scared expression. I still did not want to kill him, and am sorry to-day that I did, for I believe I could have captured him, but I fired, and I saw the blood spurt all over his face. He was the prettiest youth I ever saw. When I fired the Yankees broke and run, and I went up to the boy I had killed, and the blood was gushing out of his mouth. I was sorry.[22]

Watkins seems to confirm the modern company commander's assertion that killing an enemy is more traumatic than watching a friend die. He devotes very little space to the latter event and a good deal to the former, and unlike several other soldiers quoted earlier, he does not cite the death of his comrade as justification for killing the Yankee. Beyond these omissions, the noteworthy elements of this passage are Watkins's repeated emphasis on the youth's beauty, his odd (perhaps phylogenetic) feeling of acquaintance with him, his numerous reiterations of his reluctance to shoot the young lieutenant, and his graphic description of the dead man's face. Contrasted with these details, his bare statement of feeling sorry seems less a resolution of his emotions than an indication of his awareness of the inadequacy of that response.

This unresolved distress is even clearer in a comparison of Watkins's memoirs, written at two different times, about another episode in which he kills someone he has met before. Writing in 1882 about the battle of Dead Angle, fought against Sherman's forces on the Kennesaw line on June 27, 1864, Watkins recalls, with evident satisfaction, that the fight was essentially a slaughter as the well-entrenched Confederates cut down the attacking Yankees in windrows. "I am satisfied," he says, "that on this memorable day, every man in our regiment killed from one score to four score, yea, five score men. . . . All that was necessary was to load and shoot. . . . [The Yankees] seemed to walk up and take death as if they were automatic or wooden men." Watkins feels no compunction about this carnage because, he continues, "It was, verily, a life and death grapple, and the least flicker on our part, would have been sure death to all." But evidently he does feel guilty about one particular shooting during this fight. Early on, he relates, he happened to look up from firing and saw "a beautiful flag of the Stars and Stripes flaunting right in my face, and I heard John Branch, of the Rock City Guards, . . . who were next [to] Company H, say, 'Look at that Yankee flag; shoot that fellow; snatch that flag out of his hand!'" Watkins does not explain his response to this request; his next sentence is, "My pen is unable to describe the scene of carnage and death that ensued in the next two hours." However, when he returns to this battle in another memoir, written thirty-five years later in 1917, he does describe what happened. In response to Branch's exhortation, he says, "I raised up with my gun loaded, and there stood a pale, beardless boy, the flag bearer of his regiment, looking as white as a sheet. . . . God bless the boy! I did not want to kill him. I thought I must have met him somewhere before. There he stood like a statue. Our eyes met. He gazed at me in a kind of mute entreaty. I found out afterward that it was Lieutenant Champion, who had treated me so kindly on the cars at Sandusky."[23]

Watkins's unwillingness to relate this experience in 1882 might be one indication of his distress; also, note the similarities in language between this passage and the one about killing the young lieutenant outside Atlanta. A stronger indicator of his distress is what he fails to do here: he does not describe the actual shooting or how the corpse looked; he does not explain how he confirmed his suspicion that he knew his victim (presumably by inspecting the corpse after the battle); he does not offer any details about what this young man had done for him in Sandusky (presumably Watkins means Sandusky, Ohio, but he does not elaborate); and he does not say that he was sorry for killing him. Indeed, it seems that even fifty-three years after the event, the best he can do is acknowledge that it occurred and quickly move on. And once again, he refrains from offering the death of a comrade as a justification for his action. In this case, he devotes a lengthy paragraph to eulogizing his friend Billy Hughes, who saved Watkins from the point-blank discharge of a Yankee rifle by grabbing its muzzle and thus incurring a mortal wound himself. Watkins notes that the Yankee wielding this rifle was scream- ing as he fired, "D—n you! You've killed my brothers, and now I've got you."[24] But Watkins still refuses to turn this battlefield rationale to his own advantage by casting his killing of Lieutenant Champion in its light. Instead, the two deaths remain entirely unconnected.

On the surface, Daniel Sawtelle of the Eighth Maine Volunteer Infantry seems to be the precise opposite of Sam Watkins. Far from feeling ambivalent about killing and lacking any vindication for his actions, Sawtelle routinely justifies what he does by the deaths of his friends. This rationale is most evi- dent during Sawtelle's account of his stint in a crack sharpshooting unit he joined in 1864, after two years of regular service. As a member of this force, Sawtelle spent much of the siege of Petersburg engaged in the very action that John Haley considered murder—sniping at enemy pickets. Although Saw- telle never exults over his kills, he emphatically rejects any negative moral judgment of them. "We had a pleasant job in some ways though dangerous," he says of his sniper unit, and "as to sharpshooting the Rebs, we had been shot at so much and had comrades shot down at our sides so often that we had come to have no more feeling or sentiment in regard to the matter than as if they had been wild animals."[25] Even when expressing some compassion for his foes, Sawtelle maintains this stance. At one point during the Petersburg cam- paign, he says:

> We had a West Virginian in our [rifle] pit, a young fellow who was on the watch for every chance to get a Johnny. He said the Rebs had used them so mean he wanted to kill every one he could. Just as day was breaking, a Johnny went out of his pit for something and this boy saw him and fired hitting him, for he hollered so loud the boy jumped up and down saying "I got him! I got him!" over and over again. It made me feel rather bad to hear the Reb moan and cry, but

this boy seemed to rejoice at his misery. I do not know whether he had to lie there all day, but [I] suppose he did for we watched every man and neither side dared to show even a finger above the works.[26]

However bad Sawtelle may have felt about the wounded Confederate's misery, he immediately implies that it was deserved in his next sentence: "I found out afterwards one of our boys in another pit was wounded and had to lie there all day in the hot sun."[27]

This attitude apparently served Sawtelle well. While sniping at Petersburg he wrote to his sister about military life: "I am bound to improve all I can and when I look back (if I should out live this) there will be some bright spots, some pleasant reminisances . . . and I trust I shall never commit an act for which I need to blush."[28] Writing his memoirs in 1912, impelled to do so partly by his active involvement in the Grand Army of the Republic, he seems to indicate that this trust was borne out, since his valediction in that volume is "all's for the best." However, some omissions in Sawtelle's recollections for the record suggest that this pronouncement was not entirely true. His postwar life consisted of a series of restless westward movements, false starts, and failed efforts at farming in Wisconsin, Minnesota, South Dakota, and finally Oregon. Sawtelle blamed his failures on chronic physical disabilities resulting from his military service, but he was never wounded and appears to have suffered only the usual maladies afflicting Civil War soldiers, such as frequent diarrhea. We might speculate, then, that some of his problems were psychological, that his bouts of chills and fever, his "sickly sallow complexion," and the frequent periods "when he would be unable to do any work at all," according to a Wisconsin neighbor, had psychosomatic origins. Also note his characterization by a government pension agent in 1898: "morose, irritable, despondent, sour, indolent, cynical."[29]

It is, of course, unwarranted to take such slim evidence from more than a hundred years ago and impose a diagnosis of posttraumatic stress disorder on Daniel Sawtelle, Sam Watkins, or any other Civil War veteran. It is also important to bear in mind that, in the view of James Marten, author of an extensive study of this cohort, "we know little about the interior lives of veterans."[30] However, in the face of this evidence, it seems equally unwarranted to assert that such men were entirely free of psychological damage, that they bore absolutely no resemblance to contemporary war veterans like Carl Cranston. Indeed, Marten acknowledges this point, noting that it is entirely possible that Civil War veterans suffered from posttraumatic stress disorder in numbers equal to Vietnam veterans.[31] Similarly, Drew Gilpin Faust says that "in the Civil War, it was killing, not dying, as Orestes Brownson observed in 1862, that demanded 'the harder courage,' for it required the more significant departure from soldiers' understanding of themselves as human beings and . . . Christians"; for this departure, she speculates, "they may have paid for decades after the war ended, as we know twentieth- and twenty-first century soldiers from Vietnam to Iraq continue to do."[32]

Unfortunately, the people who would have been our best sources of definitive information left little record of their views on this subject. In one of his last letters, a 1923 request for an increase in his pension, Sawtelle told the pension board that "my wife has been my Dr. and nurse all these 50 years of our married life. She is 74 yrs old and badly broken down in health."[33] One wonders whether Sawtelle's wife, and perhaps many other ailing wives of her generation, would have sympathized with Mrs. Cranston's reaction to her husband's claim, "Really, though, I'm fine."

Alice Fahs provides a tantalizing example in this regard. A great deal of popular literature published during the war focused on women's suffering on the home front, but in the 1880s and 1890s, the dominant form of war writing became the veteran's memoir, focusing on manly courage and sacrifice. Fahs notes that although stories of southern women bearing up during the war continued to sell, "Northern women's war experiences became marginal in the literary marketplace," and there was even less interest in women's postwar sufferings than in the postwar tribulations of veterans.[34] Nevertheless, Fahs points to one story, Elizabeth Stuart Phelps's *Comrades*, published in 1911, that might offer some insight into the plight and opinions of veterans' wives. The story's protagonist is Patience Oak, the significantly named spouse of an ailing veteran. When she breaks custom by marching alongside her feeble husband in a Decoration Day parade, the embarrassed old man asks Patience what people will say about her joining the ranks. She replies, with her lifetime of service to him in mind, "They'll say I'm where I belong. . . . I've *earned the right to*." Patience, of course, is a fictional character, but her assertion and Phelps's description of her as embodying "all that blundering man has wrought on tormented woman by the savagery of war" may well be suggestive of an obscured actuality.[35] When real-life veteran Daniel Sawtelle said, "All's for the best," did Mrs. Sawtelle and large numbers of her peers silently mouth, "Not for the best. Not for the best"?

## Notes

1. George R. Gautier, *Harder than Death: The Life of George R. Gautier, an Old Texan, Living at the Confederate Home, Austin, Texas* (Austin: n.p., 1902), 50.

2. Quoted in Dan Baum, "The Price of Valor," *New Yorker*, July 12 and 19, 2004, 52.

3. Ibid., 49, 50.

4. Ibid., 44, 52, 44–45.

5. Cyrus F. Boyd, *The Civil War Diary of Cyrus F. Boyd, Fifteenth Iowa Infantry, 1861–63* (Iowa City: State Historical Society of Iowa, 1953), 42.

6. James I. Robertson Jr., *Soldiers Blue and Gray* (Columbia: University of South Carolina Press, 1988), 227.

7. Earl J. Hess, *The Union Soldier in Battle: Enduring the Ordeal of Combat* (Lawrence: University Press of Kansas, 1997), ix, xi.

8. Mark S. Schantz, *Awaiting the Heavenly Country: The Civil War and America's Culture of Death* (Ithaca, N.Y.: Cornell University Press, 2008), 5, 2.

9. Eric T. Dean Jr., *Shook over Hell: Post-Traumatic Stress, Vietnam, and the Civil War* (Cambridge, Mass.: Harvard University Press, 1997), 211.

10. Gerald F. Linderman, *Embattled Courage: The Experience of Combat in the American Civil War* (New York: Free Press, 1987), 266. Many other studies have examined the forces that shaped the content of veterans' memoirs in the late nineteenth century. Among the most thorough and lucid are Alice Fahs, "The Feminized Civil War: Gender, Northern Popular Literature, and the Memory of the War, 1861–1900," *Journal of American History* 85 (March 1999): 1461–94; David Blight, *Race and Reunion: The Civil War in American Memory* (Cambridge, Mass.: Harvard University Press, 2001); Joan Waugh and Alice Fahs, *The Memory of the Civil War in American Culture* (Chapel Hill: University of North Carolina Press, 2004); and James Marten, *Sing Not War: The Lives of Union and Confederate Veterans in Gilded Age America* (Chapel Hill: University of North Carolina Press, 2011). Marten makes much the same point as Linderman regarding veterans' lack of writing about postwar suffering. He notes that "the memoir literature is virtually silent on this issue," focusing on "battles and marches and comrades rather than . . . returning to civilian life," but he argues that various "psychological responses [such] as nightmares, delusions, and other manifestations of the terrors of combat must have plagued many soldiers. Conjecture based on research into the lives of modern veterans is supported by anecdotal but compelling evidence that things *were* different for countless men scarred by war" (10).

11. Hess, *Union Soldier in Battle*, 164.

12. Ibid., 184–85.

13. Two thorough and illuminating discussions of how the political, journalistic,

and literary cultures of the North and South attempted to construct the opposing side as "other" are Charles Royster, *The Destructive War* (New York: Knopf, 1991), and Ritchie Devon Watson, *Normans and Saxons: Southern Race Mythology and the Intellectual History of the American Civil War* (Baton Rouge: Louisiana State University Press, 2008).

14. William F. Plane, "Letters of William Fisher Plane, C.S.A., to His Wife," *Collections of the Georgia Historical Society* 48 (1964): 223; Borden M. Hicks, "Personal Recollections of the War of the Rebellion," in *Glimpses of the Nation's Struggle: Papers Read before the Minnesota Commandery of the Military Order of the Loyal Legion of the United States, January, 1903–08*, 6th ser. (Minneapolis, 1909), 544; Charles Blackford, *Letters from Lee's Army*, ed. Susan Leigh Blackford (New York: A. S. Barnes, 1962), 107.

15. Oliver W. Norton, *Army Letters, 1861–65* (Chicago: O. L. Deming, 1903), 106–9.

16. Samuel T. Foster, *One of Cleburne's Command: The Civil War Reminiscences and Diary of Capt. Samuel T. Foster, Granbury's Texas Brigade, C.S.A.* (Austin: University of Texas Press, 1980), 62; Bob Womack, *Call Forth the Mighty Men* (Bessemer, Ala.: Colonial Press, 1987), 369.

17. Robertson, *Soldiers Blue and Gray*, 140; Warren Lee Goss, *Recollections of a Private* (New York: Thomas Y. Crowell, 1890), quoted in Richard Wheeler, *Voices of the Civil War* (New York: Meridian, 1990), 272–73; van Lisle quoted in ibid., 356.

18. Quoted in Baum, "Price of Valor," 49–50.

19. Laforest Dunham, *Through the South with a Union Soldier*, ed. Arthur H. DeRosier Jr. (Johnson City: East Tennessee State University Press, 1969), 141.

20. John Haley, *The Rebel Yell and the Yankee Hurrah: The Civil War Journal of a Maine Volunteer*, ed. Ruth L. Silliker (Camden, Maine: Down East Books, 1985), 201, 245. Union private Robert Knox Sneden expressed a similar sentiment in a different situation: while watching Thaddeus S. C. Lowe launching observation balloons over Confederate lines during the Peninsula Campaign in early 1862, Sneden recalled that "some of our more sanguine generals want [Lowe] to cut his balloon loose . . . sail over the enemy's camps and drop live shells on the fellows below. Lowe won't do it however as it would be murder, not war." *Eye of the Storm: A Civil War Odyssey*, ed. Charles F. Bryan Jr. and Nelson D. Lankford (New York: Free Press, 2000), 18–19.

21. Sam Watkins, *Company Aytch or, a Side Show of the Big Show*, ed. M. Thomas Inge (New York: Plume, 1999), 15.

22. Ibid., 174.

23. Ibid., 131–33, 131, 237.

24. Ibid., 238.

25. Daniel Sawtelle, *All's for the Best: The Civil War Reminiscences and Letters of*

*Daniel W. Sawtelle*, ed. Peter H. Buckingham (Knoxville: University of Tennessee Press, 2001), 116.

26. Ibid., 158–59.

27. Ibid., 159.

28. Ibid., xvi.

29. Ibid., xxvii, xxviii.

30. Marten, *Sing Not War*, 73.

31. Ibid., 90.

32. Drew Gilpin Faust, *This Republic of Suffering: Death and the American Civil War* (New York: Knopf, 2008), 32, 60. Two other relatively recent studies offer similar speculations. In *To Appomattox and Beyond: The Civil War Soldier in War and Peace* (Chicago: Ivan R. Dee, 1996), Larry Logue takes a line similar to that of Earl Hess, asserting that "Confederate soldiers came home battle-toughened but not fundamentally altered" (103–4); however, he acknowledges evidence that some veterans from both sides "showed the long-term stress disorders that we associate with modern wars" (147). In *The Gentlemen and the Roughs: Violence, Honor, and Manhood in the Union Army* (New York: New York University Press, 2010), Lorien Foote concentrates mainly on the war itself but notes that "the soldiers and officers who returned to civilian life lived with a complicated reality in the years after the war" (179).

33. Sawtelle, *All's for the Best*, 338.

34. Fahs, "Feminized Civil War," 1491.

35. Elizabeth Stuart Phelps, *Comrades* (New York: n.p., 1911), 43, 40.

# 2

# Traumatized Manhood

## Confederate Amputees in History, Memory, and Hollywood

*Brian Craig Miller*

In the 1959 film *The Horse Soldiers*, members of the Union cavalry ride into Newton Station, where Colonel John Marlowe (John Wayne) and Major Kendall (William Holden) interact with a Confederate prisoner named Colonel Johnny Miles (Carleton Young). Major Kendall recognizes the prisoner from their time fighting Indians together along the Platte River prior to the Civil War. He also notices that his former comrade has lost his right arm. "Sorry about the arm, John. When did that happen?" Kendall asks. "I want neither your solicitude nor to recall our association," responds the defiant Confederate, who then asks Marlowe, "Have I your permission to retire, sir?" Marlowe casually orders some of his men to take the prisoner to his holding cell. As Marlowe and Kendall watch Miles recede into the background, Kendall says, "I can't figure a man like Miles giving up that easy. He's West Point. Tough as nails." "Maybe losing that arm took a lot out of him," remarks Marlowe. Kendall quickly responds, "The man I knew could lose both arms and still kick you to death."[1]

Images of wounded men and amputees have dominated Hollywood's memory of the Civil War era. Numerous Civil War films utilize a hospital scene to remind viewers of the horrors of warfare. In *Dances with Wolves*, Lieutenant John Dunbar (Kevin Costner) musters up the courage to escape amputation and ride toward enemy lines in an apparent suicide mission (which he survives), as Confederate soldiers cheer him. In *Gone with the Wind*, Scarlett O'Hara is ordered to assist in an amputation on an injured soldier, despite a lack of chloroform. The soldier cries out, "No, no you won't. You can't do it. I won't let you do it to me," and then screams, "Don't cut! Don't cut!" The camera remains squarely on Scarlett's face, revealing her horror and disgust as she witnesses the act of butchery. She then exits the hospital as she declares, "I don't want any more men dying and screaming. I don't want anymore." In the carriage ride back to her temporary home, the dashing Rhett Butler asks Scarlett if she has grown tired of seeing "men chopped up."[2]

Most recently, the horrific nature of Civil War medicine makes another stunning appearance in Steven Spielberg's *Lincoln*. As Lincoln and his son Robert embark on a carriage ride through the streets of Washington, they debate Robert's desire to enlist in the war effort. When the carriage parks in front of a military hospital, Robert refuses to follow his father inside, knowing that he plans to use the wards full of Union amputees to dissuade him from military service. But as Robert passes by the hospital door, a bloody wheelbarrow navigated by several black workers races past in frantic fashion. Curious, Robert follows the wheelbarrow, like Alice in pursuit of the white rabbit. When the wheelbarrow halts at the top of a hill, its contents are revealed: a pile of severed hands, feet, arms, and legs. The workers dump the bloody appendages into a pit filled with other festering limbs. The image visibly disturbs Robert. It also sent a gasp through the sold-out crowd in the theater where I viewed the film.[3]

Despite Hollywood's best attempts to recognize the plight of wounded soldiers, few Civil War historians have followed suit. In 1989 Maris A. Vinovskis called on historians to look at "the effects of the war on everyday life in the United States." In the last few years, some historians have examined the effects on Union amputees returning from battle. For these northerners, the perseverance and preservation of the Union, the destruction of slavery, and the triumph of liberty, freedom, and equality ensured that their sacrifices would be recognized, memorialized, and cherished for generations. However, can the same be said for southern amputees who returned from the war scarred, disillusioned, and defeated?[4]

In many ways, injured southern white soldiers faced a crisis in defining their own manhood. Prior to the war, southern men defined their masculine worth through multiple avenues. As historian Lorri Glover explains,

"Manhood was a social, not simply a biological designation, and it required testing." Men tested and asserted their male identity through the mastery and control of their women and children, slaves, land, and households, as well as their horses, guns, and liquor. Other men defined their manhood through honor, or an internal recognition of self-worth that could be revealed to the public by dressing, acting, eating, and socializing like a proper man and displaying the suitable set of emotions and facial expressions. Furthermore, the male physique had to be maintained through proper weight and an appropriate outward appearance. Men also participated, from time to time, in certain honorable acts and rituals, such as dueling, to solidify their masculine status among their peers. Even those men who lived outside elite society, who had no slaves or vast properties to control, identified themselves as men according to societal constructs determined by elite men.[5]

This essay examines how Confederate men contemplated their own masculine worth when forced to decide whether to accept amputation as a medical procedure. The Civil War fundamentally altered how southerners defined manhood. Antebellum notions of mastery and slavery vanished in the midst of emancipation and female sacrifices that altered the dynamics of the southern household. The South's failure to secure victory meant that men lost "the right to construct their sense of manhood exactly as they pleased," notes historian LeeAnn Whites. And as historian Megan Kate Nelson recently argued, "As the ruins of men dispersed throughout the country, their fragmented bodies became sites of debate about both wartime and post-war masculinity." Thus, when a wounded Confederate soldier entered the hospital tent and faced the daunting prospect of losing a limb, he had no idea how southern society would view his empty pant leg or sleeve.[6]

While a vast majority of soldiers accepted amputation to ensure their survival, others flat-out rejected it; they are the main focus here. Some soldiers avoided the scalpel and the saw in order to maintain their complete male physique, which, as historian Bertram Wyatt-Brown notes, serves "as [an] outward sign of inner merit." Men worried that society would recognize their missing limbs as a marker of diminished manhood. Others feared a negative backlash from potential spouses, who might find disabled men undesirable. Some men eschewed amputation in order to return to battle as quickly as possible, and still others reacted violently to the prospect of amputation and defended their limbs or decided to end their lives rather than live in a physically disabled state. Although southern men internalized their own notions of manhood, they needed others to recognize their manly and honorable status, which could be achieved through successful military service. Whatever their reasons for denying permission to amputate, these soldiers assumed major risks, including infection, permanent paralysis, pain, and even death.[7]

One of the multiple challenges when tackling the question of amputation among Confederate soldiers is the lack of documentation. Whereas there are extensive records pertaining to Union amputees, we have no concrete figures on how many Confederate amputees survived the war. The hospital records pertaining to the Confederacy are incomplete and unorganized, and many records were destroyed during the evacuation of Richmond in 1865. Confederate surgeon Joseph Jones called this destruction a "serious" loss to the medical department. Despite this loss, the available medical records contradict the widespread butchery depicted by Hollywood and some historians. The raw medical data maintained by the Confederacy indicate that surgeons exercised caution and did not purposefully amputate a limb from every man that came across their tables. Furthermore, in many cases, amputation did not automatically mean death. At the First Mississippi Hospital at Jackson, only six men underwent amputation from 1863 to 1865. In the Richmond area from June 1 to August 1, 1862, Confederate surgeons performed 580 amputations, after which 245 soldiers perished. Winder Hospital in Richmond treated 228 patients for gunshot wounds between August 1862 and November 1864. The surgeons performed 75 resections (accounting for 32.9 percent of the patients treated) and amputations on an additional 37.7 percent of patients. Among the amputees, 41 lost a leg, 22 lost some portion of an arm, 10 lost a finger, 9 lost a foot, and 4 lost a hand. According to data received by the surgeon general's office in Richmond, between June 1862 and February 1864, 1,688 amputations were performed, resulting in 599 deaths and 1,089 patients who recovered.[8]

The perfect storm of projectiles and pathogens created a medical crisis that the Confederate army seemed ill prepared to handle. However, surgeons did not enter the hospital tent void of information on how and when to perform amputations. Several surgical and instructional handbooks remained in print throughout the Civil War, offering specific guidelines on when to amputate based on the severity of the injury. When a patient arrived, the damaged limb was examined and assessed. Surgeons routinely removed the limb if it had been damaged by a cannonball or shredded on the railroad tracks or if it exhibited the horrific signs of gangrene. Any gunshot wound to a large joint (ankle or knee) generally prompted removal of the limb, as did any extensive damage to arteries, veins, or nerves.[9]

Once a limb had been condemned, the operation commenced. Surgeons routinely provided anesthesia in the form of chloroform, some whiskey, or a shot of morphine under the skin. After the anesthesia was administered, Confederate surgeons waited five minutes before starting the amputation. In addition to the surgeon, there was usually a team of three assistants. The first assistant administered the chloroform, while the second assistant applied pressure to the main artery, a tactic preferable to the use of a tourniquet. The third assistant held down the limb and prepared to support the flap that would be utilized to create the stump after the operation.[10]

If at all possible, the most experienced surgeon, or the individual with the most extensive knowledge of the surgical manual, performed the operation. As one medical manual explained, "The surgeon removes the limb, ligates the vessels, and when all the oozing has ceased, secures the stump by points of suture placed at intervals of an inch or a little less along the entire line of the wound." The most common technique, the circular method, involved making a circular (or, if the surgeon preferred, an oval) cut around the limb before utilizing a saw to cut through the bone. Doctors were advised to use the circular cut because it "required less time and care in dressing, was easily handled, seldom sloughed, . . . its discharges were less and . . . it was less frequently followed by hemorrhage," according to the medical literature. Others preferred the single- or double-flap method, which consisted of creating one or two flaps of skin to cover the stump. Although this technique resulted in a more physically attractive stump, it could be time-consuming; thus, surgeons recommended that this method be performed at hospitals away from the battlefield. Manuals simply noted, "You cannot well leave too much skin."[11]

As wounded soldiers and officers arrived at the hospital tent, their thoughts were fixed on their survival, their families, and their comrades in arms. As those men facing potential amputation waited to be treated, the religious among them tended to ask why: Had God chosen to punish them for the sins they had committed? Was God using amputation to punish the South for its sins that had sent the soldiers off to war? Other religious men saw the loss of a limb as simply God's will and considered it a blessing rather than a curse. Historian George Rable argues that "men could almost stand outside of themselves, viewing their suffering and pain as but a temporary phase during which they might glimpse the glories of heaven." One amputee from

North Carolina changed his life entirely, as he shucked "coarse and vulgar ideas" for the scriptures.[12]

While waiting for the surgeon, men had time to turn inward and assess their own masculine worth. Did they want to return home damaged? Or did they want to return to the field of battle? Should they accept amputation as a potentially life-saving medical treatment, or should they reject it and try to run away? Could they face the long-term physical and emotional ramifications? As one medical professional noted, the process of waiting for an amputation to commence produced "a variety of emotions, including depression; suicidal urges, even in those who have never considered suicide before; anger both at themselves and others; fear; worry; and in certain cases, guilt." This opportunity for internal reflection allowed the wounded men to decide what course of action they wanted to take.[13]

The time spent waiting could be a major psychological detriment, as a soldier's thoughts sometimes turned violent. At Gettysburg, Dr. Henry Miner had to deal with Captain McMay, who tried not once but twice to shoot the doctor, who had determined that the captain would need to lose a finger. As the operation commenced, McMay suddenly plunged his hand under his coat and pulled out a pistol, thrust the muzzle against the surgeon's back, and pulled the trigger. Fortunately, a fast-acting fellow surgeon intervened and saved the doctor's life. McMay tried to shoot the surgeon again when the candle that illuminated the room blew out. Miner wrote, "There we were in the dark, with the angry man trying to shoot again, the doctor struggling to hold him and to hold the pistol." Captain McMay, well aware of the dangers of amputation and the possibility that he might never return to the field of battle, resorted to violence to save his finger. Ultimately, the size of the amputation did not matter.[14]

Among others who fought amputation was William Brimage Bate, a colonel in the Second Tennessee. Both major bones in his left leg were broken by a musket ball at the Battle of Shiloh. Although the surgeons insisted on amputation, Bate refused and ordered his servant to give him his pistols, letting the surgeons know "he intended to protect that leg." He kept his pistols at his bedside for the remainder of his hospital stay. Captured Confederate T. J. McGahee found himself in the hands of a Federal physician. When the Union surgeon told McGahee his leg would have to be amputated, McGahee said, "I do not want my leg cut off, I would rather die." The surgeon sternly replied, "I don't care what you want, I am going to cut it off." McGahee refused chloroform, and as the operation commenced, he punched the surgeon in the face, sending him flying backward as his nose gushed fountains of blood. After the surgeon regained his bearings, McGahee rushed at him with one of the surgical knives and sliced him. The surgeon decided not to complete the operation, and McGahee left the hospital with his leg intact.[15]

Some men reacted to a missing limb or even the possibility of amputation by committing acts of violence against themselves. Jacob Clark, shot in the arm at Shiloh, seemed rather cheerful and in good spirits, yet he ended his life by putting a pistol to his temple while recovering in a hospital in Missouri. His wife noted that he feared losing his arm by amputation. Confederate soldier Bill Hicks was, by all accounts, "a fine young man, an Apollo in form, and a model of strong physical manhood." But according to Dr. F. E. Daniel, "Bill lost a leg in battle, and after the war, although he began the practice of law with flattering prospects, the loss of his leg so preyed on his mind, the thought of going through life such a cripple, in a fit of despondency, he blew out his brains." Charles Minnigerode sustained a gunshot wound in the leg at Appomattox in 1865. Although doctors allowed Minnigerode to keep his leg, he limped for the rest of his life. With his business endeavors failing and a mountain of debt consuming his ever-growing family, Minnigerode took his own life in 1888. In another case, A. G. Ewing, a Confederate cavalryman living in Nashville after the war, decided that he could no longer live as a one-legged man. Ewing had sacrificed his leg at Fort Pillow, Tennessee, in 1862 and took his own life via an overdose of chloroform in 1872.[16]

Suicide was an extreme reaction to amputation or the perception of altered manhood. Some officers simply worried that amputation would affect their ability to prove their masculine worth by commanding on the battlefield. Time spent in a hospital recovering from surgery was time lost leading men into combat. Dr. Henry Miner treated a Confederate officer who initially refused to allow the amputation of part of his finger, arguing that "if he took chloroform, he would not be able to command his men the next day and . . . he was sure there would be another fight the next day." Eventually he relented and declared, "Cut this damned finger off." The patient recovered immediately and returned to the battlefield. The next day, the officer was tossed from his horse and became "lame in both legs, [along] with a ragged finger." Dr. Miner reexamined the snarled finger and insisted on complete amputation this time, but the officer refused any major surgery so that he could command his regiment "until all the fighting was over."[17]

Confederate officers who defined their manhood by their performance in battle sometimes gambled their lives in order to stay in command. While commanding soldiers at the Battle of Spotsylvania Court House in May 1864, Major Joseph McGraw had his left arm torn away by a solid shot that left "only a stump in the shoulder socket." Some of the men rushed to assist their commander, but McGraw held them at bay, shouting, "Don't mind me, men. I'm alright. Give 'em hell!" McGraw passed out in his saddle immediately after giving the command, but he later regained consciousness and underwent surgery. McGraw refused all anesthetics, as he thought requiring chloroform was unmanly. Instead, he endured the operation without "eliciting a groan" as he puffed away on his pipe. He glibly quipped to his physician, "I reckon I'll be off duty thirty days."[18]

In a similar display of bravado in the face of grave injury, Brigadier General Michael J. Bulger sustained several gunshot wounds during the war. When he was shot in the arm, he simply tied it off and remained in command. When he was shot in the leg, he put a corncob on each side of the wound and used his suspenders to hold it all together. He fought to the point of exhaustion, and a surgeon recommended the removal of his leg. Bulger refused and later commanded at Gettysburg, where he suffered another wound to his chest. Brigadier General Brickett Davenport Fry received a devastating wound to his arm at Antietam in 1862. When Confederate medical personnel recommended amputation, Fry asked, "What are the chances of my living without the operation?" The surgeon responded, "One in three hundred." Fry, who knew an amputation would hinder any chance he had of military success, briefly pondered his options and proudly declared, "Then I will take it," and returned to command. He was wounded again at Chancellorsville and at Gettysburg during Pickett's ill-fated assault on July 3, 1863. After a recovery period and a short stint at Johnson Island as a Union prisoner, he survived the war, without any amputations.[19]

Rejecting amputation did not always guarantee survival and an immediate return to the battlefield. Captain J. Frederick Cooper, an officer from Georgia, arrived on the operating table with a smashed knee. Although the physician recommended immediate amputation, Cooper cried, "Stop, doctor. Can't you save my leg?" The physician, Dr. Miller, responded, "No, it is impossible. It must come off, I tell you." Cooper rephrased his entreaty: "Doctor, is there a possible chance for me to save this leg?" The surgeon paused and then said, "Perhaps, one chance in a hundred, but I warn you now that if it is not speedily cut off you will be a dead man in two weeks." "Doctor, I will take that chance," replied Cooper. The physician called for the next patient. Cooper perished seven weeks later.[20]

The desire to avoid amputation and maintain physical wholeness sometimes resulted in survival and a return to military service, but it sometimes resulted in death. Chaplain Charles Holt Dobbs recalled the case of a soldier at Spotsylvania Court House in May 1864 who took a minié ball in the knee joint. The attending surgeon recommended amputation, but the patient violently protested, despite the surgeon's statement that recovery was simply unattainable without amputation. Dobbs tried to convince the soldier, but his pleas fell on deaf ears. The patient told Dobbs he knew of one soldier who had rejected amputation and survived, and he fervently believed the same fate would befall him. A month later, Dobbs ran into the patient in a Richmond hospital. He wrote, "He was a living skeleton, the flesh seemed all gone; he was full of bed sores. His wounded limb was swung up in a cloth; it was four times its natural size and full of worms." Yet the patient continued to reject amputation and died "in great anguish," according to Dobbs, who said the man "deeply regretted his folly when it was too late."[21]

Others who died included Private T. J. Hobson, a member of the Thirty-Second Tennessee. Rather than undergoing amputation, Hobson had bone fragments removed to shorten his leg after being shot at Kennesaw Mountain on June 24, 1864. He died three days later. Private A. Simms refused amputation after being shot in the knee at Antietam. The knee continued to swell, and Simms, a member of the Nineteenth Georgia, died six weeks later. One surgeon declared, "This man's life would no doubt have been saved had an immediate amputation of his limb been made." J. W. Shettles, a private in the Second Mississippi, also received a knee injury at the Battle of Antietam on September 17, 1862; complications sent the private to his grave on November 9, 1862. Surgeon J. H. Rauch reported, "Had this man been operated upon, I am satisfied his life would have been saved." Private W. West, of the Fifty-First Georgia, sustained a gunshot wound to his leg at South Mountain on September 14, 1862. He rejected his surgeon's recommendation for amputation and declared his "readiness and willingness to incur all risks of that course." He died a month later. Although these men avoided amputation and their bodies remained physically intact, it came at a great price.[22]

Yet death guaranteed the recognition of a soldier's manhood when he died honorably in defense of his family or his country. As Lieutenant Colonel

Henry Watkins Allen proclaimed, "A man ought always to expect to be killed in battle, and should be willing and prepared for death always before he goes into it." Allen refused amputation after being wounded in the leg at Baton Rouge on August 2, 1862. Prepared to die, Allen awaited a fate that never materialized. He slowly recovered and eventually returned—on crutches—to visit members of the Fourth Louisiana, his old regiment. The "scarred men" applauded, seized his hands, kissed him, and then "picked him up in their arms, embraced him, and bore him aloft through their camp, cheering and weeping as they went." Allen also wept.[23]

Heroic tales and reminiscences of soldiers who charged forward, even while under severe physical duress, cemented the manhood of southern military personnel. At the Battle of Chickamauga on September 19, 1863, Lieutenant John E. Wilson, a member of the Sixth Florida, charged up a hill and was hit in the leg by a cannonball. One witness remembered, "With the blood flowing from the wound, he shouted to us to come on, and he led that charge to victory, crawling on his hands and one knee." With victory at hand, Wilson told his men, "We have gained the needed time. I am willing to die." Physicians removed Wilson's leg, and he spent time recovering in an Atlanta hospital. His brother arrived a month later to transport him home, but Wilson died on the train ride from Atlanta to Columbus, Georgia, on October 16, 1863.[24]

Not all Confederates were willing to die an honorable death on the field of battle. Honor gained through military service could be lost when soldiers decided to desert from the army. The stigma and shame of desertion damaged a soldier's manhood in the eyes of his fellow soldiers, his peers, and other members of southern society. Throughout the war, soldiers trumpeted the fact that they did the manly thing by sticking it out. A soldier from Georgia remarked, "I would rather die on the battle field than to disgrace myself and the whole family." Another from Tennessee proclaimed, "I did not disgrace our name." Carroll Henderson Clark, a soldier from the Sixteenth Tennessee, endured a gunshot wound at Atlanta that oozed with pus and made his fingers and hand swell. Initially, surgeons applied a simple dressing to try to save the hand, which failed. After Clark moved to another hospital in Macon, Georgia, the wound still failed to heal. When his surgeon there recommended amputation, Clark refused and deserted from the army rather than lose his hand. He ended up in Dawson, Georgia, where he survived without losing his limb. Clark viewed fleeing as a physically complete man more desirable than remaining in the war as a disabled individual.[25]

While some southern soldiers worried that desertion might sap them of their manhood, others wondered how society would view their newly acquired injuries. When he was shot through the foot at the Battle of Chickamauga, Private William Fletcher arrived at a field hospital to receive medical attention. During his wait, Fletcher met a comrade who had been disfigured by a shot in the face. Fletcher joked with the soldier, stating that he would have "better success courting when he got back, with his back to the girls." The soldier replied, "That will be better than you; as you can't turn any way to hide your wooden leg." "Yes, if I had one," replied Fletcher. In fact, the lighthearted conversation struck a chord with Fletcher, who also witnessed another soldier's "foot cast in [a] scrap heap." When the doctor approached Fletcher and examined his wound, he kicked at the doctor and almost knocked him off balance. The surgeon stated, "I will leave you alone, without treatment." Fletcher replied, "Doc, that is what I want, and the fellow that I considered most to blame would make the mistake of his life if treated without my sanction, as that man (calling his name) has been treated, put under influence of something and when he comes to, his foot gone."[26]

After Fletcher refused amputation, the surgeons tried an acid treatment on his foot, which forced him to walk on his toes. The doctors suggested either breaking the foot or amputating it, since they estimated only a 10 percent chance of saving it. Fletcher wrote, "I said I would prefer life with a crooked leg and walking on toes, to an artificial foot; so they said they would consider it no more." Fletcher's final decision to reject amputation was made with the words of his fellow injured soldier ringing clearly in his mind. He feared returning home an incomplete man, unable to hide his disability from potential romantic partners. So he chose to remain physically whole, despite the horrific pain.[27]

Men who were spared the ordeal of amputation still required an adjustment period to cope with shortened or damaged limbs. At Gaines's Mill in June 1862, Lieutenant H. B. Myatt, a member of the Fourteenth Louisiana, was shot in the groin. As an ambulance team removed him from the front lines to a field hospital, a random artillery shell shattered his left elbow. Surgeons suggested amputating his left arm, but Myatt refused because he could still move his fingers. Instead, the physicians excised the elbow joint and removed some of the shattered bone. He had some initial pain and swelling in his hand but recovered quickly on a solid diet and twice-a-day brandy regimen. Although the operation shortened the arm by about two inches, he had full functionality and could, according to his physician, "hold a fork, a knife or any other small object in that hand; he lifts up a bucket full of water; sensibility and mobility of the fingers are perfect." Myatt noted, "It seems to me my arm is gaining every day, I can now bend it almost at right angle without the use of the other hand; I can carve my food, tie my cravat, and write a few words with my left hand."[28]

Men valued the opportunity to save an injured limb. Captain Charles Knowlton, a member of the Tenth Louisiana, might have lost his leg but his surgeon, Dr. Reid, jettisoned amputation in favor of trying to save it. One nurse remarked, "Out of many cases of the kind, this was the only one recorded where amputation was avoided and the patient's life was saved." C. L. Sayre, a member of the Confederate Marine Corps, also lucked out after being injured during an engagement at Santa Rosa Island, Florida, in 1861. Surgeons decided not to amputate his leg; instead, he wore an elaborately constructed frame that stabilized the limb during healing. Sayre was thankful "that I saved my leg," even though it ended up being an inch shorter. James William Howard, a member of the Ninth Arkansas, was struck by a projectile during the Atlanta campaign on May 13, 1864. Three different doctors probed his wound with their fingers to discover that the ball had cracked his arm in half and lodged just under the shoulder blade. Howard refused amputation and also refused to let the doctors remove the ball when they inquired again on May 28. He complained of constant pain and sleepless nights but remained steadfastly determined to save his arm. He survived with his arm intact and a bullet in his shoulder as a souvenir of the war.[29]

What would happen if a soldier lacked the strength to reject the amputation on his own accord? After the Battle of Chickamauga, Bishop Charles Todd Quintard discovered a weeping soldier. When Quintard asked why he was weeping, the soldier replied, "The surgeon has been examining my wound and says that my leg must be amputated. I would not care for myself, but my poor mother." The soldier worried that his mother would be unable to accept his disability. Quintard took it upon himself to end the soldier's crying and assisted him to a hospital, where his leg remained intact. Years later, the chaplain ran into the soldier, who thanked him. The soldier was working as a railway conductor, and he noted that his damaged leg had healed "as good as the other."[30]

Away from the battlefield, other wounded Confederates rejected amputation because they were worried about their ability to make a living after the war. The removal of a limb could prevent a man from continuing an occupation that had been pivotal in providing for his wife and children. Colonel M. D. L. Stephens, a member of the Thirty-First Mississippi Infantry, was wounded in the upper leg at the Battle of Franklin. After an assemblage of surgeons deemed amputation a necessity, Stephens called for Dr. Wall, the chief surgeon of the makeshift hospital. Stephens beseeched, "I am a physician and have a wife and two children at home. Everything is swept away in our country and the Negroes free. I will be compelled to practice my profession if I live to get back there. You know that I cannot practice medicine in my hill country when I am quartered up." Stephens emphatically declared, "I will go with my leg and my leg will go with me." Dr. Wall offered his own assessment, stating, "I think it best for you to let your leg go." As tears swelled in his eyes, Stephens begged Wall to prevent the amputation, and the surgeon finally agreed. The decision prompted a sharp rebuke from another physician who vociferously disagreed with Wall, and the two nearly came to violence over the proper course of treatment. Wall, a complete stranger to Stephens, was willing to shoot the surgeon who was threatening amputation. He well understood Stephens's plight. Although amputation would remove the damaged limb, it would also diminish Stephens's stature as a physician in his community and compromise his ability to support his family. As a man, and as a doctor, Wall understood this.[31]

In that hospital room in Tennessee, a surgeon and his patient defined and battled for their manhood in separate but overlapping avenues. Stephens defined his manhood through the maintenance of his entire male physique, which would preserve his status as a medical professional. With Union victory imminent, Stephens calculated a forthcoming transition in both his livelihood and his family. Without slavery to buttress his household income, Stephens's medical practice had to remain profitable if his family were to survive. He did not think a one-legged doctor could sustain a reputation that would guarantee a bounty of potential clients. He needed both legs to keep his honor, protect his reputation, and provide for his family. Wall, in turn, acted honorably by promising to save his patient's leg, a pledge he was willing to support with violent means, if necessary.

In some cases, Confederate soldiers did not let amputation impede their ability to continue the war and prove their manhood and valor on the battlefield. Brigadier General Adley Hogan Gladden of South Carolina was wounded on the first day of Shiloh, and a surgeon removed his left arm. Instead of going to a quiet location to recuperate, Gladden mounted his horse and headed back to the field to give orders and consult with his staff. After the battle ended, he rode to Corinth, Mississippi, where he underwent a second surgery on his arm. General Braxton Bragg sent a replacement to take over while Gladden recuperated, but the brigadier stated, "Give General Bragg my compliments, and say that General Gladden will only give up his command to go into his coffin." Gladden continued to command until lockjaw killed him shortly after the second operation.[32]

William Jackson, who lost an arm at Seven Pines, stated, "Thank God I have another arm with which to shoot the Yankees." Major R. E. Wilson enlisted with the Eleventh and then the Twenty-First North Carolina in April 1861. He went on to serve with the First North Carolina battalion of sharp-shooters, failing to let three gunshot wounds end his military service. However, on April 2, 1865, he lost his left leg at Petersburg and underwent medical treatment at a Baptist church in Richmond, Virginia. The next day Union forces flooded the city, and Wilson found himself a prisoner of war. He remained in prison, both in Richmond and later in Raleigh, North Carolina, until December 20, 1865, and during his captivity he allegedly killed three Union soldiers. According to one account, Wilson might have been the final Confederate veteran to return home.[33]

In an address to the Southern Historical Society after the Civil War, Major H. B. McClellan of Kentucky recalled seeing a young soldier at Chancellorsville "whose right arm was dangling from the elbow by some shreds of flesh." The soldier said, "Mister! Can't you cut this thing off? It keeps knocking against the trees, and it's mightily in my way." Although McClellan had no medical experience, he tied a tourniquet above the arm and used a pocketknife to remove the limb. McClellan recalled, "Brave boy! I directed him to the rear, where he no doubt soon met with skillful attention from our surgeons. I saw him no more, but I trust that his sturdy spirit sustained him and ensured his recovery. Such boys grow into men who are an honor to any country." Despite his shattered body, the soldier attained a high level of manhood, according to McClellan, because he had lost the limb while serving an honorable and manly cause. The missing limb failed to hinder his transition from boyhood to manhood.[34]

Hollywood's depiction of Civil War medicine acknowledges the brutality of war but not the delicate decisions and debates about the prospect of amputation. Hospital scenes in films have constructed a collective memory of butchering surgeons, screaming and helpless patients, and decrepit piles of mangled and bloodied limbs. In reality, accidents, gunshots, and artillery projectiles created a medical and social dilemma for wounded Confederate soldiers. Some soldiers used violence to avoid amputation, sending the surgeon off to the next bedside. Men refused amputation to preserve their physical wholeness, to maintain their mental alertness in order to return to the battlefield, or simply because they did not know how their families or society would perceive them if they gave up a limb. Damaged men hobbled about with shortened, crooked, or deformed limbs and endured chronic pain and emotional distress, wondering whether they had made the right decision. Others accepted amputation and returned to military service or simply returned home, believing that an incomplete man is surely better than no man at all. Either accepting or rejecting amputation involved the possibility of death, which would secure honor for the fallen soldier. The contours of the Civil War, combined with the Union victory, created an earthquake that shook and crumbled the pillars of southern society. The South jettisoned traditional antebellum definitions of manhood and womanhood to create an honorable place on the shelf of southern society. Damaged men earned the respect of their wives, their colleagues, and their states, which later reached out to provide financial assistance and artificial limbs to their wounded warriors.

## Notes

The author would like to thank Steven Berry, Amy Murrell Taylor, Diane Miller Sommerville, Nicholas Messing, Wendy Venet, Lawrence Kreiser, Randal Allred, and the anonymous readers for their helpful and insightful comments and assistance.

1. *The Horse Soldiers* (Metro Goldwyn Mayer, 1959).

2. *Gone with the Wind* (MGM Studios, 1939). Recent films, including *Cold Mountain*, contain riveting and graphic hospital sequences.

3. *Lincoln* (DreamWorks Studios, 2012), viewed on November 16, 2012.

4. Maris A. Vinovskis, "Have Social Historians Lost the Civil War? Some Preliminary Demographic Speculations," *Journal of American History* 76 (June 1989): 34–58. Some historical studies that touch on amputation include Lawrence W. Friedmann, *The Psychological Rehabilitation of the Amputee* (Springfield, Ill.: Charles C. Thomas, 1978); Daphne Frick, "Soldiers with Empty Sleeves: The Minié Ball and Civil War Medicine," *Proceedings and Papers of the Georgia Association of Historians* 14

(1993): 46–53; Valerie DeBrava, "The Offending Hand of War in *Harper's Weekly*," *American Periodicals* 11 (2001): 49–64; Faye Lewellen, "Limbs Made and Unmade by War," *America's Civil War* (September 1995): 38–45; Jennifer Davis McDaid, "With Lame Legs and No Money: Virginia's Disabled Confederate Veterans," *Virginia Cavalcade* (Winter 1998): 14–25; Stephen Berry, "When Metal Meets Mettle: The Hard Realities of Civil War Soldiering," *North and South* 9, no. 4 (August 2006): 12–21; Ansley Herring Wegner, *Phantom Pain: North Carolina's Artificial-Limbs Program for Confederate Veterans* (Raleigh: Office of Archives and History, North Carolina Department of Cultural Resources, 2004), ix; Brian Matthew Jordan, "Living Monuments: Union Veteran Amputees and the Embodied Memory of the Civil War," *Civil War History* 57, no. 2 (June 2011): 121–52; James Marten, *Sing Not War: The Lives of Union and Confederate Veterans in Gilded Age America* (Chapel Hill: University of North Carolina Press, 2011), 75–123; Megan Kate Nelson, *Ruin Nation* (Athens: University of Georgia Press, 2012); Alfred Jay Bollet, "Amputations in the Civil War," in *Years of Change and Suffering: Modern Perspectives on Civil War Medicine*, ed. James M. Schmidt and Guy R. Hasegawa (Roseville, Minn.: Edinborough Press, 2009), 57–67; Frances Clarke, "'Honorable Scars': Northern Amputees and the Meaning of Civil War Injuries," in *Union Soldiers and the Northern Home Front: Wartime Experiences, Postwar Adjustments*, ed. Paul A. Cimbala and Randall M. Miller (New York: Fordham University Press, 2002).

   5. Lorri Glover, *Southern Sons: Becoming Men in the New Nation* (Baltimore: Johns Hopkins University Press, 2007), 3, 91, 97, 101; Craig Thompson Friend and Lorri Glover, "Rethinking Southern Masculinity: An Introduction," in *Southern Manhood: Perspectives on Masculinity in the Old South*, ed. Craig Thompson Friend and Lorri Glover (Athens: University of Georgia Press, 2004), x, xi; Bertram Wyatt-Brown, *Southern Honor: Ethics and Behavior in the Old South* (New York: Oxford University Press, 1982), 14; Laura F. Edwards, "The Problem of Dependency: African Americans, Labor Relations and the Law in the Nineteenth-Century South," *Agricultural History* 72, no. 2 (Spring 1998): 315; Jane Dailey, *Before Jim Crow: The Politics of Race in Post Emancipation Virginia* (Chapel Hill: University of North Carolina Press, 2000), 90–95; Stephen W. Berry II, *All that Makes a Man: Love and Ambition in the Civil War South* (New York: Oxford University Press, 2003), 12, 20–21. Lee-Ann Whites has termed the Civil War a "crisis in gender"; see her book *The Civil War as a Crisis in Gender: Augusta, Georgia, 1860–1890* (Athens: University of Georgia Press, 1995). For more on how the image of the whole man equates with manhood, see Kenneth S. Greenberg, *Honor and Slavery: Lies, Duels, Noses, Masks, Dressing as a Woman, Gifts, Strangers, Humanitarianism, Death, Slave Rebellions, the Proslavery Argument, Baseball, Hunting, and Gambling in the Old South* (Princeton, N.J.: Princeton University Press, 1996). For more on gender notions in the antebellum and wartime South, as well as how men defined themselves in that period, see Kathleen M.

Brown, *Good Wives, Nasty Wenches and Anxious Patriarchs: Gender, Race and Power in Colonial Virginia* (Chapel Hill: University of North Carolina Press, 1996); Laura Edwards, *Scarlett Doesn't Live Here Anymore: Women in the Civil War Era* (Urbana: University of Illinois Press, 2000); John Mayfield, "'The Soul of a Man!' William Gilmore Simms and the Myths of Southern Manhood," *Journal of the Early Republic* 15 (1995): 477–500.

6. Whites, *Civil War as a Crisis in Gender*, 8; Nelson, *Ruin Nation*, 178.

7. Wyatt-Brown, *Southern Honor*, 48–49.

8. "Description of the Last Campaign of the Civil War," box 24, Joseph Jones Papers, Tulane University, New Orleans, La.; records of First Mississippi Hospital at Jackson, 1863–1865, Mississippi Department of History and Archives (the six amputees were A. D. Saddler, Twenty-First Mississippi; Jonathan Green, Forty-Fourth Alabama; J. A. McGowan, Forty-First Mississippi; John Bini; F. Kepler, Thirtieth Louisiana; and Wyatt Feflin, Ninth Louisiana); H. H. Cunningham, *Doctors in Gray: The Confederate Medical Service* (Baton Rouge: Louisiana State University Press, 1958), 222; Medical and Hospital Series, box 2, Winder Hospital, Eleanor S. Brockenbrough Library, Museum of the Confederacy, Richmond, Va.; James O. Breeden, *Joseph Jones, M.D.: Scientist of the Old South* (Lexington: University Press of Kentucky, 1975), 222. Cunningham also lists amputations performed in Constantinople in 1855 and discovered a comparable number of amputations with a slightly higher mortality rate (46 percent compared with 42 percent around Richmond). The Crimean War had a mortality rate of nearly 62 percent for amputations. Dixon Wecter estimates the number of Confederate amputees at 25,000; see *When Johnny Comes Marching Home* (Cambridge, Mass.: Houghton Mifflin, 1944), 209. Union numbers are more precise: there were 29,980 recorded amputation operations during the war, with a 25 percent mortality rate. However, that number does not include amputations performed on officers in private homes or by family physicians. Nor does the Union total include amputations occurring after the war, so the number was undoubtedly higher. See *The Medical and Surgical History of the War of the Rebellion*, pt. 3, vol. 2 (Washington, D.C.: Government Printing Office, 1883), 877.

In terms of historians noting the butchery of the war, see Peter J. Parish, *The American Civil War* (New York: Holmes and Meier, 1975), 147; David J. Eicher, *The Longest Night: A Military History of the Civil War* (New York: Simon and Schuster, 2001), 789; James M. McPherson, *Battle Cry of Freedom: The Civil War Era* (New York: Oxford University Press, 1988), 486; James M. McPherson, *Ordeal by Fire: The Civil War*, vol. 2 (New York: McGraw-Hill, 2001), 418; Eric T. Dean Jr., *Shook over Hell: Post-Traumatic Stress, Vietnam, and the Civil War* (Cambridge, Mass.: Harvard University Press, 1997), 48–53; and Allen Guelzo, *Fateful Lightning: A New History of the Civil War and Reconstruction* (New York: Oxford University Press, 2012), 267, 273. Charles P. Roland, *An American Iliad: The Story of the Civil War* (New York:

McGraw-Hill, 1991), 64, argues that "gore-daubed surgeons, overwhelmed by multitudes of casualties, cut and sawed and ligatured, creating ghastly mounds of severed arms and legs" after the Battle of Shiloh. He describes amputations taking place "continuously, followed in most instances by death." Not all historians agree with this negative assertion, but David Goldfield, in his recent *America Aflame: How the Civil War Created a Nation* (New York: Bloomsbury Press, 2011), 269, argues that "surgeons were careless in their amputations and unmindful of even the limited sanitary knowledge of the time." Bruce Catton, *The American Heritage Picture History of the Civil War* (Avenel, N.J.: Wings Books, 1982), 360, contends that no one should be blamed for soldiers' poor medical treatment, as both sides tried their best in an age of bad care. The same can be said for Terry L. Jones, *The American Civil War* (New York: McGraw-Hill, 2010), 439, 441, 461, who does not believe that surgeons deserved their poor reputations; he argues that medical care improved during the Civil War as medical personnel utilized new techniques and devices and implemented more sanitary conditions that led them down the road to medical modernity. James I. Robertson Jr., *Soldiers Blue and Gray* (New York: Warner Books, 1988), 158–59, notes that surgeons did not deserve the negative nicknames given to them by Civil War soldiers; he contends that medical professionals worked hard and were devoted to the care of their patients. Thomas B. Buell, *The Warrior Generals: Combat Leadership in the Civil War* (New York: Three Rivers Press, 1997), 360, notes that armies evolved during the war and moved beyond "primitive and haphazard" medical care.

9. S. D. Gross, *A Manual of Military Surgery or Hints on the Emergencies of Field Camp and Hospital Practice* (Augusta, Ga.: Steam Power Press Chronicle and Sentinel, 1861), 11; Samuel Gross, Confederate Pamphlet-Manual of Military Surgery, 11, 34–37, Perkins Library, Duke University, Durham, N.C.

10. J. Julian Chisolm, M.D., *A Manual of Military Surgery for the Use of Surgeons in the Confederate Army* (Richmond: West and Johnston, 1862), 426, courtesy of the Virginia Historical Society.

11. Ibid., 420–21, 427–28; Edward Warren, *An Epitome of Practical Surgery for Field and Hospital* (Richmond: West and Johnston, 1863), 103–8. For more on the differences between the circular and flap methods, see Samuel D. Gross, *A System of Surgery: Pathological, Diagnostic, Therapeutic and Operative*, vol. 1 (Philadelphia: Blanchard and Lea, 1862), 541–46.

12. George C. Rable, *God's Almost Chosen Peoples: A Religious History of the American Civil War* (Chapel Hill: University of North Carolina Press, 2010), 171–72. Rable presents several examples of soldiers (mostly Union) who connected the loss of a limb with a religious sacrifice. These men would rather enter heaven as amputees than be condemned to hell as physically complete specimens. Some soldiers viewed their lost limbs as markers of their sacrifice for both the nation and their savior, Jesus Christ.

13. Friedmann, *Psychological Rehabilitation*, 24.

14. Eugene Ferris Collection, box 2, folder 1, University of Mississippi Archives, University, Miss.

15. Park Marshall, *A Life of William B. Bate: Citizen, Soldier and Statesman* (Nashville: Cumberland Press, 1908), 54; Frank R. Freemon, *Gangrene and Glory: Medical Care during the American Civil War* (Cranbury, N.J.: Associated University Presses, 1998), 157; *Confederate Veteran* 1, no. 4 (April 1893): 118.

16. Letter from Mary Jane Vaughn Clark, May 7, 1862, Missouri Historical Society Archives, St. Louis, Mo.; F. E. Daniel, M.D., *Recollections of a Rebel Soldier (and Other Sketches) or In the Doctor's Sappy Days* (Austin, Tex.: Von Boeckmann, Schutze, 1899), 32–33; Diane Miller-Sommerville, "'Will They Ever Be Able to Forget?' Suicide, Mental Illness and Civil War Soldiers in the Defeated South" (paper presented at Weirding the War Symposium, Athens, Ga., October 24, 2009), 17; *Columbia (Mo.) Herald*, November 29, 1872.

17. Ferris Collection, box 2, folder 1. For more on the desire to fight to the bitter end, see Grady McWhiney and Perry D. Jamieson, *Attack and Die: Civil War Military Tactics and the Southern Heritage* (Tuscaloosa: University of Alabama Press, 1982).

18. *Confederate Veteran Magazine* 32 (1924), 59–60.

19. Gen. Clement A. Evans, ed., *Confederate Military History*, vol. 8, *Alabama* (New York: Broadfoot, 1987), 395–97, 409–11.

20. Warren Wilkinson and Steven E. Woodworth, *A Scythe of Fire: A Civil War Story of the Eighth Georgia Infantry Regiment* (New York: William Morrow, 2002), 90–91.

21. John Wesley Brinsfield Jr., *The Spirit Divided: Memoirs of Civil War Chaplains, the Confederacy* (Mercer, Ga.: Mercer University Press, 2006), 89.

22. *Medical and Surgical History of the War of the Rebellion*, 93, 380–83.

23. Sarah A. Dorsey, *Recollections of Henry Watkins Allen* (New Orleans: M. Doolady, 1866), 12–13, 74, 144–47; Jack D. Welsh, *Medical Histories of Confederate Generals* (Kent, Ohio: Kent State University Press, 1995), 5.

24. David Hartman and David Coles, *Biographical Rosters of Florida's Confederate and Union Soldiers, 1861–65*, vol. 2 (Wilmington, N.C.: Broadfoot, 1995), 644.

25. Freemon, *Gangrene*, 157; Welsh, *Medical Histories*, 15–16; James McPherson, *For Cause and Comrades: Why Men Fought in the Civil War* (New York: Oxford University Press, 1997), 80. See also Victoria Bynum, *Unruly Women: The Politics of Social and Sexual Control in the Old South* (Chapel Hill: University of North Carolina Press, 1992), 141.

26. William A. Fletcher, *Rebel Private: Front and Rear, Memoirs of a Confederate Soldier* (New York: Meridian, 1997), 102–3.

27. Ibid., 104–6.

28. Felix Formento Jr., *Notes and Observations on Army Surgery* (New Orleans: L. E. Marchand, 1863), 51–53.

29. Fannie A. Beers, *Memories: A Record of Personal Experience and Adventure during Four Years of War* (Philadelphia: J. B. Lippincott, 1888), 215; letter to Major A. J. Foard, November 30, 1861, Samuel Hollingsworth Stout Papers, Manuscript, Archives and Rare Book Library, Emory University, Atlanta, Ga.; James William Howard Journal, entries for May 13 and 28, 1864, Auburn University Archives, Auburn, Ala.

30. Sam Davis Elliott, ed., *Dr. Quintard, Chaplain in C.S.A. and Second Bishop of Tennessee: The Memoir and Civil War Diary of Charles Todd Quintard* (Baton Rouge: Louisiana State University Press, 2003), 79.

31. M. D. L. Stephens manuscript, University of Mississippi Archives, University, Miss.

32. *An Impressed New Yorker, Thirteen Months in the Rebel Army, Being a Narrative of Personal Adventures in the Infantry, Ordnance, Cavalry, Courier and Hospital Services* (New York: A. S. Barnes and Burr, 1862), 179–80.

33. Nelson, *Ruin Nation*, 181; *Lost Cause* 7, no. 5 (December 1902): 74, in United Daughters of the Confederacy Records, Kentucky Historical Society.

34. J. William Jones, ed., *Southern Historical Society Papers*, vol. 8 (Richmond, 1880), 445–46.

# Section II

# Reunions and Battlefield Preservation

# 3

# Relics of Reunion

## *Souvenirs and Memory at Chickamauga and Chattanooga National Military Park, 1889–1895*

*Daryl Black*

At noon on September 19, 1895, General J. S. Fullerton, chairman of the Chickamauga Park Commission, stepped to the rostrum on a temporary stage set up at the foot of Snodgrass Hill.[1] The former Union officer and veteran of the Chickamauga and Chattanooga Campaigns welcomed the audience—more than 12,000 people—to the dedication ceremony for the Chickamauga and Chattanooga National Military Park. Charged with providing a "simple" introduction for Vice President Adlai Stevenson, Fullerton found himself inspired by "the scenes of this battlefield around us, and the many old comrades into whose faces we now look for the first time since the war cloud went down." Fullerton's "swelling of memory" led to a lengthy discourse recounting the battle and conjuring images of those "youthful soldiers" who had contested the field at Chickamauga. But after recalling the events of 1863, and as he reached the end of his remarks, Fullerton declared, "this celebration, the inauguration of this park and commemoration of the grand and noble idea—marks the beginning of a regenerated national life." Barely "thirty years have passed," he noted, "since the most desperate of battles was fought, and now survivors of both sides harmoniously and lovingly come together to fix the battle lines and mark the places now and forever to remain famous as monuments to the valor of the American soldier."[2]

Speaker after speaker reiterated General Fullerton's theme. Chattanooga mayor George Ochs called the park a "symbol of the Nation's second birth."[3] Former Confederate general John B. Gordon declared that the battlefield park was a demonstration of the "brotherhood, and unity between the soldiers who fought and between their children who are the heirs of their immortal honors." And, he said, "the warriors' blood spilled on the battlefields" contributed "to the upbuilding of a loftier American manhood for the future defense of American freedom."[4] Addressing the former Confederates in the audience, John Palmer, commander of a Union division at Chickamauga and a corps at Missionary Ridge, claimed, "I never allowed myself to forget that you were Americans, freely offering your lives in the defense of what you believed to be your rights and in vindication of your manhood."[5] These speeches and dozens more like them delivered at the dedication ceremony marked a major transition in the dominant cultural memory of the Civil War. Conflict was forgotten, cause and result downplayed, and unity among white Americans celebrated. In the days before audio and film recordings, the words spoken at these ceremonies of remembrance were transitory, while the written versions of these comments remained deep in the shadows of late-nineteenth- and early-twentieth-century literature. Yet the meanings expressed by the speakers, writers, and monument builders penetrated to the core of white American culture and became a dominant template for thinking about the Civil War.[6]

This essay examines how the souvenirs created to commemorate the park's dedication advanced a version of the Civil War that focused on the valor of white men in combat and simultaneously marginalized the wartime roles of African Americans and overlooked the experiences of the freed people who had to fight for inclusion in the new nation after the war. These objects also domesticated women's experience and confirmed a bourgeois model of female dependency. Finally, these souvenirs erased any lingering examples of sectional animus and created a visual culture that homogenized the national narrative of the Civil War and transformed it into a story that celebrated nationalism, muscular manhood, and white supremacy.

As Sherry Turkel argues, "objects help us make our minds, reaching out to us to form active partnerships."[7] Thus, the programs, songbooks, and ribbons given to visitors at Civil War reunions in the 1880s and 1890s were portable carriers of the memory that defined and reproduced with mechanical consistency a new narrative created on the Chickamauga battlefield. These were new kinds of products—products of the new industrial age that spoke in a repeatable, consistent visual and symbolic language. Thousands of these mass-produced and mass-distributed objects made their way into the personal collections of families across the North and South and operated to help Americans "make their minds" about how to recall and interpret the Civil War. At the same time, they helped link the remembered war to the nation's expanding commercial interests and, in so doing, created a connection between mass consumption and visions of the national future.[8]

This survey of objects is limited to those held in the permanent collection of the Chattanooga History Center, which has been a local repository for the community's material culture since 1979. In this collection are more than 100 objects created to commemorate the various reunions held in and around the city between 1889 and the 1930s. This essay analyzes objects created between 1889, when the formation of the memorial committee was announced at the famous Blue and Gray Bar-B-Que, and the park's formal dedication in 1895. Broadly, there were two distinctive sets of objects during these early reunion years: printed and decorative souvenirs that specifically commemorated an event, such as pamphlets, booklets, badges, and ribbons; and printed materials that promoted commercial ventures. Although these objects can be separated in hindsight, during the time they were in circulation, they all existed and functioned as part of a network of symbols and ideas that blurred the lines between mass production, mass culture, memory of the Civil War, and definitions of national identity. Thus, this essay examines the pieces chronologically to show patterns of representation, while paying careful attention to the occurrence of overt commercialization.

To chart the visual themes and imagery of race, nation, and gender communicated through these Civil War remembrances and mass-produced souvenirs, I chose three particular objects that, both visually and textually, capture the broad themes of the early reunion period. The first is the visually rich program from the 1889 Blue and Gray Bar-B-Que. It clearly illustrates the intention of the event—reunion. Images of elderly veterans sharing a game of cards and gleefully preparing to roast a pig appear in the top corners of the program. Unlike their younger selves who shot, stabbed, and maimed their opposite numbers, these idealized, smiling, old white veterans appear to relish one another's company as they prepare for a feast and a celebration. Two "peace pipes"—one bearing the initials of the Army of the Cumberland (AC) and the other the initials of the Confederate Veterans (CV)—are literally tied together with gray and blue ribbon.

The representation of smoking works in two ways. First, it brings to mind the camaraderie of a shared smoke—a common form of relaxation during the war. It no doubt conjured images of the informal truces during the siege of Chattanooga, when pickets from the opposing armies met between the lines to trade and socialize. A shared bowl of southern tobacco was a hallmark of these meetings. At the same time, the pipes have a second, contemporary meaning. As the United States became a society of urban dwellers who worked in offices or factories and who consumed rather than produced the necessities of life, many commentators looked for ways to connect to the primal, natural state that exemplified a stronger and more virtuous era in the nation's history. One of the ways they did this was to appropriate Native American symbols as references to elemental aspects of authentic American culture. As a metaphor that harks back to a more primitive, masculine experience, the pipes speak to a double regeneration—one that created a new nation, and one that created a new manhood. The appearance of the pipes on the cover of the program was not coincidental. In the first lines of text the visual reference on the cover is made clear: "Chattanooga Welcomes the Blue and the Gray to a Barbecue to Be Given on Veterans Day on the Chickamauga Battle Field, Where They Will Smoke the Pipe of Peace, and Bid Each Thought of Conflict Cease." To carry the metaphor further, the seventh act of the event was to "Light the Pipe of Peace. Made with Wood Cut on Chickamauga Battlefield." Immediately afterward was the formal organization of the committee that would create the plan for the park and seek congressional appropriations for land acquisition and preservation.

In the background, without the slightest hint of irony, chugs a locomotive. The railroads had certainly been one of the main reasons for the clash at Chickamauga and Chattanooga—the town was the railroad gateway to the Deep South. But the railroads, which were barely ten years old when war broke out in 1861, had increasingly knit the nation together in the 1870s and 1880s, collapsing distance and regional distinctions. The railroads were the archetypal symbol of modern America. "Those who saw themselves as modern manipulated these new interfaces," writes William G. Thomas. In fact, "the control of them, and of knowledge about them, was an important and highly contested arena of modernity." Many self-delusions, Thomas argues, developed out of the massive changes wrought by the railroad, most notably a faith that technology would create moral progress.[9] Indeed, this technology helped destroy the Native American people in the West, thus domesticating and making safe the Native symbols and rituals being used to symbolically remake the nation. In very real ways, the victory over space and distance and the victory over Native American resistance made it possible for Americans to come together under one flag. Throughout the nineteenth century, the railroads represented the physical drawing together of the United States.

This emphasis on unity is symbolized on the program's cover, which depicts only the Stars and Stripes. At later reunions, both the national flag and the battle flag of the Confederacy were displayed, but at the 1889 event, there was room for only one flag. As the program reiterates, "And here upon our sacred sod, with one proud nation, flag, and God, we welcome Dixie's veteran band, and greet the Army of the Cumberland; and prayer on prayer comes from each mouth, to closer bind the north and south. We'll fan to life the patriot flame, and build an altar to each hero's name—their deeds of bravery thus to mark in Chickamauga National Park, a nation's charge from this great day, in memory of both blue and gray."

A year later (July 3–5, 1890) the United Confederate Veterans (UCV) held their reunion in Chattanooga. Among the commemorative newspapers, flags, and ribbons that marked the occasion was a songbook produced by the Woolson Spice Company, with offices in Kansas City, Missouri, and Toledo, Ohio. Called *War Songs Dedicated to the United Confederate Veterans First Annual Convention*, the pocket-sized volume blurs the line between remembering the war and advertising. Words and images juxtapose nostalgia for the war and promotion of Woolson's Lion Coffee, mingling representations of Union and Confederate generals with wartime songs of northern and southern origin. The message bears two potentially unifying themes—a blend of sentimental war-era lyrics in a hazy reunionist fantasy of causeless strife, and the national experience of consumption. Together, these ideas result in reminders that "Veterans of the North and South drink Lion Coffee."

The authors of the songbook were direct in their instructions: "Take this little Souvenir Book of War Songs home with you," they wrote, "in remembrance of the days when we fought, died, and bled. With this little volume you can brush up the Old Songs, and around the Camp-fire the old time fervor and enthusiasm will make the walls ring." This invocation demonstrates two major threads in the reunion movement: the masculine suffering of the soldier as the primary remembrance, and the sentimentalization of the war. This performance of manhood was translated into a sentimentalized campfire scene in which the actions, real or imagined, of soldierly suffering were constantly reenacted. The war experience was carried into the domestic campground as a means of asserting a martial identity that fit the context of a burgeoning culture of the outdoors—an attempt to rescue the weakened American man who was enervated by urban living and mass consumption. Thus, as Jackson Lears has observed, the Civil War was turned into a touchstone of a more authentic form of American manhood that could be called forth to create connections with traits lacking in late-nineteenth-century men.[10]

In 1895 the Chickamauga and Chattanooga National Military Park was ready for dedication. Thousands traveled to the field for a two-day celebration on the thirty-second anniversary of the battle. The speeches made during the event pointed to an increasingly broad acceptance of a de-sectionalized memory in which reunification was the primary celebratory motif. In a ribbon designed for the dedication, the Confederate battle flag and the Stars and Stripes are crossed in union; at the point of crossing, the two staffs are joined by a ring. By giving them equal visual weight, the ribbon's designer represented a growing sense of equality among white soldiers and their descendants, who were coming to view the war as a dispute that had no beginning and whose only meaning was the celebration of each side's manhood. To confirm this simple idea, the designer employed a pair of hands clasped in a handshake, denoting the emerging agreement between the two sides to forget the essence of the conflict and the essential changes it brought.

This brief survey of three objects suggests the types of images used to link major sites of memory with communities across the nation. Perhaps more significant than what these objects contain is what they exclude and marginalize. None of the objects in the Chattanooga History Center's collection represents African Americans, whether as slaves, as self-emancipated individuals, or as free people. This omission amplifies the physical invisibility and marginalization of black veterans, their families, and members of the black community during reunion ceremonies. Despite the presence of an African American Grand Army of the Republic post (Chickamauga Post 22) and an active black political class in the city, no black veterans or politicians gave speeches during the dedication ceremony, no blacks sat on the platform, and no groups dedicated monuments to black soldiers. Chattanooga held a parade during the welcoming ceremonies in September 1895, and the only black participants were a group of schoolboys who marched at the very end. Given the city's importance to slaves who sought refuge there in 1864–1865, the presence of four regiments of African American volunteers during the war (two of which were raised out of the refugee camps established by the freed people), and the large, politically active and influential black community in Chattanooga in the 1880s and 1890s (some 40 percent of the total population), this was a glaring omission. The marginalization of African Americans was planned, and it helped move the story of emancipation and the postwar campaigns for civil rights out of the dominant culture. In Chattanooga—and across the nation—white political and economic leaders were pushing African Americans physically, politically, and legally to the edges of public life.[11]

This erasure of a black memory at Chickamauga and Chattanooga was part of a broader movement that joined racism and mass culture to help ease the way toward white reunification. As Robert Rydell and Rob Kroes point out, the terms *racism* and *mass culture* were coined at approximately the same time. And both, they argue, were "absolutely essential to the manufacturing [of] a new national identity" for white Americans. Advertising played on racial stereotypes and visually degraded blackness, casting African Americans as either simple buffoons or subservient labor. These new images—reproduced and broadly circulated in everyday life—represented whites' deeply held assumptions about blacks' incapacity to participate in the nation's public life and helped confirm the emerging caste system of Jim Crow America. By erasing images of blacks' contributions to the defense of the Union and blacks' assertions of national citizenship through military service, those who produced reunion ephemera effectively wrote the black community out of the confirming moment of postwar nationhood and out of any national future communicated through mass-produced and mass-circulated objects. The creation of a white version of the Civil War was both literally and figuratively manufactured in the form of souvenirs.[12]

While these souvenirs expressed a white national memory and identity, they also marginalized women's roles in defending the Union or the Confederacy and in remaking the nation. Women had been central participants in making memory and memorial spaces during the 1860s, 1870s, and into the 1880s, but the creation of the national military park at Chickamauga highlighted a distinctly gendered version of the Civil War.[13] Only one of the objects in the Chattanooga History Center's collection contains any reference, in either text or image, to women. The Woolson Spice Company's UCV songbook includes a brief narrative that positions women as passive receivers of the war's action and as domestic consumers whose role in the new nation is to choose the best mass-produced goods for their families. As the introduction puts it, "This little book of War Songs will reach none more interested in patriotic songs than our mothers and sisters. These noble women inspired their sons, lovers, and husbands when fighting the battles and with unwearied hands prepared useful and necessary articles for field and hospital use." This work by women was linked back to the home, where they "gathered around the fireside and thought of the dangers—not only in war's destruction of killed and wounded, but hardships of marching and exposure and uncertainty of the safe return of the absent ones." Thus, the only object that represents women at all casts them in naturalized, domestic roles. Women's work was an extension of their role as keeper of the home, and their proper posture was one of patient waiting. This vision of stable households defies historical reality and erases the wartime contributions of women, who took on the farmwork while their husbands and sons were absent, went into hospitals as nurses, sewed uniforms for mass-production factories, worked in Union and Confederate ammunition plants, and rioted in the streets, encouraging their men to abandon the army and, in the South, resisting the impressment of officers. Instead, women are depicted as contented housewives whose "spirit of constancy" provides an idealized middle-class image of succor and safety. The songbook clearly states the intent of the broader, memorialized, and represented masculine version of the war: women should consume the war as a form of manly heroism.

The songbook makes the domestic and consumptive role of women clear as the advertising text shifts from a paean to women of the 1860s to an advertising pitch: The Woolson Spice Company is "appreciative of your share in the sorrows of war, congratulates you in being partakers of the joys of peace, and trusts when in need of a pure and wholesome roasted coffee in your home you will remember and ask for Lion Coffee. You assume no risk, for it is the best package coffee in the United States and will certainly please the old veteran." As shared consumers of "the best package coffee in the United States," the wives and daughters of "old veterans" can help bring the nation together by enjoying not a local brew but a national one.

As Caroline E. Janney points out, however, sectional discord persisted "in both the planning and dedication of the battlefield." Confederate veteran William C. Oates delivered "divisive remarks" that "were more than a rejection of the reconciliatory language—they were a rejection of the Union cause."[14] Union veteran and future president William McKinley and Illinois governor John P. Altgeld emphasized emancipation and reminded the audience that great change had resulted from the war. Such a corrective is important to acknowledge and helps us see the complexity of putting together a new imagined community in the late nineteenth century. However, it is problematic to assert that isolated examples of resistance to the reunionist theme and passing mentions of emancipation constitute a significant counternarrative to the dominant interpretive mode identified by David Blight.[15] Indeed, the marginality of the speeches by Oates and McKinley bolsters the view that most white Americans' memory of the war was predominantly controlled by a reunionist language and a visual idiom that separated emancipation from ideas of racial equality or justice.

As philosopher Paul Riceour has argued, sites of memory are "fundamentally vestiges" that exist liminally and possess "the capacity to produce another history."[16] The speeches given in September 1895 demonstrated the remembered significance of the place, including the battles of 1863. At the same time, however, the place and the objects connected to it became something new through a complex retelling, both in word and in visual shorthand. At this moment when the events of the battlefield were separated from cause and consequence, a new history transpired that mobilized the symbols and biases of the past to renarrate and retell stories and thus forge a new national unity. The souvenirs that circulated at Chickamauga helped confirm a new way of knowing the meaning of both the past and the future that could grow out of that memory. As Marita Sturken points out, time is arrested yet is in constant replay in such objects.[17] The objects distributed during reunions in Chattanooga both simplified the meaning of a war of incomprehensible scale and violence and created an interpretive field in which the replayed event was not the war itself. Rather than recalling the trauma of civil division and war, the souvenirs at Chickamauga created a continuous past in which national unity existed uninterrupted throughout the nineteenth century and the white republic remained in place. This knowledge established new lines of race and gender by diminishing the social significance of emancipation and the transformative power of a narrative that possessed the potential to create new lines of national identity rooted in equality and civil rights.

The cause and effect of the trauma or rupture were redefined and reinterpreted in these objects of mass culture and carried into the realm of mass consciousness. This consumer culture created an imaginative link to the comforts of home and the practices of consumption—of both the objects and the advertisements accompanying them—providing reassurance, stability, and protection. Consumers were reassured that a unified household had been re-created in the images of camaraderie that were common in reunion souvenirs. Even the concept of a "reunion" provided a reassuring feeling of communion and domestic connection—a link to a nostalgic past defined by protection and safety. When linked to a sense of nationalism, these objects helped create an individualized sense of protection and domestic connection within the national community. They forged a link to an imagined nation that defined the Civil War as a continuity rather than a rupture, providing a nostalgic sense of a harmonious home that had never been in meaningful conflict.

The act of remembering through the objects collected at reunions was also a conscious effort to forget.[18] To remember a narrative of white reconcili-ation, of valor and drama on the battlefield, meant that some stories must necessarily be forgotten. The memory of emancipation, of African American men and women claiming their freedom and fleeing southern plantations, and of their efforts to carve out a social and political space in the United States demanded a different set of forgettings and rememberings.[19] The damaging effects of this willful erasure of African American agency during the war were compounded by the active forgetting of how white southerners used violence and intimidation to reassert political control in the former Confederate states during the 1860s and 1870s. As Riceour writes of the elision of Vichy mem-ory in France, "politics will be founded anew on the forgetfulness of sedition." Such forgetfulness worked to "reaffirm national unity by a liturgy of language, extended by the ceremonies of hymns and public celebrations." Such forget-fulness can have dire consequences. As Riceour puts it, "is it not a defect in this imaginary unity that it erases from the official memory the examples of crimes likely to protect the future from the errors of the past and, by depriv-ing public opinion of the benefits of dissensus, of condemning competing memories to an unhealthy underground existence?"[20] Historian Jackson Lears points out that Americans "evaded the tragic significance of the war. Public moralists, North and South, wanted to turn it into a melodrama—and they succeeded."[21] The souvenirs circulated at Chickamauga and Chattanooga reinforced this melodramatic rendering while affirming a patriarchal and white supremacist vision of the nation. They helped stunt the process of acknowledgment and reconciliation that recognized multiple experiences of the war, defined by race and gender, and replaced it with a comforting visual rhetoric that promised future harmony and national consensus.

Yet the meanings ascribed to objects of national veneration do not remain fixed in time. Their survival in museums and in private collections across the nation demonstrates that these ephemera have meaning to those who keep them and pass them down through multiple generations. Their survival helps us identify how a patriarchal, white supremacist national consensus took form and allows us to better understand the constant making and remaking of American nationalism. By examining objects that represent a national narrative, we become aware of the codes of mass culture and the ways ideology penetrates mass society. The Civil War as an event has no stable meaning. The texts that explain it are all expressions of an imaginative act of recalling through snapshots of memory or shards of recollections given shape by mundane, mass-produced objects. The war's meanings and signs are assigned not by an inherent reality but by a subjective construction of meaning. These meanings are in constant flux and open to interpretation. Thus, memories of the war are unstable and subject to interruptions that make claims to power and authority—often in the guise of objective truth—in the present for future actions.[22]

The best way to search for meanings and to better understand competing meanings is not simply to analyze the comings and goings of armies and politicians—although studying these events remains an important part of explaining the war as it unfolded. Rather, one should study the many ways people consumed, imagined, and communicated memories of the war and its consequences. By examining the mundane objects associated with reunions between 1889 and 1895, we gain critical insight into the depth and breadth of an emerging narrative of power that invokes the Civil War as a touchstone of American memory, a basis for politics, and a template for an American future.[23] This view also encourages an awareness of how images and representations of the Civil War continue to operate as a field of social, cultural, and political power in contemporary America. And it challenges us to rethink how we view and how we are shaped by the physical objects produced by a culture predicated on white supremacy.

### Notes

1. Timothy B. Smith, *A Chickamauga Memorial: The Establishment of America's First Civil War National Military Park* (Knoxville: University of Tennessee Press, 2009), xvii; Caroline E. Janney, "'I Yield to No Man an Iota of My Convictions':

Chickamauga and Chattanooga National Military Park and the Limits of Reconcili-ation," *Journal of the Civil War Era* 2, no. 5 (September 2012): 394–420.

2. H. V. Boynton, *Dedication of the Chickamauga and Chattanooga National Military Park, September 18–20, 1895, Report of the Joint Committee to Represent the Congress at the Dedication of the Chickamauga and Chattanooga National Military Park* (Washington, D.C.: Government Printing Office, 1896), 25–26.

3. "Address of George Ochs," in Boynton, *Dedication*, 44–45.

4. "Address of John B. Gordon," ibid., 37–40.

5. "Address of John Palmer," ibid., 35.

6. David Blight, *Race and Reunion: The Civil War in American Memory* (Cam-bridge, Mass.: Harvard University Press, 2001); Gaines Foster, *Ghosts of the Confed-eracy* (New York: Oxford University Press, 1988); Charles Reagan Wilson, *Baptized in Blood: The Religion of the Lost Cause, 1865–1920* (Athens: University of Georgia Press, 1987).

7. Sherry Turkel, "What Makes an Object Evocative?" in *Evocative Objects: Things We Think With*, ed. Sherry Turkel (Cambridge, Mass.: MIT Press, 2007), 308.

8. According to Thomas Brown, the remembrance of the war years "has pro-duced a vast sea of monuments, speeches, poems, reenactments, motion pictures and other works." The purpose behind these forms of commemoration, Brown points out, "is not only to understand a single historical event or to explore American mem-ory; it is also to recognize issues that continue to play a dynamic role in our society. Understanding how the Civil War has been told and retold, often with different emphases and different goals, sheds light on the issues and ideas that have affected American culture for the better part of a century and a half." Thomas J. Brown, *The Public Art of Civil War Commemoration: A Brief History with Documents* (Boston: Bedford/St. Martin's, 2004), vii.

9. William G. Thomas, *The Iron Way: Railroads, the Civil War, and the Making of Modern America* (New Haven, Conn.: Yale University Press, 2011), 10.

10. T. J. Jackson Lears, *Rebirth of a Nation: The Making of Modern America, 1877–1920* (New York: Harper Perennial, 2010).

11. *Chattanooga Times*, September 19, 1895; Barbara A. Gannon, *The Won Cause: Black and White Comradeship in the Grand Army of the Republic* (Chapel Hill: University of North Carolina Press, 2011); Janney, "I Yield to No Man." Janney spec-ulates that black veterans participated in some ways during the celebrations; however, her analysis brushes past the direct evidence that African Americans were largely excluded from *public* performances. For an analysis of Chattanooga's African Ameri-can experience in the late nineteenth century, see Michelle R. Scott, *Blues Empress in Black Chattanooga: Bessie Smith and the Emerging Urban South* (Urbana: University of Illinois Press, 2008).

12. Robert W. Rydell and Rob Kroes, *Buffalo Bill in Bologna: The Americaniza-
tion of the World, 1869–1922* (Chicago: University of Chicago Press, 2005), 3.

13. See Nina Silber, *The Romance of Reunion: Northerners and the South, 1865–
1900* (Chapel Hill: University of North Carolina Press, 1997), for ways that middle-
class gender conventions shaped reunion. William Blair, *Cities of the Dead: Contesting
the Memory of the Civil War in the South, 1865–1914* (Chapel Hill: University of
North Carolina Press, 2004), 79–81, 86, 116; Caroline E. Janney, *Burying the Dead
but Not the Past: Ladies' Memorial Associations and the Lost Cause* (Chapel Hill: University of North Carolina Press, 2008), 167–94.

14. Janney, "I Yield to No Man," 407–10.

15. See Blight, *Race and Reunion*.

16. Paul Riceour, *Memory, History, Forgetting*, trans. Kathleen Blame and David
Pellauer (Chicago: University of Chicago Press, 2004), 405.

17. Marita Sturken, *Tourists of History: Memory, Kitsch, and Consumerism from
Oklahoma City to Ground Zero* (Durham, N.C.: Duke University Press, 2007), 1–34.

18. Riceour, *Memory, History, Forgetting*, 452.

19. Ibid.

20. Ibid., 454–55.

21. Lears, *Rebirth of a Nation*, 17.

22. Michel de Certeau, *The Practice of Everyday Life*, trans. Steven Rendall
(Berkeley: University of California Press, 1984).

23. Blair, *Cities of the Dead*, 1–10.

# 4

# The Graying of Gettysburg National Military Park

## Race, Erasure, Ideology, and Iconography

*Robert E. Weir*

Modern-day Americans remember the Civil War in many ways, most of them historically inaccurate. Humorist Austin O'Malley (1858–1932) once quipped, "Memory is a crazy woman that hoards colored rags and throws away food." Frederick Douglass agreed. In his 1871 Memorial Day address at Arlington National Cemetery, Douglass lambasted those seeking to rewrite the meaning of the Civil War: "May my tongue cleave to the roof of my mouth if I forget the difference between the parties to that bloody conflict. . . . If this war is to be forgotten, I ask in the name of all things sacred what shall men remember?"[1]

What indeed? Until recently, Gettysburg and other former Civil War battlefields were largely collections of "colored rags"—repositories of moldering uniforms, rusty muskets, frayed regimental banners, and spent ammunition. The material culture of conflict was stripped of specificity, as if the only causes for which men died on the battlefield were abstractions such as glory, honor, and union. Starkly missing amid the rifles, banners, and uniforms was the mention of slavery or emancipation. Alas, as this essay argues, this was by design. It would take more than a century before the sort of memory Douglass referenced made its way into the narrative at Gettysburg National Military Park.

Gettysburg, a small town of just 7,620 residents located in southern

Pennsylvania, has profited handsomely from displaying colored rags. Since the National Park Service (NPS) began gathering attendance figures in 1934, there have been more than 123.5 million visitors to Gettysburg. These numbers dwarf those of its closest competitor for tourists, Chickamauga in northern Georgia.[2] For many Americans, a trip to Gettysburg is their most in-depth exposure to the Civil War. Historian James Horton notes that 80 percent of all Americans receive no formal training in history beyond high school. For good or ill, historical tourism shapes what is remembered.[3]

When President Abraham Lincoln dedicated a cemetery at Gettysburg just four months after the terrible events of July 1–3, 1863, he proclaimed that the "unfinished work" of the war was to bring forth "a new birth of freedom."[4] During his second inaugural speech, Lincoln reiterated the view that human bondage lay at the heart of secession: "One-eighth of the whole population were colored slaves, not distributed generally over the Union, but localized in the southern part of it. These slaves constituted a peculiar and powerful interest. All knew that this interest was somehow the cause of the war."[5]

Yet until Gettysburg National Military Park (GNMP) unveiled its new visitor center on April 14, 2008, visitors would have been hard-pressed to find evidence of Lincoln's thesis. The battlefield's 1,328 monuments honor the sacrifice of white soldiers, but one gets little sense of the "difference between the parties" that clashed there. A single representation of nonwhite Americans exists: the Forty-Second New York Infantry memorial is topped with Native Americans, but only because they were the mascots of the Tammany Regiment.

Historians have documented the quickness with which the Civil War's emancipation themes gave way to reconciliation narratives that were thinly veiled bastions of what Canada's *National Post* labeled "southern bias."[6] Even as Reconstruction unfolded, Gettysburg was burying its rich black past.

No black regiments fought at Gettysburg, but African Americans were visible before, during, and after the battle. Of the town's 2,400 residents in 1863, about 8 percent (189) were black.[7] The all-black St. Paul African Methodist Episcopal (AME) Zion Church hosted the Slave Refugee Society and was a stop on the Underground Railroad.[8] Local residents resisted the Fugitive Slave Act and were outraged when Confederate raiders carried off 250 African Americans in the weeks preceding Lee's entry into Gettysburg. They applauded black volunteers who repulsed Major General Jubal Early's attempt to cross the Susquehanna River and attack Harrisburg days before the clash at Gettysburg.[9]

However one parses the war's initial causes, the conflict was about slavery by the time armies met at Gettysburg. As James McPherson, a nationally recognized historian, asserts, the Emancipation Proclamation "changed the war from one to restore the Union into one to destroy the old Union and a build a new one purged of human bondage."[10] African Americans served as teamsters at Gettysburg and took up arms during the battle; several black residents died at the hands of invading Confederates.[11] When the battle ended, Basil Biggs headed the crews of local black men that collected and buried putrefying bodies. In October, Biggs oversaw the grimmer task of disinterring corpses for reburial in the new Soldiers' National Cemetery.[12]

Gettysburg celebrated emancipation only briefly. Six years after Lincoln's Gettysburg Address, at the commemoration of Gettysburg's first monument, the Soldiers' National Monument, Indiana governor Oliver Morton declared, "The rebellion was . . . brought on by the pernicious influence of human slavery."[13] But the American public soon forgot Morton's remarks. Virginia journalist Edward Pollard's *Lost Cause: A New Southern History of the War of the Confederates* (1866) had reconfigured the war as a chivalric but unsuccessful southern defense of states' rights. Ladies' memorial associations in the South repatriated more than 3,300 Confederate bodies from Gettysburg shortly after Morton's speech.

Sectional wounds were so raw that the Gettysburg Battlefield Memorial Association (GBMA) downplayed ideological differences in favor of somber memorials to the dead.[14] Most early monuments represented three politically neutral themes: allegory, commemoration of sacrifice, and didacticism. The GBMA avoided Roman- and Napoleonic-type memorials imbued with the teleological and ideological undertones that scholars dub "the cult of the fallen soldier."[15] A handful of equestrian statues suggest martial nobility, but Gettysburg has just six elaborate pre-1917 memorials, four of which subsume conflict under more universal metaphors. The Soldiers' National Monument, for instance, is a 60-foot-tall allegorical composition, carved by Randolph Rogers, that personifies History, War, Labor, and Peace on its base. The Genius of Liberty holds a sword in one hand and a laurel wreath in the other. Ground-level panels excerpt Theodore O'Hara's "The Bivouac of the Dead" and invite musings about war's human cost. The nearby New York Monument (1893) is comparable in design. The Monument to the United States

Regulars (1909) and the Lincoln Speech Memorial (1912) are similarly somber. Only the Highwater Mark of the Rebellion Monument (1892) directly references a specific battle, but its nonpartisan design lists those from *both* sides who died on July 3, 1863. The only memorial that approaches the grandeur of monuments built in Europe to commemorate Roman or Napoleonic victories is the Pennsylvania Monument (1910). The dome soars to 110 feet and is topped by the Goddess of Victory and Peace. In keeping with Greco-Roman design, the monument contains carved marble battle friezes and partisan statuary of Lincoln, Governor Andrew Curtin, and Pennsylvania-born Union generals.[16]

Most early monuments simply record where particular units saw action and the names of the commanders. This prosaic pattern is found on all 13 of New Jersey's regimental monuments. New York's lack of iconography is even more startling: just 16 of its 110 monuments and markers (exceeding those of any other state) integrate uniformed soldiers into their design, and only 5 suggest active combat. New York's most controversial monument is that of the Forty-Fourth and Twelfth Infantry at the crest of Little Round Top, because the 44-foot granite castle's design is jarringly different from adjacent structures.[17]

The GBMA insisted on decorum in both memorial design and dedication ceremonies. Typical was a speech delivered by Captain Samuel Fullwood on September 11, 1889, which merely highlighted the action seen by his 102nd Pennsylvania Infantry.[18] The GBMA imposed such rigid standards that it clashed with state monument commissions and hastened Gettysburg's transference to federal control. In 1891 a planned New York State memorial engendered so much opposition from other states—for its 93-foot height, not its content—that the association delayed its approval.[19]

Daniel Sickles, who had lost his leg at Gettysburg, headed the New York State Gettysburg Monument Commission. He was elected to Congress two years later and sponsored the bill that created Gettysburg National Military Park in 1895 and placed it under the control of the War Department. State memorial associations remained powerful, however. The War Department steered clear of design disputes and confined itself to developing park infrastructure. Designs were mostly noncontroversial, though, as nearly all came from northern states and were funded through public channels. Commemorating individual regiments was an easier sell than reaching consensus on delicate political topics.

Sickles dictated the early shape of the GNMP. He had little sympathy for emancipated slaves but even less for the southern planter class.[20] When he attended a Grand Army of the Republic (GAR) encampment at Gettysburg in 1888, Sickles was appalled to find commercial development at the battlefield and lobbied for its preservation.[21] When Congress designated Chickamauga, the site of a Confederate victory, as the nation's first national military park in 1895, Congressman Sickles promptly introduced a bill to give Gettysburg the same status.[22] The Supreme Court's 1896 ruling in *United States v. Gettysburg Electric Railway* upheld eminent domain rights and accelerated preservation efforts. Sickles was so influential in Gettysburg's preservation that when an associate noted there was no statue of him, Sickles snarled, "The whole damn battlefield is my monument."[23]

But where was race at Gettysburg? The importance of emancipation faded because even former firebrands like Sickles had become reconciliationists. Battlefield reunions fueled the shift. The GAR, a fraternal order of Union veterans formed in 1866, held yearly "national encampment" reunions, such as the one Sickles attended in 1888. Early gatherings commemorated Union victory, but by the 1880s, veterans mostly reminisced and fraternized, often with like-minded groups such as the United Confederate Veterans and various Blue and Gray Associations. Blue-Gray reunions, in historian David Blight's words, "buttressed the non-ideological memory of the war. The great issues of the conflict—slavery, secession, emancipation, black equality, even disloyalty and treason—faded from the national consciousness as the nation celebrated reunion."[24]

Yet reconciliation *was* ideological, in that it indirectly embodied Lost Cause ideals. The first important GAR encampment at Gettysburg took place in 1878, and subsequent gatherings grew increasingly larger as the silver anniversary drew near.[25] The 1888 encampment—nearly 1,000 strong—set the tone by making the battle itself the focal point. The Civil War's larger questions gave way to songs, revelry, war stories, and battleground artifacts.[26] This became Gettysburg's interpretive template for the foreseeable future.

By the 1890s, the Civil War had been transformed—in scholar Benedict Anderson's words—into "a great civil war between 'brothers' rather than between . . . two sovereign nation-states."[27] Former adversaries and their offspring took up arms against Native Americans, Hawaiians, Spaniards, and Filipinos and became comrades in wars to reinforce the belief in Anglo-Saxon superiority. McPherson notes that within a single generation of the war's end, schoolchildren were routinely taught that southern secession had little to do with slavery.[28] Young readers poring over the novels of Thomas Page and Oliver Optic or articles in youth magazines would have drawn similar conclusions.[29] Even reconciliation—inherently a positive ideal—assumed a southern bias.

When Sickles attended Gettysburg's fiftieth anniversary commemoration in 1913, reconciliation had obliterated emancipation. More than 50,000 veterans—aged 61 to 112—braved 100-degree heat to attend. Many bivouacked in the 280-acre Great Camp, complete with electricity, 173 field kitchens, medical facilities, and 2,000 cooks.[30] President Woodrow Wilson opened his July 4 speech by stating, "I need not tell you what the Battle of Gettysburg meant"; he then proceeded to ignore secession, slavery, and Reconstruction. In Wilson's telling, Gettysburg brought "peace and unity and vigor, and the maturity and might of a great nation. We have found one another again as brothers and comrades. . . . Enemies no longer . . . our battles long past, the quarrel forgotten."[31]

Forgotten? Not quite! Former Confederate general James Longstreet's widow, Helen, served as a reunion correspondent for the *New York Times* and reported hearing the "rebel yell" throughout the weekend. One son of a Confederate general slashed seven men with a knife when they took umbrage at his anti-Lincoln remarks.[32] If Wilson was reluctant to mention race, Mrs. Longstreet was not. When asked whether she was happy with the war's outcome, she replied, "I'm glad so far as the war itself is concerned, but not for the reconstruction days. . . . Nothing saved us from utter ruin but the Ku Klux Klan, and I'm proud to say that I was a member of it."[33] Reconfiguring Reconstruction as abuse of the South obscured the fact that Gettysburg was a Jim Crow town in 1913 and that African Americans were confined to roles as cooks, porters, and servants. Black residents faced outrages ranging from stereotyping and insult to abuse and assault.[34]

With African Americans confined by Jim Crow and Reconstruction recast as a failure, Lost Cause advocates launched a frontal assault. On June 8, 1917, Virginia became the first former Confederate state to erect a memorial at Gettysburg—a battle scene topped by Robert E. Lee astride a horse.[35] Virginia governor Henry Carter Stuart opened the dedication by assuring, "We are not here to consider the reasons for [this] conflict."[36] Keynote speaker Leigh Robinson had no such qualms. A renowned orator, Robinson called the southern cause "sacred" and thundered, "We assemble to commemorate catastrophe." His rambling twenty-one-page speech compared attempts to limit slaveholding to pre-Revolutionary taxation without representation, cat-aloged alleged states' rights violations, and made the astonishing claim that Virginia would have abolished slavery in the 1840s "but for the intemperance of northern fanatics." He even asserted that slavery had been a positive expe-rience and declared that the slave *trade* was evil, not bondage itself. "The South did not desert the Union," Robinson insisted. "The Union deserted the South."[37]

The Virginia memorial rose during a spate of Confederate monuments so extensive that McPherson quipped, "If the Confederacy had raised propor-tionately as many soldiers as the postwar South raised monuments, the Con-federates might have won the war."[38] Unlike publicly funded and vetted northern monuments at Gettysburg, southern tributes were financed by overtly partisan groups such as Sons of Confederate Veterans and United Daughters of the Confederacy, which imposed Lost Cause readings on events they never witnessed. Needless to say, no monuments honored black soldiers, remembered the victims of postwar lynching in the South, or praised Reconstruction.[39]

Lost Cause ideology resonated with cultural and intellectual trends in American society. The Supreme Court's 1896 ruling in *Plessy v. Ferguson* granted constitutional legitimacy to post-Reconstruction segregation, and Lost Cause motifs such as those in the 1915 film *Birth of a Nation* were ubiq-uitous in American popular culture. Academic interpretations of the war's meaning fell under the interpretive sway of William Archibald Dunning. A professor at Columbia University, Dunning argued that Reconstruction was an utter failure that fostered the tyranny of carpetbaggers and scalawags and poisoned southern racial relations.[40] Slavery scholarship was similarly biased. Ulrich B. Phillips, a prominent early-twentieth-century historian, asserted that slavery was an inefficient economic system maintained beyond its useful life by benevolent and paternal masters.[41] Although Dunning and Phillips had detractors—including W. E. B. Du Bois and Herbert Apthecker—their views held intellectual dominance until Kenneth Stampp published *The Pecu-liar Institution: Slavery in the Ante-bellum South* in 1956.

Southern bias was literally chiseled in stone at Gettysburg. In 1929 North Carolina unveiled a monument sculpted by Gutzon Borglum, of Mount Rushmore fame. It depicts ragged but robust lads gazing toward the enemy, their faces etched in determination. At the dedication, North Carolina gover-nor O. Max Gardner insisted that "the bitterness engendered by [the] terrible struggle . . . has been forgotten" and that "the heritage of our race is imperish-able." Former governor Angus McLean praised the United Daughters of the Confederacy (UDC), which had bankrolled the monument. Both men struck themes in accordance with the prevailing scholarship: that the Civil War had been a valiant conflict among brothers moved by differing senses of duty.[42]

Alabama dedicated a Gettysburg monument on November 12, 1933. A bronze statue commissioned by the UDC portrays two soldiers flanking a scantily draped female representation of Alabama. The wounded combatant hands his ammunition belt to the other soldier, who represents Determina-tion. Determination gazes toward Little Round Top, as the female Alabama points in that direction. The assemblage pays tribute to a Confederate assault on Little Round Top, and its very existence exemplifies the changing views at Gettysburg. During the early 1900s, Alabama had sought to locate a monu-ment *on* Little Round Top and *behind* the Twentieth Maine monument—a position it never attained. Joshua Chamberlain, commander of the Twentieth Maine, complained bitterly, and the War Department denied Alabama the opportunity to place *any* monument on the grounds.[43]

In 1938 the Gettysburg battlefield hosted a seventy-fifth anniversary encampment. Given that the average age of veterans was ninety-four, any future gathering of survivors was unlikely. Speakers again emphasized national unity rather than sectional discord. Today, the gathering is best remembered for the dedication of Gettysburg's most famous "fallen soldier" memorial, the Eternal Peace Light Monument. At a ceremony attended by roughly 150,000 spectators, President Franklin Roosevelt evoked Lincoln's call for "malice toward none, with charity for all," and consecrated the memorial "in the spirit of brotherhood and peace." Speaking of the combatants, Roosevelt intoned, "All of them we honor, not asking under which flag they fought then—thankful that they stand together under one flag now."[44] Roosevelt ignored race, mindful of the southern wing of the Democratic Party. The 1938 reunion was less overtly Jim Crow than that of 1913, and at least one black army veteran, Frank Lilley, took part in the encampment.[45] Still, Afri-can Americans were most visible as porters helping the elderly veterans from trains and as cooks in the mess tents.

Duty, sacrifice, and interfamilial conflict dominated battlefield interpre-tation in the post–World War II decades. Gettysburg buffered itself from pre-vailing social and intellectual winds even as the civil rights movement waxed and revisionist historians—inspired by Stampp and Stanley Elkins—

challenged racist scholarship.[46] The park's visitor center was chockablock with musketry, uniforms, ammunition, and text boards emphasizing martial glory. One display, titled "Brother Fought Brother," told of two former Gettysburg residents—William Culp, who fought in a Pennsylvania regiment, and his brother Wesley, a Virginia infantryman who was killed at Gettysburg.

Brotherly sentimentality was dramatized in the Friend to Friend Masonic Memorial (1993), a tribute to Confederate general Lewis Armistead and Union general Winfield Scott Hancock. Both generals suffered wounds during Pickett's charge, and Armistead's was fatal. Captain Henry Bingham is depicted cradling the dying Armistead, who uses his last breath to command that his watch be delivered to his Masonic brother, Hancock. At the dedication ceremony, Edward Fowler Jr., the grand master of Pennsylvania Masons, implored, "Is there anyone . . . who can look upon this larger-than-life statue . . . without . . . feeling the compassion and charity that comes from the Fatherhood of God and a Brotherhood of Man! Can't you see . . . a compassion that surpasses personal allegiances [and] even the harsh political differences of a bitter war?[47]

The Culp and Armistead stories are compelling, but also telling. The Masonic Memorial is located behind a row of high-traffic tourist shops, and the Culp panel was located on the main floor of the old visitor center. The center's only panel dealing with African Americans—mostly black soldiers— is located in the poorly lighted basement corridor.[48]

During the 1960s the park's biggest outlay was to open a cyclorama housing a decidedly late-nineteenth-century artifact: Paul Philippoteaux's 377-foot mural-in-the-round depicting the final day's conflict at Gettysburg.[49] The painting—though popular among visitors—reinforces a martial romanticism that was fueled by battle pageants conducted by numerous Civil War reenactor organizations that formed between 1961 and 1965. These groups meticulously researched military minutiae, but few seriously engaged the roots or social implications of the Battle of Gettysburg.

More troubling were southern monuments that stoked controversy during a delicate time in U.S. race relations. Between 1961 and 1973—a period of high visibility for the civil rights movement—Arkansas, Florida, Georgia, Louisiana, Mississippi, South Carolina, and Texas all dedicated monuments on Gettysburg's Confederate Avenue. The NPS discouraged racially divisive speeches, but several states embedded provocative messages in their monument designs. The Mississippi and Louisiana monuments are especially suggestive.

The Louisiana monument (1971), designed by sculptor Donald De Lue, is surely the eeriest memorial on the battlefield. From the rear it appears to be the angel Gabriel resting on a splintered tree and gazing at a dead soldier—suitable commentary on the carnage of war. In fact, the muscular figure is St. Barbara, the patron saint of artillery, and she holds a flaming cannonball in her palm. The fallen soldier clutches a Confederate flag, and the assemblage embodies "The Spirit of the Confederacy."[50] The adjacent Mississippi monument (1973), also designed by De Lue, depicts a nearly barefoot Confederate soldier about to use his rifle butt to dash out the brains of a prostrate Union soldier. Marker text speaks of the "righteous cause" and "sacred heritage of honor" for which Mississippians fought, and the site is routinely seeded with fresh Confederate flags when old ones are pilfered.

Other memorials are equally telling. The epitaph on Georgia's monument (1961) reads: "We Sleep Here in Obedience / When Duty Called, We Came / When Country Called, We Died." Here, "Country" refers to the Confederate States of America. South Carolina's memorial (1963) uses a verse by Henry Timrod that speaks of an "abiding faith in the sacredness of States Rights."[51] Florida's memorial (1963) reminds visitors that Floridians fought "for the ideals in which they believed." Of all the Confederate state monuments, only that of Texas (1964) is in keeping with the didactic nature of most Union monuments, perhaps because the Lone Star State's President Lyndon Johnson supported African American civil rights.

By 1990, the GNMP was so thoroughly soaked in the brine of the Lost Cause that an administrative report dealt almost entirely with conservation and monument preservation. According to that document, the major "interpretive issues" facing Gettysburg were outdated regulations and a shortage of guides. A parenthetical nod to the battle's "impact on the community and the country" is the only mention of a review of content.[52] Inattention to interpretive problems is especially surprising, given the dip in park attendance. In 1979 just 994,035 visitors came to Gettysburg, a shocking decline from the 6.8 million who poured in during 1970.[53] In administrative circles, it was as if the civil rights movement and the new social history had never occurred.

But they did. By the 1980s, social historians raised an alarm over the erasure (or rosy depiction) of race in southern plantation museums, and even venerable sites such as Mount Vernon and Monticello were pressured to integrate their narratives.[54] In 1989 Congress linked battlefield funding to reinterpretations "in the larger context of the Civil War and American history, including the causes and consequences of the Civil War and including the effects of the war on all the American people."[55] In August 1990 Gettysburg officials were given their ultimatum.

The initial response was an awkward mix of reconciliation and political correctness. On July 1, 1997, Gettysburg hosted a pageant in which Civil War reenactors and a military honor guard transferred the remains of an unknown Civil War soldier from Arlington National Cemetery to the Soldiers' National Cemetery in Gettysburg. Two "Civil War widows" served as guests of honor: Daisy Anderson, a ninety-six-year-old black woman from Denver, and ninety-year-old Alberta Martin, a white Alabaman. The wheelchair-bound women embraced, and each laid a rose on the grave. Anderson commented that the ceremony "made me think about slavery and what the war was about," but, she added, "We need to keep unity." Martin also stressed unity, and the Reverend Daniel Hans of Gettysburg Presbyterian Church added a histrionic flourish. Of the remains, Hans exclaimed, "We do not know if he wore blue or gray. But we do know he bled red. We do not know if he sang 'John Brown's Body' or whistled 'Dixie.' But . . . as we remember him now, we can all hum 'Amazing Grace.'"[56]

The ceremony was laden with tokenism. Anderson offered a racial balance to Martin, a minor celebrity who toured the South as the "last Confederate widow" and appeared at Sons of Confederate Veterans events. Historian Wayne Flynt remarked, "She became a symbol like the Confederate battle flag," which, Martin insisted, "I don't see nothing wrong with . . . flying."[57] The event at Gettysburg was thoroughly contrived. Neither woman was a "Civil War widow"; both their husbands survived the war, and neither woman was alive when the conflict raged. The Andersons married in 1922, when the bride was twenty-one and Robert Ball Anderson, an escaped Kentucky slave who had served with the 125th U.S. Colored Troops, was a prosperous seventy-nine-year-old Nebraska farmer.[58] Martin's first husband died in 1926, leaving her penniless and with a young son. She moved into her father's house in Opp, Alabama, where she met widower William Jasper Martin, who had fought with the Fourth Alabama Regiment and had a $50-per-month Confederate pension. They married on December 10, 1927; she was twenty-one and he was eighty-one. Martin died on July 8, 1931, and two months later Alberta married his grandson![59]

This was not what revisionists had in mind. The *New York Times* proclaimed, "National Parks Get Low Marks in History," noting that interpretations were "one-sided and disturbingly out of date." Historian Eric Foner complained that there was not "a single mention of slavery" at Gettysburg.[60] The *Boston Globe* sardonically observed: "The willingness to address sharpshooting but not slavery at battlefields is an example of the way American history, a chronicle of the struggle to establish and expand human rights, has become antiseptic in the telling."[61]

Barbara Barksdale conducted black history tours of Gettysburg but caustically noted, "99 percent of the time, I'm the only [black person] there. [The parks] are not ready for blacks to come." When Barksdale made those remarks in 2000, Gettysburg had twenty-three tour rangers, none of whom was black. Congressman Jesse Jackson Jr. took direct aim at racial amnesia by inserting language into an NPS bill that would make *all* funding contingent on integrating slavery into battlefield interpretations.[62]

In Gettysburg, though, more concern was voiced about commercialization—and efforts to tear down a 307-foot observation tower and defeat a casino proposal—than about developing a slavery narrative.[63] As late as 2002, a *Central PA Magazine* story about Gettysburg began: "There's a long-standing joke among American historians that the South may have lost the Civil War, but it won the memory." Katie Lawhon, a battlefield public relations specialist, admitted, "For years, we've been limited to who shot who where." John Latschar, the park's official historian, was more candid: "Our interpretative programs had a pervasive, although unintended, southern sympathy. By . . . emphasizing the heroism of the soldiers, without discussing why they were fighting, we were presenting the reconciliationist memory of the Civil War . . . to the exclusion of the emancipationist vision."[64] When Latschar cited slavery as a cause of the Civil War during a public lecture, the Southern Heritage Coalition sent 1,100 postcards to the secretary of interior demanding his dismissal.[65] It reiterated that demand when Latschar told Canadian interviewers: "Our current museum is absolutely abysmal. . . . It's a curator's museum with no rhyme or reason."[66]

Gettysburg was counting on its new visitor center to address concerns detailed in a 2005 report titled "Presenting Race and Slavery at Historic Sites," which was deeply critical of the slow implementation of mandated interpretive revisions.[67] A brochure for a black history driving tour was developed, but it was not displayed, and visitors had to know of its existence to request it. Private fee-for-service black history tours were available, but they too required special inquiry.[68] The park's most explicit foray into racial dialogue was website curriculum material designed for elementary schools. To access it, one had to log on to the homepage and click the link labeled "For Teachers." This took one to a new page labeled "Curriculum Materials," where one had to search for activities, biographies, and documents pertaining to black history. (A 2008 website redesign was even less intuitive.)[69]

The opening of Gettysburg's visitor center suffered numerous delays, several of which were occasioned by outside opposition. As renowned historians labored to write slavery into new displays, conservative commentator Patrick Buchanan blasted "political correctness at Little Round Top." Historians James McPherson and Eric Foner were denounced as "Marxists" by conservative blogger Gail Jarvis.[70] In another rant, Buchanan denounced new interpretations as "propaganda" and charged the NPS with converting "every battlefield into an endless seminar on the evils of slavery and the South." Buchanan pledged that "the old battlegrounds will become the new battlegrounds of the culture war."[71]

Local controversy fueled conservative wrath. In 2004 Gettysburg College hosted "The Proper Way to Hang a Confederate Flag," a politically charged exhibit. African American artist John Sims placed the Confederate battle flag inside a hangman's noose, suspended it from a makeshift gallows, and announced his intent to "resurrect" the Confederate flag "on my terms." Gallery director Molly Hutton was more forthright: "To John and a lot of African Americans it's a symbol of white power and the hate groups who have adopted it. It's a symbol of visual terror."[72] The Sons of Confederate Veterans declared that southern "heritage" had been "impugned," and the Ku Klux Klan rallied on the battlefield in September 2006 to protest illegal immigration, political correctness, and desecration of the Confederate flag.[73]

The new visitor center finally opened in 2008. It indeed places race within the overall narrative of the Battle of Gettysburg. The films and text boards are informative and in keeping with recent scholarship, as one would expect, given the input from such accomplished historians as Foner, McPherson, Gabor Borrit, Gary Gallagher, Scott Hartwig, Harold Holzer, and Nina Silber. Rooms are organized around themes from Lincoln's Gettysburg Address, and there is a superb twenty-two-minute introductory film narrated by actor Morgan Freeman titled *A New Birth of Freedom*. Most of the information it contains is repeated elsewhere in the museum, but few visitors ducking the film will be able to reassemble Freeman's coherent narrative on race.[74]

The number of items exhibited has been pared from 6,633 to just 1,338.[75] But displays have the pell-mell feel of the food islands popular in college cafeterias, and they encourage more á la carte grazing than intellectual dining. What will visitors infer if they randomly view items such as slave manacles, a playbill for *Uncle Tom's Cabin*, a text board on Dred Scott, a sound bite of "Babylon Is Falling," a fugitive slave handbill, and a portrait of a black man (Lloyd Watts) active in the local AME Zion Church?

The new building's gallery space is 3,000 square feet larger, and its sheer size and remoteness from the battlefield entrance present interpretive challenges. I asked several visitors what they thought of the new center, and they admitted to being confused by the displays; they also thought the center took too long to navigate and said they were anxious to get to the battlefield. Does this impatience mean they will spend little time in the "They Shall Not Have Died in Vain" exhibit, whose superb slide show details slavery and its aftermath?

Once visitors get to the battlefield, a major problem remains: many monuments praise the righteousness of the Confederate cause, but none deals with African Americans.[76] Gettysburg cannot bear the entire burden of engaging the public in the larger issues of war, slavery, Reconstruction, reconciliation, and race, but because it is the most publicly identified symbol of the Civil War, it must do more to take on the issues raised by Lincoln and Douglass.

There is still too much attention to "colored rags" and not enough to people of color. Nearly $15 million was spent to restore the archaic Philippoteaux mural, a sum that could have been used more appropriately. In 2002 the park unveiled a statue of Elizabeth Thorn, the wife of Evergreen Cemetery's caretaker. This statue is the first to honor the women of Gettysburg, another glaring oversight whose rectification is long overdue. But why is Thorn, a white woman, honored for burying more than a hundred bodies following the Battle of Gettysburg when there is no monument for Basil Biggs and his African American crews?[77] Could this be one of the reasons why African Americans seem to be underrepresented among visitors to the park?

Gettysburg remains more attractive to military buffs than to minorities. More than 15,000 reenactors staged Pickett's Charge on July 3, 2008, and an estimated 60,000 people watched a 2011 reenactment, but there were few black faces in the photographic record of the events.[78] Gettysburg's visitor center speaks to "The Unfinished Work of the Declaration of Independence," but no battlefield monument parallels that of Robert Gould Shaw and the Massachusetts Fifty-Fourth Volunteer Infantry that graces Boston Common or the African American Civil War Memorial in Washington, D.C. Gettysburg's presentation of race is tepid when compared with nearby Harpers Ferry, West Virginia, where one can find displays not only on John Brown's raid but also on slavery, black education, Reconstruction, the Niagara Movement, and the twentieth-century civil rights movement. Until Gettysburg manifests race with something more substantive than a Tammany regimental monument, its staff will receive periodic reminders that the civil rights movement and the new social history *did* occur.

## Notes

1. Quoted in David Blight, *Beyond the Battlefield: Race, Memory, and the American Civil War* (Amherst: University of Massachusetts Press, 2002), 96.

2. "National Park Service," http://www.gettysburg.travel/media/news_detail .asp?news_id=197 (accessed June 24, 2010); "National Park Service," http://www .nature.nps.gov/stats/ (accessed June 24, 2010). In 2009 there were 1,013,002 official visitors to Gettysburg. Chickamauga had the second highest total at 992,448, followed by Fredericksburg and Spotsylvania, Fort Sumter, Vicksburg, Manassas, Shiloh, and Antietam. The NPS listed 1,031,554 visitors to Gettysburg in 2010, but local and state tourism boards regularly claim that more than 3 million people visit annually. For 2010 NPS figures, see "National Park Service," http://www.nature.nps .gov/stats/viewReport.cfm (accessed September 14, 2011).

3. James O. Horton, "A Look at How We Think about Slavery," *Washington Post*, November 22, 1998.

4. Abraham Lincoln, "The Gettysburg Address," November 19, 1863, http:// americancivilwar.com/north/lincoln.html (accessed January 16, 2009).

5. Abraham Lincoln, "Second Inaugural Speech," http://www.bartleby .com/124/pres32.html (accessed January 7, 2009).

6. Alan Elsner, "Parks Service Puts New Face on U.S. Civil War," *National Post* (Toronto), December 24, 2002.

7. Peter Vermilyea and William Tally, "War for Freedom: African American Experiences in the Era of the Civil War: Gettysburg," http://www.nps.gov/gett/ forteachers/upload/GETT%20War%20for%20Freedom%20Complete.pdf (accessed February 3, 2009).

8. James Paradis, *African Americans and the Gettysburg Campaign* (Lanham, Md.: Scarecrow, 2005).

9. Ibid. See also Victoria Donohoe, "The Black Soldiers at Gettysburg," *Philadelphia Inquirer*, November 28, 1999. African Americans helped build earthworks on the Wrightsville side of the river, which delayed Early's advance. When Early broke through on June 28, 1863, they burned the mile-long bridge connecting Wrightsville to Columbia, thereby thwarting a possible attack on Harrisburg.

10. James M. McPherson, *Crossroads of Freedom: Antietam* (New York: Oxford, 2002), 139.

11. Margaret Creighton, *The Colors of Courage; Gettysburg's Forgotten History: Immigrants, Women, and African Americans in the Civil War's Defining Battle* (New York: Basic, 2005); Donohoe, "Black Soldiers at Gettysburg."

12. Paradis, *African Americans and the Gettysburg Campaign.*

13. David Blight, "Decoration Days: The Origins of Memorial Day in North and South," in *The Memory of the Civil War in American Culture*, ed. Alice Fahs and Joan Waugh (Chapel Hill: University of North Carolina Press, 2004), 104.

14. "An Act to Incorporate the Gettysburg Battle-Field Memorial Association," April 30, 1864, appendix to Harlan Unrau, "Administrative History: Gettysburg National Military Park and National Cemetery" (NPS report, 1991).

15. George Mosse, *Fallen Soldiers: Reshaping the Memory of the World Wars* (New York: Oxford, 1990); Susan-Mary Grant, "Landscapes of Memory," *Today's History*, March 2006, 18–20; Edward T. Linenthal, *Sacred Ground: Americans and Their Battlefields* (Urbana: University of Illinois Press, 1991).

16. To view the monuments mentioned in this essay, go to http://gettysburgmonuments.com/.

17. My on-site battlefield observances were cross-referenced with D. Scott Hartwig and Ann Marie Hartwig, *Gettysburg: The Complete Pictorial of Battlefield Monuments* (Gettysburg: Thomas Publications, 1995).

18. "Dedication of the Gettysburg Monument 102nd Regiment Infantry," address by Samuel L. Fullwood, September 11, 1889. See also "Several Pennsylvania Monuments Dedicated Yesterday," *New York Times*, September 12, 1889.

19. "New York at Gettysburg: The Monument Question Settled at Last," *New York Times*, March 1, 1891. New York contributed and lost more soldiers to the Battle of Gettysburg than any other state.

20. Thomas Keneally, *American Scoundrel: The Life of Notorious Civil War General Dan Sickles* (New York: Nan Talese, 2002); W. A. Swanberg, *Sickles the Incredible: A Biography of Daniel Edgar Sickles* (New York: Scribner's, 1956). Sickles's youthful admiration of the South soured when his wife had an affair with Marylander Philip Barton Key, the son of Francis Scott Key. In 1859 Sickles killed Key, allegedly in a duel, although many viewed it as murder. Sickles left Congress in 1861 and quit the Democratic Party; he rose through army ranks during the war and was a major general in 1863. His leg was shattered by a cannonball near Little Round Top during a

controversial maneuver he led that countermanded General Meade's orders. Sickles insisted that his actions prevented Lieutenant General James Longstreet from taking Little Round Top; critics argued that he so weakened the Union position that Longstreet almost broke through.

After the war Sickles became a Republican Party stalwart. During Reconstruction he commanded the Second Military District until he was fired by President Andrew Johnson. Sickles viewed this as an act of revenge by his southern Democratic enemies. In November 1876 Sickles sent telegrams to the Republican governors of Florida, Louisiana, and South Carolina and advised them not to certify their states' presidential ballots, thereby tipping the electoral balance from Samuel Tilden to Republican Rutherford B. Hayes.

21. Keneally, *American Scoundrel.*

22. "An Act to Establish a National Military Park at Gettysburg, Pennsylvania," 28 Statute 651, February 11, 1895.

23. Daniel Eicher, *Gettysburg Battlefield: The Definitive Illustrated History* (San Francisco: Chronicle Books, 2003), 274.

24. Blight, *Beyond the Battlefield*, 103.

25. Richard W. Sears, "Pilgrim Places: Civil War Battlefield, Historic Preservation, and America's First National Military Parks, 1863–1900," *CRM: The Journal of Heritage Stewardship* 2, no. 1 (Winter 2005), http://crmjournal.cr.nps.gov/04_article.cfm?issue=Volume%202%20Number%201%20Winter%202005 (accessed January 8, 2009).

26. James Weeks, *Gettysburg: Memory, Market, and an American Shrine* (Princeton, N.J.: Princeton University Press, 2003), 84–115.

27. Benedict Anderson, *Imagined Communities: Reflections of the Origins and Spread of Nationalism* (London: Verso, 1991), 201.

28. James McPherson, "Long-Legged Yankee Lies: The Southern Textbook Crusade," in Fahs and Waugh, *Memory of the Civil War in American Culture*, 64–78; Nina Silber, *The Romance of Reunion: Northerners and the South, 1865–1900* (Chapel Hill: University of North Carolina Press, 1993).

29. Alice Fahs, "Remembering the Civil War in Children's Literature in the 1880s and 1890s," in Fahs and Waugh, *Memory of the Civil War in American Culture*, 79–93; James Marten, ed., *Lessons of War: The Civil War in Children's Magazines* (Wilmington, Del.: SR Books, 1999).

30. "The Great Reunion of 1913," http://www.nps.gov/archive/gett/getttour/sidebar/reunion13.htm (accessed February 3, 2009).

31. Woodrow Wilson, "Address at Gettysburg," July 4, 1913, in John T. Wooley and Gerhard Peters, *The American Presidency Project*, http://www.presidency.ucsb.edu/ws/ (accessed February 3, 2009).

32. "Mrs. Longstreet with Blue and Gray," and "Old Soldiers Defy Gettysburg

Heat," *New York Times*, July 2, 1913; "Seen by Mrs. Longstreet" and "Stabbed at Gettysburg," *New York Times*, July 13, 1913.

33. "Old Soldiers Defy Gettysburg Heat."

34. James Weeks, "A Different View of Gettysburg: Play, Memory, and Race at the Civil War's Greatest Shrine," *Civil War History* 50, no. 2 (June 2004): 175–91. Gettysburg sponsored such unsavory events as "coon dunks" and watermelon-eating contests.

35. The monument was designed and sculpted by F. William Sievers of Richmond and cost $50,000 (the equivalent of more than $842,400 in 2010 dollars).

36. Henry Carter Stuart, "Address at the Dedication of the Virginia Memorial at Gettysburg," June 8, 1917, http://www.civilwarhome.com/gettysburgvamemorial .htm (accessed February 3, 2009).

37. Leigh Robinson, "Address at the Dedication of the Virginia Memorial at Gettysburg," June 8, 1917, ibid.

38. McPherson, "Long-Legged Yankee Lies," 64.

39. For a graphic account of the violence unleashed against African Americans, see Stephen Budiansky, *The Bloody Shirt: Terror after Appomattox* (New York: Viking, 2008).

40. William Dunning wrote *Reconstruction—Essays on the Civil War and Reconstruction* (1898) and *Reconstruction, Political and Economic, 1867–1877* (1907). His students produced dozens of works (mostly state studies) largely reiterating the myth of the benevolent southern planter class.

41. Ulrich Phillips first made his mark with a 1901 book on the states' rights debate. Key works such as *American Negro Slavery* (1918) and *Life and Labor in the Old South* (1927) were preceded by articles articulating the benevolent slave owner thesis.

42. "Ceremonies Attending the Presentation and Unveiling of the North Carolina Memorial on the Battlefield of Gettysburg," July 3, 1929, http://www.gdg.org/ Research/Monuments/ncmon.html (accessed January 9, 2009).

43. Glenn LaFantasie, *Gettysburg Heroes: Perfect Soldiers, Hallowed Ground* (Bloomington: Indiana University Press, 2008), 80–82.

44. Franklin D. Roosevelt, "Address at the Dedication of the Memorial on the Gettysburg Battlefield, Gettysburg, Pennsylvania," July 3, 1938, in Wooley and Peters, *The American Presidency Project*.

45. "The Horse Soldier," http://www.horsesoldier.com/catalog/reunion.html (accessed February 3, 2009). Lilley, aged ninety-five, did not fight at Gettysburg. He enlisted in the 124th U.S. Colored Troops on September 21, 1864.

46. Stanley Elkins's *Slavery: A Problem in American Institutional and Intellectual Life* was first published in 1959. Aspects of this work have proved contentious, but it may be the most influential book written on slavery. Elkins inspired myriad scholars

to defend or attack his ideas, and his work anticipated the "new social history" that emerged in the 1960s.

47. "Friend to Friend Masonic Memorial," http://www.masonicworld.com/education/files/jun03/friend_to_friend_masonic_memoria.htm (accessed February 3, 2009).

48. The corridor was dark all eight times I visited between 2000 and 2007.

49. The cyclorama was praised when it opened in 1961, but design flaws necessitated expensive patchwork. When the Philippoteaux mural was removed from public view in 2005, it required intensive conservation work. Critics blasted the decision to build a new cyclorama and to restore the mural as money wasted on an outmoded concept.

50. Frederick Hawthorne, "Gettysburg: Stories of Men and Monuments," http://www.gdg.org/Research/Authored%20Items/monmen.html (accessed February 3, 2009).

51. Ibid. Henry Timrod (1828–1867) was known as the "Poet Laureate of the Confederacy," and his verses allegedly inspired men to volunteer. Poor health limited his own military activity; he died of consumption at age thirty-eight.

52. Unrau, "Administrative History," 353–57.

53. "National Park Service," http://www.nature.nps.gov/stats/viewReport.cfm (accessed January 28, 2009).

54. Jennifer Eichstedt and Stephen Small, *Representations of Slavery: Race and Ideology in Southern Plantation Museums* (Washington, D.C.: Smithsonian Press, 2002).

55. The quote is from Public Law 101-214m, December 11, 1989, and is cited in Dwight Pitcaithley, "'A Cosmic Threat': The National Park Service Addresses the Causes of the American Civil War," in *Slavery and Public History: The Tough Stuff of American Memory*, ed. James Oliver Horton and Lois E. Horton (New York: New Press, 2006), 169–86.

56. "Battlefield Burial," *Gettysburg Times*, July 2, 1997.

57. "Alberta Martin, Last Widow of Civil War Veteran, at 97," *Boston Globe*, June 1, 2004.

58. "Daisy Anderson, 97, Widow of Former Slave and Union Soldier," *New York Times*, September 26, 1998. Robert Anderson was killed in an automobile accident in 1930.

59. "Alberta Martin, Last Widow." William and Alberta Martin had a son just ten months after their marriage. Alberta also outlived her third husband, Charlie Martin (William's grandson), who died in 1983.

60. *New York Times*, November 15, 1997. Technically, Foner was incorrect: the panel in the basement of the visitor center mentioned "slavery."

61. David Shribman, "New Reality for Civil War Sites," *Boston Globe*, May 9, 2000.

62. Melia Bowie, "Seeking More Diversity in Telling Gettysburg," *Philadelphia Inquirer*, October 31, 2000.

63. See George Archibald, "House Puts Brakes on Gettysburg Mall Plan," *Washington Times*, February 12, 1999; Mary Leonard, "Strife Revisits Gettysburg," *Boston Globe*, February 23, 1999; "Waging War for Gettysburg's Soul," *Guardian* (London), June 21, 1999; David Eldrige, "Tall Observation Tower Felled in Gettysburg," *Washington Times*, July 4, 2000; Frederick Kunkle, "Preservationists Insist Battlefields Sell Themselves," *Washington Post*, October 5, 2005; Teresa Mez, "At Gettysburg, a New Battle: Urban Sprawl," *Christian Science Monitor*, August 24, 2007.

64. Lori Myers, "Beyond the Battlefield," *Central PA Magazine*, September 2002. This publication is mailed to subscribers of WITF, a public television station broadcasting from Harrisburg and Hershey.

65. James O. Horton, "Slavery in American History: An Uncomfortable Dialogue," in James O. Horton and Lois E. Horton, *Slavery and Public History*, 35–56.

66. Elsner, "Parks Service Puts New Face."

67. Sandra Heard, "Presenting Race and Slavery at Historic Sites: A Cooperative Research Project between the National Park Service and the Center for the Study of Public Culture and Public History at the George Washington University," July 25, 2005.

68. The NPS is not supposed to promote private enterprises, although there has never been a shortage of information at Gettysburg concerning private lodging, dining, and retail opportunities. In 2008 I obtained a copy of a brochure titled "The Underground Railroad in Adams County." It is a promotion piece for a private tour and, like the driving tour map, must be requested specifically.

69. See http://www.nps.gov/features/warforfreedom/ (accessed January 9, 2009).

70. Gail Jarvis, "Political 'History,'" http://www.lewrockwell.com/jarvis/jarvis30 .html (accessed January 7, 2009).

71. Patrick Buchanan, "Gettysburg about to Become Politically-Correct," http:// www.rense.com/genera133/gts.htm (accessed August 31, 2008).

72. Deborah Fitts, "Gettysburg College to Host Confederate Flag, Lynching Exhibit," *Civil War News*, September 2004.

73. Deborah Fitts, "SCV Keeps Focus on Gettysburg College after Flag Exhibit," *Civil War News*, December 2004; Deborah Fitts, "KKK Plans Sept. 2 Rally at Gettysburg Battlefield," *Civil War News*, August 2006.

74. When I visited on a hot day in August, the center was packed but *A New Birth of Freedom* was sparsely attended, perhaps because the admission fee of $10.50 for adults and $6.50 for children (aged six to eighteen) is steep for such a short film.

The price includes entry into the refurbished cyclorama. The fee was $7.50 while the cyclorama was closed.

75. Deborah Fitts, "Gettysburg Museum; Visitor Center Opens April 14," *Civil War News*, April 2008.

76. John Heiser to Robert Weir, November 27, 2007.

77. Kathryn Jorgensen, "Gettysburg Civil War Women's Memorial Dedication Nov. 16," *Civil War Times*, November 2002; Paradis, *African Americans and the Gettysburg Campaign*.

78. *Hanover Evening Sun*, June 30, 2008. For the 2011 reenactment, see "Gettysburg Daily," http://www.gettysburgdaily.com/?p=11540 (accessed September 14, 2011).

# 5

# Civil War Battlefields for Future Generations

## *The Relationship between Battlefield Preservation and Popular Culture*

*Susan Chase Hall*

In 2007 noted author, economist, actor, and pop icon Ben Stein stood before an audience at the National Press Club in Washington, D.C. He did not look out onto a crowd of uninterested students and discuss the science of volcanoes or call out for "Bueller" in his famous monotone. Instead, he enthusiastically addressed the importance of battlefield preservation as a powerful educational tool. He stood as a spokesperson for the Civil War Preservation Trust (CWPT), a private nonprofit dedicated to the preservation of Civil War battlefields. At the unveiling of the CWPT's report on the most endangered Civil War battlefields, Stein announced, "Our children's children will be able to walk these sacred fields and just have a hint of an idea of the sacrifice it took to build this glorious nation." Stein highlighted the concepts and rhetoric central to the CWPT's mission—battlefields are sacred, physical, and authentic artifacts of the Civil War, documenting where soldiers sacrificed their lives for the nation's future. If preserved, they can give future generations of Americans direct access to the Civil War and its legacy.[1]

Stein's presence at the CWPT's press conference suggests a certain rapport between battlefield preservation and popular culture. However, popular culture has a long, complicated relationship with Civil War sites. In the latter half of the nineteenth century, preservation served as a reactionary tool against modernity, popular culture, and change. Its national resurgence in the latter decades of the twentieth century indicated a similar relationship. When the CWPT was established in 1999, however, the organization took a new, proactive approach to popular culture, using it, ironically, as a tool to help mobilize the masses in support of historic preservation. This budding relationship between former foes was not without setbacks, pitfalls, and concerns, however. The nation's popular trends had a deeply contentious history with battlefield preservation that could not be easily shaken.

Historian Timothy Smith describes the 1890s as the "golden age" of battlefield preservation. Congress and Civil War veterans targeted the battlefields of Antietam, Gettysburg, Shiloh, Chickamauga/Chattanooga, and Vicksburg for preservation and interpretation, introducing them as "natural," undisturbed reminders of a glorified Civil War past. They promoted battlefields as physical embodiments of historical memory—visibly documenting the Civil War, its heroic soldiers, and their gallant military maneuvers. In other words, the preserved sites acted as patriotic memorializations of the Civil War.[2]

Although focusing on the past, battlefield preservation responded specifically to the uncertainties of the modern industrial society that developed at the end of the nineteenth century. Americans were excited by the increase in mass production, mass consumption, and mass entertainment. To some, however, modernity threatened life as they knew it, ushering in an increasingly foreign and urban population. Preservationists argued that people were not just faceless masses crowded into the urban environs of factories, tenements, and nickelodeons. According to historian Mary Abroe, battlefield sites counteracted modernity by announcing "to industrial America the power of individualism in shaping history." In commenting on the early preservation efforts at Antietam, a *New York Post* writer exclaimed, "The increase of population and the march of material progress have not disturbed Antietam . . . which today looks about as it did in 1862." Yet Marguerite Shaffer's examination of tourism and nationalism in *See America First* finds selectivity and exclusivity in the preservation and presentation of the nation's historic sites—attracting Civil War veterans and the nation's elite. Preservationists' motivations rested on a romantic theory of nationalism that excluded the working class, immigrants, and urban hubs.[3]

Nearly 100 years later, Civil War battlefields experienced a second wave of preservation. This resurgence in the 1980s and 1990s resulted, in part, from the conflict over teaching standards and historical memory known by scholars as the Culture Wars. Historians Gary Nash and Edward Linenthal, among others, define the Culture Wars as a heated conflict between conservatives and liberals, as well as academics and the public, over history, political correctness, and memory. Debates included who has a right to determine what the public learns, why, and how. In October 1994 Lynne Cheney, chairwoman of the National Endowment for the Humanities, argued that Americans had developed a case of "historical amnesia"—forgetting their roots. Cheney and her supporters placed some of the blame on popular culture. In a speech on the Senate floor, Republican senator Slade Gorton questioned, what "is a more important part of our nation's history for our children to study—George Washington or Bart Simpson?" Cheney argued that popular culture—television, video games, and the like—desensitized the American people to what made the nation great and special.[4]

In reality, her accusation of historical amnesia was misleading. The American people had not lost their connection with the past. Instead, they had lost touch with a past that Cheney viewed as appropriate—one that tended to be exclusive and selective. They had lost touch with "traditional," patriotic history that glorified and sanitized America's superiority. Textbooks *and* television lacked a positive tone of affirmation, emphasizing social conflict, encouraging debate rather than celebration, and introducing new minority figures rather than highlighting the traditional white male leaders.[5]

In the context of the Civil War, the Culture Wars fueled a dispute over how the war and its battlefields should be defined and remembered. Some people continued to argue that battlefields could be tools of patriotic education and remembrance, providing visitors with a visual account of military heroism and tactical achievements. Others believed that preserved battlefields could account for the larger narrative of the war, including the role of slavery as one of its causes.

Despite its origins in the divisive culture debates, the second wave of battlefield preservation was a more inclusive movement than the first. Preservationists did not necessarily agree on *why* the battlefields should be preserved, but they often agreed on a common enemy: popular culture. Conservatives and liberals; upper, middle, and working classes; academics and the general public united against popular culture because it threatened to destroy these physical tools of remembrance and education. They saw Civil War battlefields as instruments of memory making—whether patriotic or controversial—and these sites were being threatened by large-scale commercial consumerism. This trend toward commercialism encouraged the construction of shopping centers to support consumption and nearby housing developments to create a demand base.

By the end of the 1980s, strong reactionary measures against large-scale commercial consumerism and suburban development had begun. In 1987 the Association for the Preservation of Civil War Sites was organized in Fredericksburg, Virginia, in response to the loss of battlefield land at Ox Hill/Chantilly in Fairfax County. The association received a fair amount of attention in 1988 as a result of the "Third Battle of Manassas"—an effort to prevent the Hazel-Peterson Company from constructing a shopping mall adjacent to the Manassas National Battlefield. The Civil War Trust—a private, nonprofit organization headquartered in Hagerstown, Maryland—was organized by the secretary of the interior to combat Hazel-Peterson and prevent development more quickly than the federal government's bureaucracy could move.[6]

After the strip-mall crisis near Manassas, the preservation predicament peaked in the mid-1990s with the emergence of a new threat. The public debate resulting from this threat reiterates the truly complex relationship between battlefield preservation and popular culture. In the fall of 1993, Michael Eisner, chairman and CEO of the Walt Disney Company, announced that Disney planned to open a new theme park thirty-five miles southwest of Washington, D.C. Disney's America would consist of 3,000 acres in Prince William County, Virginia, where Disney planned to "[celebrate] the nation's richness of diversity, spirit and innovation." In addition to its spin on history, Disney highlighted the economic benefits to the state and county. Local and state governments supported the project because it provided employment opportunities and encouraged suburban growth. However, there was backlash from people who feared changing the region's landscape—specifically, the sprawl a theme park would create in northern Virginia.[7]

While the antidevelopment argument reflected the sentiments of the nineteenth century's preservation elite, the debate over Disney's America introduced battlefield preservation to a national audience—many of whom loved Disney—by challenging the company's ability to accurately present history. The *New York Times* argued that Disney "excels at creating artificial wonderlands aimed at 10-year-old, television-nurtured sensibilities. Nothing wrong with that, in Anaheim or Orlando." Together, opponents formed

Protect Historic America—dedicated to publicly contesting Disney's America. Well-known figures such as author Shelby Foote, Richard Moe of the National Trust for Historic Preservation, and Ken Burns, creator of PBS's *Civil War* series, brought their names to the fight. Scholars James McPherson, C. Vann Woodward, and John Hope Franklin also contributed. Pulitzer Prize–winning author David McCullough traveled across the country lecturing against "MickHistory," which would destroy the "authentic" and "real" battlefields of Manassas. He argued, "The very idea of bulldozing the land of Lee, Stonewall Jackson, . . . [and] the legions who fought and died there . . . exposes those who want to do it as having no heart for the history they want to exploit." Rex Ellis, the director of museum programs for the Smithsonian Institution, announced that he was opposed to "having fun at the expense of slavery." Disney could not properly convey the nation's uncomfortable and unpleasant history because of its slant toward entertainment.[8]

Importantly, not everyone spoke out against Disney's America. To gain support for its project, Disney publicized that some noteworthy historians and preservationists had been recruited as consultants, among them Eric Foner, James Oliver Horton, and the Association for the Preservation of Civil War Sites. Although they did not necessarily endorse the project wholeheartedly, these consultants wanted to ensure that Disney did not create another artificial wonderland. Rather, they hoped Disney would use its status as a pop icon to provide historical sensitivity and accuracy for public consumption. If used correctly, popular culture had the power to introduce the Civil War and its history to a much larger audience.[9]

Despite the consultants' receptive attitude toward popular culture, most of the growing preservation community remained reticent. Even though they differed on the battlefield's meaning, opponents agreed that Disney's venture epitomized popular culture's threat to battlefield preservation and interpretation. In October 1994 the company dropped its plans for Disney's America—a huge victory for the battlefield preservation community. Yet the complicated battle involving popular culture, commercial development, and historic preservation was just heating up. It grew at a dramatic rate in the late 1990s and early 2000s as preservationists pitted themselves against popular culture. Many believed only one side could win the fight.[10]

To more effectively counter the threats to America's Civil War battlefields, the Civil War Trust and the Association for the Preservation of Civil War Sites merged in 1999 to form the Civil War Preservation Trust. Under the guidance of its president, Jim Lighthizer, the CWPT is dedicated to preserving "America's significant Civil War battlefields by protecting land and educating the public about the vital roles those battlefields played in directing the course of our nation's history." Picking up the battle flag of its predecessors, the CWPT emphasizes the hallowed nature of the battlefields where Union and Confederate soldiers lost their lives. At a 2001 press conference, Lighthizer announced, "These battlefields are the last tangible reminders of sacrifices made by those who wore the blue and gray. When we destroy the land, we destroy the memory of that sacrifice." The CWPT has also vowed to combat elements of popular culture—most notably mass consumer commercial development and cookie-cutter houses. As Lighthizer argued, "A strip mall or townhouse development can be built practically anywhere. An historic battlefield cannot." Significantly, the CWPT appropriated a tool introduced in the fight against Disney's America: grassroots mobilization. Through the establishment of coalitions, the CWPT has reasserted that battlefield preservation is not an elite, exclusive, or academic endeavor; although targeting the culture of the "masses," the CWPT's preservation program simultaneously promotes the active involvement of the general public.[11]

The CWPT's first grassroots campaign focused on Spotsylvania County, Virginia, located fifty-five miles south of Washington, D.C. The county has been—and continues to be—a hotbed for developers. In 2002 the CWPT learned that the Dogwood Development Group wanted to purchase and develop the Mullins property—core battlefield land next to the Fredericksburg and Spotsylvania National Military Park. The Mullins property included the Chancellorsville battlefield, which witnessed the flanking of General Oliver Howard's Eleventh Corps and the mortal wounding of Confederate general Thomas "Stonewall" Jackson. Dogwood's plan, known as the "Town of Chancellorsville," called for the construction of more than 2,000 homes and 2.3 million square feet of commercial space. Developer Ray Smith argued that the "town" would boost the area's economy; its three hotels and other tourist-friendly amenities would bring more visitors to the nearby battlefield parks. But the plan threatened the land involved in the first day of fighting at Chancellorsville, which served as key open space for the national park and nearby Route 3. To counter the proposal and protect the battlefield, the CWPT, other preservationists, environmentalists, concerned local citizens, and historians joined forces and formed the Chancellorsville Coalition.[12]

In late March 2003 Spotsylvania County's Board of Supervisors unanimously voted against rezoning the Mullins property to accommodate the "town." That vote ended Dogwood's grand plan and gave the Chancellorsville Coalition and the CWPT a win in their battle to protect history from sprawl. It did not, however, prevent the development of the important battlefield land. In an effort to protect at least some of the acreage, the coalition worked with Tricord, a conservation-friendly development group. The CWPT preserved 140 acres of core battlefield, while Tricord developed the remaining acreage in a preservation-friendly manner. The victory over Dogwood confirmed the CWPT's capabilities and became a model for grassroots efforts in future preservation fights. However, it also articulated the need to be flexible and to work with preservationists' supposed foes.

In 2003 South Carolina put the lessons learned at Chancellorsville to the test. The city of Charleston, known for its historic architecture, was facing the threat of new housing developments on Morris Island. On July 18, 1863, African Americans in the Fifty-Fourth Massachusetts Regiment volunteered to spearhead an assault on Battery Wagner on Morris Island in Charleston Harbor. It was their first large-scale battle, and for many, including Colonel Robert Gould Shaw, it was their last. In 2003 developers requested that the island be rezoned to permit the building of houses on the secluded, scenic space. This led to the formation of the Morris Island Coalition to oppose its development. Although Charleston denied the rezoning request, the fight did not end. Another developer's proposal included twenty million-dollar homes—considered high density on the small island. The CWPT and other preservationists believed that construction on this historic island would destroy the view, disrupt the wildlife sanctuary, and cause erosion.

Despite the city government's refusal to rezone the land, Morris Island succumbed to the pressures of popular culture two years later. In January 2005 the owner of Morris Island's development rights, Harry Huffman, placed it on eBay with an asking price of $12.5 million. His intention was to sell Morris Island to someone looking to buy a private island and build one home. By the winter of 2005, however, Florida-based Ginn Company, a firm specializing in resort development, had purchased the property from the eBay developer. Ginn intended to develop 300 acres on the north end of the island. Although a preservation-friendly developer eventually purchased that acreage, a portion of Morris Island still remained vulnerable. In May 2008 a coalition of preservationists that included the CWPT, the Trust for Public

Land, the state of South Carolina, and the city of Charleston raised $2.9 million to purchase the land still owned by Ginn. Lighthizer sent a letter to members explaining that the other coalition partners were counting "on CWPT to be the 'final dollars in' ($100,000) for this amazing pact." CWPT members came through, making the sale possible and preserving the remaining acreage on Morris Island.[13]

In addition to theme parks, subdivisions, commercial developments, and resorts, the CWPT has opposed another form of popular culture: gaming. In 2005, when investors proposed the construction of a casino at Gettysburg, Pennsylvania—site of the Union's famous July 1863 victory—Lighthizer lamented that "Gettysburg is such an inappropriate location for a casino it is hard to believe that the proposal is receiving serious consideration." Governor Ed Rendell agreed: "I wouldn't want a casino two blocks from the Liberty Bell in Philadelphia and . . . I wouldn't want it anywhere close to . . . Gettysburg." The CWPT and other preservationists established the No Casino Gettysburg and Stop the Slots coalitions, fighting for twenty months to sway the Gaming Board's vote. When the board rejected the casino in December 2006, this prompted Lighthizer to enthusiastically exclaim, "It is no exaggeration to say that this is the most significant battlefield preservation victory since the defeat of Disney's proposed theme park at Manassas." Although this victory was monumental, it did not mark the end of the threat to the Gettysburg battlefield.[14]

A few years later another group proposed the construction of the Mason-Dixon Gaming Resort a half mile from the battlefield park. The CWPT again partnered with local and national preservation organizations to oppose the development. In the spring of 2011, when the Gaming Board voted against the proposed resort, Lighthizer announced, "By stating that the hallowed ground of America's most blood-soaked battlefield is no place for this type of adults-only enterprise, they have reiterated the Commonwealth of Pennsylvania's commitment to its priceless history." The CWPT and its coalition reminded Pennsylvania residents that it was their obligation to protect Gettysburg so that the legacy of the Union and Confederate soldiers who fought there would not be lost to "wanton and unnecessary" entertainment.[15]

In an effort to maintain its loyal members, the CWPT relies on traditional patriotic language highlighting the heroism and sacrifice of both Union and Confederate soldiers—the same rhetoric used by veterans in the 1890s.

Battlefields are hallowed grounds that deserve preservation rather than sacrifice to the whims of commercial development and consumer trends. This language appeals primarily to Civil War buffs, history-minded individuals who live near battlefields, and those with a Civil War ancestry. The larger, national population of potential supporters, donors, and members does not necessarily respond to such rhetoric. Although unwilling to go as far as using a history-themed amusement park to spread its message, the CWPT has recognized the need to reach more people through mass entertainment. As demonstrated by Ben Stein's act of affirmation, the trust is using new, creative tools to gain a wider base of support. Under the direction of Jim Campi, the director of policies and communication, the organization relies on television, film, music, social networking, and smart phone technology to garner national attention and new members. Ironically, popular culture and mass consumerism benefit the preservation community even while working against it.

In 1994 Lynne Cheney pointed an accusatory finger at the film and television industry, blaming it, in part, for America's "historical amnesia." But for the CWPT, film and television are key tools in garnering support. It relies heavily on well-known networks, names, and faces to attract attention to its cause. In 2001 the History Channel's *Save Our History* created an episode focusing on endangered battlefields and featuring CWPT president Jim Lighthizer. In 2002, twelve years after its first airing, PBS and Ken Burns rebroadcast the *Civil War* series, which held more than 27 million viewers' interest over five consecutive days. Strategically situating itself among students and Civil War buffs, the CWPT placed regional ads during commercial breaks. During the campaign to save Morris Island, the CWPT used the popularity of the 1989 film *Glory* to gain support. Numerous movie and television stars also came out to back the preservation community's efforts at Gettysburg. In addition to David McCullough and Ken Burns, composer John Williams and actors Matthew Broderick, Stephen Lang, and Sam Waterston spoke out against the gaming casino. Waterston lent his famous voice to an anticasino television ad that featured dramatic violin music as he listed the sites and legacies that would be lost if the casino was built. He asked viewers, "Will you save this for your children? What about your grandchildren? . . . Will you take the offer or choose to save Gettysburg for future generations? . . . Save Gettysburg today. What will be your legacy?" Like Ben Stein in 2007, Waterston used his famous persona to circulate the message posed and promoted by the CWPT.[16]

The CWPT also relies on new films and TV shows to draw in supporters. In 2003 the nonprofit released its report on the most endangered battlefields to coincide with the premiere of Ted Turner's *Gods and Generals*, starring Robert Duvall and Jeff Daniels. Director Ron Maxwell, actor Stephen Lang, and author Jeff Shaara appeared at the press conference to bring awareness to the cause. Maxwell adamantly defended the CWPT, proclaiming, "Those who cannot understand or appreciate the awesome importance of sacred or hallowed places should not be allowed to forever destroy these treasures and to deprive them from those who do, the living and the yet unborn." Their popularity helped spread the CWPT's message to a wide audience. Six years later Duvall spoke out against the construction of a Walmart near the Wilderness battlefield in Orange County, Virginia. At a press conference, Duvall announced that "the Walmart Corporation has it within its power to be a savior of the Wilderness Battlefield . . . they have the ability to protect this critical piece of American history for generations to come." The CWPT used Duvall's star power to put the Wilderness front and center in the organization's efforts.[17]

In 2009 the CWPT added the Wilderness battlefield to its list of most endangered battlefields. The press conference unveiling its report included Academy Award–winning actor Richard Dreyfuss. Like others before him, Dreyfuss used his celebrity to gain supporters. Although his face was new to the cause, his message was not: "These hallowed battlegrounds should be national shrines, monuments to American valor, determination and courage. Once these irreplaceable treasures are gone, they're gone forever." The rhetoric was the same, but after the press conference, Dreyfuss and Lighthizer made their way to the African American Civil War Memorial in Washington, D.C., to lay a wreath. By doing so, the CWPT honored the memory of African Americans during the Civil War, but it also encouraged present-day African Americans to join its organization.[18]

Along with film and television personalities, the CWPT turns to famous musicians and singers for support. Country music star Darryl Worley appeared at the trust's annual conference in Nashville in 2004. Made famous by his patriotic, post-9/11 hit "Have You Forgotten?" (2003), Worley had been the featured entertainer at the Republican National Convention and the U.S. Army All-American Bowl. He grew up near the Shiloh battlefield, so the Civil War was near and dear to the singer's heart. Because Tennesseans knew Worley well, he could help the CWPT build credible relationships with local landowners. Jim Campi explained, "Part of [the CWPT's] mission is to go out and talk to landowners who own historic land and try to convince them to sell to [the organization], but there's a big difference between us doing it and Darryl Worley doing it." Other music stars who have gotten involved in the CWPT's cause include Vince Gill and his wife Amy Grant, who performed at a benefit concert at the Carnton Plantation to raise money to preserve the Franklin battlefield at the Country Club of Franklin. Trace Adkins helped the CWPT introduce its report on the most endangered battlefields in March 2008. He observed that, "as a father of five, I believe it is critical that I protect a legacy that belongs not just to my family but to our entire nation." In true CWPT fashion, Adkins wanted to preserve Civil War battlefields not just for his own children but for all future generations.[19]

The CWPT also reaches out to the public through popular literature. In 2004 best-selling author Jay Winik spoke out in favor of the CWPT. The author of *April 1865: The Month that Saved America* described battlefields as "living breathing monuments that tell us stories about the war and the people who fought it . . . they deserve to be saved and cherished." In its April 2005 edition, *National Geographic* magazine featured an article titled "Civil War Battlefields: Saving the Landscape of America's Deadliest War." Author Adam Goodheart acknowledges that America's commercialism hindered his Civil War experience in Spotsylvania County, Virginia: "I sit in backed-up traffic along Route 1, a fumy strip of asphalt lined with gas stations, fast-food joints, and car dealerships. As I enter the once sleepy, now suburban village of Spotsylvania, my first glimpse of the battlefield is of the neat headstones of a Confederate cemetery—behind the parking lot of a 7-Eleven." Although Goodheart laments the nation's fast-food, retail-chain trend, *National Geographic* itself uses another popular trend to share its stories: the Internet.[20]

The CWPT also depends heavily on the Internet in its offensive approach. Most notably, it relies on the World Wide Web to reach a wide audience of possible supporters via online networking and marketing. In 2002 the CWPT used funding from the HTR Foundation to redesign its website (www .civilwar.org). The new website featured an online shop, online donations and memberships, and a Political Action Center where individuals could write to their local and state representatives about battlefield preservation issues. Through this website, the CWPT accessed a wider, more tech-savvy support base and expanded its grassroots efforts.[21]

Within just a few years, however, this cutting-edge website was out of date. So in 2008 the CWPT announced plans to redesign its website again. The new website includes animated battle maps, video messages, and the CWPT's Amazon bookstore. It is a key component of grassroots advocacy as well—being used in conjunction with the Stop the Wilderness Walmart and No Casino Gettysburg websites. For the first time, contestants in the CWPT's annual photography contest could submit their entries digitally, "allowing more people to participate than ever before." As Lighthizer explained, "Viewing stirring images enhanced by today's technology will help all Americans see what precious resources our historic sites are, and why we must work to preserve them." The CWPT is committed to using the latest twenty-first-century technology to help preserve the nineteenth-century past.[22]

In an effort to keep up with developing technology without having to update its website every few years, the CWPT relies on other well-known online media, media marketing, and social networking sites. In March 2009 the CWPT joined the world of online television when it created the CWPT Battlefield Channel on YouTube, where it posts numerous video clips of press conferences, battlefield tours, and television ads. The CWPT can also be found on Twitter, Flickr, and Facebook, where it hopes to reach a younger audience.

By 2011 the CWPT was not just using technology in its proactive approach to battlefield preservation; it was speaking out in favor of it and suggesting that twenty-first-century technology goes hand in hand with the nineteenth-century past. Modernization need not be the foe of battlefield preservation. In fact, digital communication via phones and computers is key to proactive preservation and awareness. In January 2011 the CWPT officially changed its name back to the Civil War Trust (CWT), and Jim Lighthizer unveiled the new name and logo in a digital video message to members. He announced that the change modernizes the organization's look, making it accessible to more Americans.[23]

The modernization effort also includes the CWT's new "text to give" program. In explaining its significance, Lighthizer notes that texting is a way to "marry modern technology to the events of the past. . . . We believe that by embracing technology history will come alive for a new generation of preservationists." Singer and CWT board member Trace Adkins put the program to the test—encouraging his concert fans to "text to give" via a promotional video. Texting, Adkins explained, allows his fans to give to battlefield preservation anywhere and at any time.[24]

Ultimately, embracing the modern technology that defines popular culture will enable the CWT to reach a wider audience—stepping far outside its original boundaries and its reliance on Civil War buffs, local landowners, and academic historians. This new approach—actively working with popular culture through twenty-first-century technology—coincided with the beginning of the Civil War sesquicentennial (2011–2015). The CWT's social networking presence grew even stronger when it founded the Civil War Sesquicentennial Network, creating a special 150th anniversary website (www.civilwar150. org) that, with the help of Google Marketing, became the most popular sesquicentennial site online. The network's Facebook page became the second most popular Civil War–dedicated Facebook site. As of June 2013, more than 27,000 people had "liked" the network.[25]

Perhaps the most forward-thinking use of modern technology was the development of the CWT's iPhone "battle app" in honor of the sesquicentennial. The application uses GPS technology to follow users as they tour battlefields and provides pertinent information about the sites. More than 21,000 iPhone users have downloaded the apps for the Gettysburg, Fredericksburg and Spotsylvania, and Manassas battlefields. Because of their popularity, the CWT added a Chancellorsville and Malvern Hill app at the end of 2011 and an Antietam app for its 150th anniversary in September 2012. The newest additions include apps for the Vicksburg battlefield and Appomattox Court House.[26]

iPhones—along with iPads, iPods, and iTunes—define today's popular culture. In fact, the teenagers who grew up with Apple's technological advances are known as the iGeneration. This generation does not know a world without mobile devices, text messaging, and social networking. They define themselves primarily through today's ultimate product of popular culture: the smart phone. The Civil War Trust is now turning to this iGeneration as the next cohort of members and financial supporters. It believes this generation will help solidify a relationship with popular culture, demonstrating that battlefield preservation does not have to work against popular culture to preserve the past.

Yet, as the iGeneration becomes the standard-bearer of the CWT, new concerns emerge. The benefits of technology and popular culture are clear in terms of CWT membership, donations, and preserved acreage. However, the benefits of technology raise new questions regarding the very fabric and authenticity of the battlefield experience the CWT promotes. Do these new products enhance visitors' experiences, or do they encourage visitors to interact with their smart phones rather than the landscapes around them? Will technology such as 3-D imaging eliminate the need to visit battlefields in person, making preservation and the CWT obsolete? Only time will tell if a strong reliance on popular culture will devalue the very efforts preservationists intend to support.

## Notes

The following notes indicate the influence of popular culture, particularly the Internet, on the CWPT and its efforts.

1. Ben Stein, Civil War [Preservation] Trust, "Testimonials," http://www .civilwar.org/take-action/membership/testimonials.html (accessed December 1, 2011).

2. Timothy Smith, *The Golden Age of Battlefield Preservation: The Decade of the 1890s and the Establishment of America's First Five Military Parks* (Knoxville: University of Tennessee Press, 2008), 114.

3. Mary Abroe, "'All the Profound Scenes': Federal Preservation of Civil War Battlefields, 1861–1990" (PhD diss., Loyola University of Chicago, May 1996), 162; *New York Post* quote from "Antietam Unchanged," *Butte (Mont.) Weekly Miner*, April 7, 1898, 13; Marguerite S. Shaffer, *See America First: Tourism and National Identity, 1880–1940* (Washington, D.C.: Smithsonian Institution Press, 2001), 168.

4. Gary Nash, Charlotte Crabtree, and Ross E. Dunn, *History on Trial: Culture Wars and the Teaching of the Past* (New York: Vintage Press, 2000); Edward T. Linenthal and Tom Engelhardt, *History Wars: The Enola Gay and Other Battles for the American Past* (New York: Holt Paperbacks, 1996), 232.

5. Roy Rosenzweig and David Thelen's publication of *Presence of the Past: Popular Uses of History in American Life* (New York: Columbia University Press, 1998), demonstrates the falsehood of Cheney's statements.

6. A. Wilson Greene, "Association for the Preservation of Civil War Sites," *CRM Bulletin* 13, no. 5 (1990): 3; "Group Fights Developers for Civil War Sites," *Bangor (Maine) Daily News*, June 4–5, 1988, 11.

7. Walt Disney Company, "Plans Unveiled for 'Disney's America' Near Washington, D.C.," news release, November 11, 1993; "Virginia, Say No to the Mouse," *New York Times*, February 24, 1994.

8. "Virginia, Say No to the Mouse"; Bob Hohler, "For Disney, Civil War Battle," *Boston Globe*, May 12, 1994, 3; Michael Janofsky, "Learned Opposition to New Disney Park," *New York Times*, May 12, 1994; Bentley Boyd, "Disney Learns History Lesson," *Sun Journal* (Lewiston, Maine), October 3, 1994, 27.

9. "Noted Historians and Prominent Civil War Preservation Organization to Join Disney's America," *PR Newswire* (Burbank, Calif.), February 14, 1994.

10. Boyd, "Disney Learns History Lesson."

11. CWPT Mission Statement; CWPT, "Civil War Preservation Trust Unveils Most Endangered Battlefields Report," February 27, 2001, http://www.civilwar.org/aboutus/news/news-releases/2000-news/civil-war-preservation-trust-6.html (accessed December 1, 2011).

12. Matthew Barakat, "Civil War Development Site Draws Fire," *Morning Star News* (Wilmington, N.C.), January 1, 2003.

13. Associated Press, "Historic Morris Island Is up for Sale on eBay," *Beaufort (S.C.) Gazette*, January 28, 2005, 3A; CWPT, "Historic Morris Island Battlefield Again under Threat," December 21, 2005, http://www.civilwar.org/aboutus/news/news-releases/2005-news/historic-morris-island.html (accessed December 1, 2011); Fergus M. Bordewich, "Preservation or Development at Morris Island?" *Smithsonian Magazine*, July 2005, http://www.smithsonianmag.com/history-archaeology/glory.html (accessed December 1, 2011); letter from James Lighthizer to Members, n.d., http://www.civilwar.org/battlefields/batterywagner/jim-lighthizers-letter-on.pdf (accessed December 1, 2011); CWPT, "From the President," in *2008 Annual Report* (Washington, D.C., 2008), 6.

14. CWPT, "Civil War Preservation Trust Condemns Plan to Build Casino at Gettysburg," May 7, 2005, http://www.civilwar.org/aboutus/news/news-releases/2005-news/civil-war-preservation-trust-4.html; CWPT, "Civil War Preservation Trust Applauds Rendell's Remarks about Gettysburg Casino," September 17, 2005, http://www.civilwar.org/aboutus/news/news-releases/2005-news/civil-war-preservation-trust-7.html; CWPT, "Gaming Control Board Rejects Slots Parlor Near Gettysburg Battlefield," December 20, 2006, http://www.civilwar.org/aboutus/news/news-releases/2006-news/gaming-control-board-rejects.html (all accessed December 1, 2011).

15. CWPT, "Proposed Gettysburg Casino Location Rejected by Pennsylvania Gaming Control Board," April 14, 2011, http://www.civilwar.org/aboutus/news/news-releases/2011-news/gettysburg-casino-rejected.html (accessed December 1, 2011).

16. PBS News, "PBS's Rebroadcast of Ken Burns's 'The Civil War' Resonating with Viewers across the Country," October 1, 2002, http://www.pbs.org/aboutpbs/news/20021001_civilwarperf.html (accessed December 1, 2011); CWPT, "Proposed Gettysburg Casino Location Rejected"; "Save Gettysburg—Television Ad," November 16, 2010, http://www.youtube.com/cwptbattlefields#p/search/0/G4n93XD9Bt4 (accessed December 1, 2011).

17. CWPT, "Civil War Preservation Trust Unveils Most Endangered Battlefields Report," February 11, 2003, http://www.civilwar.org/aboutus/news/news-releases/2003-news/civil-war-preservation-trust.html (accessed December 1, 2011); CWPT, "Duvall, Lawmakers Speak out against Proposed Walmart at Virginia's Wilderness

Battlefield," May 4, 2009, http://www.civilwar.org/aboutus/news/news-releases/2009-news/duvall-lawmakers-speak-out.html (accessed December 1, 2011). In January 2011 Walmart dropped plans to build a supercenter near the battlefield.

18. CWPT, "Richard Dreyfuss Joins Civil War Preservation Trust to Unveil Report on Endangered Battlefields," March 18, 2009, http://www.civilwar.org/aboutus/news/news-releases/2009-news/richard-dreyfuss-joins-civil.html (accessed December 1, 2011).

19. John Gerome, "Using Music to Aid Preservation," *Free Lance-Star* (Fredericksburg, Va.), November 1, 2004, D3; CWPT, "Celebrity Supporters," in *2004 Annual Report* (Washington, D.C., 2004), 9; CWPT, "Trace Adkins Joins CWPT to Unveil Report on Endangered Battlefields," March 12, 2008, http://www.civilwar.org/aboutus/news/news-releases/2008-news/trace-adkins-joins-cwpt-to.html (accessed December 1, 2011).

20. CWPT, "Civil War Preservation Trust Unveils Most Endangered Battlefields Report," February 24, 2004, http://www.civilwar.org/aboutus/news/news-releases/2004-news/civil-war-preservation-trust-2.html (accessed December 1, 2011); Adam Goodheart, "Civil War Battlefields: Saving the Landscape of America's Deadliest War," *National Geographic*, April 1005, http://ngm.nationalgeographic.com/ngm/0504/feature5/index.html (accessed December 1, 2011).

21. The author was the webmaster of this new website.

22. CWPT, "CWPT Vows to Use the Latest Modern Technology to Save Historic Land," April 23, 2008, http://www.civilwar.org/aboutus/news/news-releases/2008-news/cwpt-vows-to-use-the-latest.html (accessed December 1, 2011); CWPT, "Civil War Goes Digital through New Civil War Preservation Trust Photography Contest," June 3, 2008, http://www.civilwar.org/aboutus/news/news-releases/2008-news/civil-war-goes-digital.html (accessed December 1, 2011).

23. CWPT, "National Preservation Group Unveils New Name, Logo to Mark Beginning of Civil War Sesquicentennial," January 10, 2011, http://www.civilwar.org/aboutus/news/news-releases/2011-news/civil-war-trust-announcement.html (accessed December 1, 2011).

24. CWT, "Join Country Superstar Trace Adkins and 'Text to Give' in Support of Historic Preservation," August 18, 2011, http://www.civilwar.org/aboutus/news/news-releases/2011-news/trace-adkins-text-to-give.html (accessed December 1, 2011). See the video at http://www.civilwar.org/video/support-the-civil-war-trust.html.

25. As of August 2011, the website was second only to the *New York Times* Civil War page. Jim Campi, e-mail correspondence with the author, August 18, 2011; CWT, "Civil War Sesquicentennial Network," https://www.facebook.com/profile.php?cropsuccess&id=742497655#!/civilwar150network.

26. Jim Campi to author, August 18, 2011, and November 4, 2012.

# Section III

# The Memory of the Civil War over Time

# 6

# The Cultural Politics of Memory

## Confederate Women and General William T. Sherman

*Jacqueline Glass Campbell*

Conventional wisdom about wartime tells us that men are both the protectors and the threat. The army regulates the exercise of violence against an enemy, and it exacts kudos and support from the protected. Logically, then, if noncombatants find their guarantees of protection gone, they will withdraw their support and help end the war. During the American Civil War, Union general William T. Sherman recognized this relationship of battlefront and home front. And although fighting had occurred on home ground before, Sherman deliberately targeted the southern home front as a means of simultaneously destroying both military resources and the morale of the southern people. There is perhaps no greater villain than Sherman in the popular memory of the Civil War, particularly among southerners.[1]

It was in the wake of a major turning point in the war that Sherman devised his plan to bring the fight to the southern home front. In September 1864 Ulysses S. Grant and Robert E. Lee were entrenched around Petersburg, Virginia. In Georgia, Sherman's campaign to take Atlanta was being frustrated by a determined Confederate force that, despite sustaining heavy losses, still clung to the city. This apparent stalemate in the field, coupled with increasing war casualties, escalated a downward slide of morale in the North that could be reversed only by a major Union victory. Sherman's capture of Atlanta could not have come at a more propitious time, and his success had major political and military repercussions. The fall of the city ensured Abraham Lincoln's election to a second term, which in turn indicated to the Confederacy that the North would continue the fight. This message was clearly brought home to the South when, on November 16, 1864, Sherman left Atlanta with an army of 60,000 handpicked men on a path to the Atlantic Ocean.

With three out of four eligible southern men in the army, the southern home front was a world of women. Into this world Sherman led an army of hardened veterans, cutting through the very heart of the Confederacy across Georgia to the sea and continuing northward through the Carolinas. Sherman believed he was sending the message that Confederate men were incapable of protecting their families, but when his soldiers brought the war into southern households, they were frequently astounded to encounter fierce, determined white women. Confederate soldiers also recognized the strength of their female kin, and many urged their wives and mothers to meet the Yankee invaders with defiance, even with firearms. Nevertheless, despite many examples of such stern female resistance, within two decades these virulent women had been recast as the defenseless victims, while Sherman and his army of demons became the personification of all Yankee atrocities.

The cultural politics of memory served the southern quest to win a postwar moral victory and also allowed white southern men to reclaim authority in a world of emancipated African Americans. This essay explores the process by which Confederate women's roles became depoliticized while Sherman became the devil incarnate in the southern mind—a process that embroiled Sherman and Confederate women in an eternal war.

Sherman's march through the Confederate heartland was an invasion of both geographical and psychological space. The Union army constructed a vision of the southern landscape as military terrain. When the invasion and punishment of the Confederacy became an invasion of homes populated mostly by women and children, many Union soldiers struggled with a series of conflicting emotions and often expressed misgivings about intruding into female domestic space. When white women faced the demons of their worst nightmares, fear frequently turned to anger as they saw the enemy destroying their homes and belongings. In fact, Union soldiers were often surprised at the intensity with which many Confederate women defended their property and dignity. When Union cavalry invaded her home in Barnwell,

South Carolina, Jane Sams determined to "remain as firm as possible." In no uncertain terms she told the soldiers that she "expected civil and polite treatment from gentlemen." One soldier tried to intimidate her by claiming that the Union army had no "gentlemen" and was composed of convicts "released for the purposes of subjugating the rebellion," but she refused to be shaken. "My strength had been given to me by an Almighty Power," she wrote, "and could not be taken from me by a Yankee's venomous tongue."[2]

It was their own venomous tongues that many white women used as their primary weapon against the Yankee invaders, eliciting responses of both reluctant admiration and moral castigation from the enemy. A New Jersey lieutenant remarked on how "determined" and "resolute" he found the white women of the South. One of his comrades commented that the "tender sex" was a match for the "roughest and most brutal" soldier when it came to the use of "obscene words." Branding them "she devils," some Union men even blamed southern women for prolonging the war, displaying a vindictiveness and a zeal for blood that seemed unprecedented.[3]

Such overt manifestations of female power disconcerted Union soldiers, who carried their own set of domestic values into the war—values based on the image of home as a "haven." One Union officer expressed sympathy for those women who sat "with grief depicted on their countenances, or tears rolling down their cheeks." But those southern women who "vent[ed] their feelings in curses and rude epithets" made it difficult for him to overlook "what the women of the South have done to keep up this war."[4]

The genesis of such a moral judgment—that some southern women were unworthy of protection—suggests a misinterpretation of what constituted appropriate female behavior in the South. Both North and South placed great importance on a woman's display of outward submission to male authority. In the South, however, this was not based on a belief that women were inherently delicate creatures; rather, they chose to restrain their inner strength for the benefit of social harmony. It was on the basis of this understanding that southern women frequently managed farms and plantations alone. Thus, when threatened by an invading army, these women saw themselves as responsible for both the material and the cultural survival of the family, while remaining within a traditional framework. The conflicting interpretations of appropriate gender behavior caused soldiers deep misgivings about their actions, while they allowed white southern women to defend themselves vigorously without fear of bodily harm.[5]

It was the ability to draw on an inner strength that allowed certain Confederate women to demand protection as their right, rather than fall into the role of defenseless victim and beseech the mercy of invading soldiers. In anticipation of the wartime roles of plantation women, southern author Daniel Hundley wrote that although the "raging tornado" would be met by men who would "march with banners flying and to the music of the fife and drum," there was "a power behind the throne greater than the throne itself." When a Confederate soldier in the Virginia trenches learned that Sherman's soldiers were an imminent threat to his family in South Carolina, he warned his female kin that they were likely to lose all their material possessions. His words expressed no concern over their physical safety; instead, he advised his mother and sisters that boldness was the key to weathering the storm. They should meet any "scoundrel" who attempted to enter their home with a gun. "Should any of them intrude or go rummaging round the place, don't hesitate to shoot," he wrote. Another Confederate soldier cautioned his wife not to become either "irritated or intimidated" but to keep "cool control" of herself and be "punctiliously polite." Yet, he cautioned, "there must be no cringing, no timidity . . . [and] if it should be necessary, speak the truth and the whole truth if you die for it."[6]

When southern white women decided to take a bold stance against enemy soldiers, they saw their roles as vital to the preservation of both the southern family and the southern nation, linking their personal survival to the larger goal of southern independence. And when threatened by an invading army, they frequently responded with a passion worthy of both mothers and warriors. In fact, Sherman's strategy of using portions of the Confederate home front as a political tool rendered civilians political actors in their own right. Many Confederate women in Sherman's path eschewed their perceived role of passive victim and demanded protection as their right rather than resorting to prayers and tears, which would have added humiliation to their predicament. In this context, moral outrage, material suffering, and strongly internalized cultural values encouraged many women to resist with whatever power they could muster.

A devastated home front was Sherman's most immediate goal. He trusted that his invasion would leave in its wake a population focused on obtaining food and shelter, rather than on supporting further political and military conflict. Many civilians were both materially and spiritually exhausted. However, disillusionment and war weariness were not enduring emotions for all citizens; these feelings were frequently just the first stage in a process of rededication to southern independence.[7]

Confederate women filled their correspondence with vows to continue the struggle, disabusing Yankees of the notion that they had been subdued. Drawing on that same sense of honor that was so vital in keeping southern soldiers in the field, many white women took pride in the fact that they had faced Sherman's army of "demons" unflinchingly, declared their enduring support for cause and country, and earned a reputation as virulent Rebels. It has been argued elsewhere that Confederate women's commitment to the cause waned in the final months of the war, as their many sacrifices seemed increasingly useless. But, having survived an invading army without the protection of their men, many now called on southern soldiers to remain at their posts and exact vengeance on the enemy. One woman wrote to "entreat" her husband not to consider returning to "give us security," ending her letter with the words "Don't Come!" Another encouraged her soldier brother to keep up his spirits and "whip Sherman." Confronting the enemy allowed these women to share in the sense of actively defending the Confederacy, with a consequent upsurge in patriotism.[8]

Having met Sherman's soldiers face-to-face, they now had an enemy on whom to vent their wrath. One young woman heard that people's spirits were even better after the Union attack. "Now that they have experienced their [the Yankees] tender mercies, they are resolved to persevere unto the bitter end," she wrote. And many women renewed their faith by focusing on the Army of Northern Virginia and, more specifically, on its leader, General Robert E. Lee, the personification of Confederate manhood. Against this image they created his nemesis in the shape of Sherman and his army of demons.[9]

Yet declarations and prayers were swept away in the maelstrom of war as the Union army overpowered Confederate forces in Virginia. When Confederate women heard the news of Lee's surrender, they mourned his demise as they would mourn the loss of a family member, and they anticipated the humiliation of defeat. South Carolinian diarist Mary Chesnut most succinctly expressed the emotions of grief and humiliation when she wrote of "Lee's tears—outsiders' sneers—Yankees' jeers."[10]

Nevertheless, even the news of Lee's defeat did not quash their hopes. Many remained convinced that although the South had been overpowered, it would never be conquered, believing that "the next generation would see the South free and independent." "Our Southern blood rose in stronger rebellion than ever," wrote one young woman, "and we all determined that, if obliged to submit, never could they *subdue* us."[11]

In Columbia, South Carolina, the city that saw the greatest devastation at the hands of Sherman, a young woman wrote that the only question remaining was "not 'what hope?' but 'what new bitterness?'" For two weeks after making this entry in her diary she felt such anger that she feared to express her sentiments in words. Finally she steeled herself to take a walk among the ruins of her once grand city. It was a moonlit night and her mind waxed poetic:

> As far as the eye could reach only
> specter-like chimneys and the shutter
> walls, all flooded over by the rich moonlight
> which gave them a mysterious but mellow
> softness, and quite took from them the
> ghastly air which they wear in the sunlight.
> They only lacked moss and lichens and tangled
> vines to make us believe we stood in some ruined
> city of antiquity.

In these romantic images lay the seeds of the Lost Cause ideology that would flourish in ensuing years.[12]

It is true that in the immediate postwar period a disparity of reactions between men and women became increasingly apparent. This was in sharp contrast to wartime, when many women had become central players in the arena of war. In the aftermath, soldiers could identify with comrades, even across enemy lines, through the mutual recognition of duty fulfilled; women were denied a similar sense of closure. But they would not go gently into their passive roles as rehabilitators of southern men and guardians of southern memory. "Why does not the President call out the women?" asked Columbia resident Emma LeConte. "We would go and fight . . . we would all better die together." One young North Carolinian committed to her journal sentiments she dared not speak aloud. "Men of the South, are you dead to all shame?" she asked. How could they accept their "present subjugated state? . . . A thousand times it were better that you had all fallen on your swords," she continued. Mary Chesnut, however, believed that women were forced to be realistic when it came to material losses, for men had the option to "die like a patriot."[13]

Some time later a South Carolina woman tried to explain the gendered nature of the healing process. All women, in her opinion, preferred "death" or "annihilation" over reunion, and she suspected most men felt the same way. But because it was impracticable for southern men to express such opinions, they associated with Yankees for purely pragmatic reasons. If women criticized their menfolk for such actions, it would only "increase their pain." Their duty, then, was to "keep pure the fire of patriotism" on behalf of a "conquered people."[14]

Scholars have noted that war simultaneously reinforces and disrupts women's roles. On the one hand, it offers men the opportunity to prove their manhood by defending a female population waiting passively on the home front; on the other, it immediately presents women with the challenge of new roles and responsibilities in the absence of their men. If this argument is extended to an examination of men's roles, however, we find a similar contradiction.[15] At its inception, the Civil War offered an opportunity for all white men to display their heroism and prove their manhood. For southern men, raised in an honor-bound society that required outside recognition, the war provided an ideal arena in which to prove themselves. War held a similar appeal for northern men, who found their path to independence increasingly obstructed by a burgeoning commercial capitalism. The reality of war did not always live up to its promise, however, as regimentation, drill, and subordination often overshadowed displays of heroism.[16]

Paradoxically, as the currents of war led women (especially those who endured invasion of the home front) into an increasingly political role that required demonstrations of courage and honor, the soldier's daily regimen consisted largely of drills, marching, and fighting, all of which focused on the male body. The most extreme case was the practice of men paying for substitutes to fight in their place, a system that historian Reid Mitchell describes as "a sort of grotesque speculation on the part of poor men; if they had nothing else to trade in, they had their own bodies." And just as horrific, it was the body parts of injured soldiers—amputated arms and legs, bandaged heads, injured knees, frostbitten fingers and toes—that increasingly represented the cost of war.[17]

Yet in the postwar years this objectification of men's bodies was reinterpreted as a celebration of masculine valor. Scholars of masculinity have argued that as the horrendous memories of mangled bodies faded, war was increasingly viewed as a vital component in shaping men's characters. By the 1880s and 1890s this new ideal aided in the reunion process, as northerners embraced those warlike qualities they had once identified as characteristic of southern men.[18]

These same decades saw an outpouring of acclaim for southern womanhood. However, those virulent women who had confronted the enemy with sharp words and vehemence had now become a classless category. In the words of Confederate general Wade Hampton, they deserved "one virtuous name." Husbands and sons, who had once urged their wives and mothers to meet the Yankee invader with defiance and even firearms, now exhorted them to "honor the brave dead and strew flowers on their graves." White women's new duty was the rehabilitation of southern men; they were urged to "reanimate their [men's] self respect, confirm their resolve and sustain their personal honor."[19] No longer vital players in their own right, southern women had become the appendages of heroes who had glorified themselves on the battlefield. This image of a dedicated and loyal southern womanhood fed into a Lost Cause rhetoric—a rhetoric the North would eventually come to embrace.[20]

Several scholars have now challenged this myth of southern womanhood, applying much more nuanced analyses to Confederate women's roles in the Civil War and in the construction of historical memory. Yet the quest to debunk this mythical image has resulted in the counterclaim that Confederate women became increasingly disillusioned and disaffected by all things military. This essay has offered an alternative interpretation—that Confederate women responded to war in diverse ways and that firsthand experience in facing the enemy often reinvigorated waning loyalty to the Confederate cause. Yet, given this range of responses, the challenge is to explain why this image of loyal but largely passive southern womanhood has been accepted for so long.[21]

As their strength and determination became abstractions, funneled into symbolic roles of sacrifice rather than active struggles for nation, white women of the South became icons to be protected by men. This depoliticization of Confederate women's roles served multiple purposes, not least of which was to reinvigorate southern manhood. In the southern mind, Yankee actions and Sherman's strategy in particular became egregious acts of war rather than noble and heroic discharges of duty on the battlefield. Southerners' military efforts, in contrast, became symbols of courage and fortitude, especially when they were outnumbered and outgunned.

The domestication of white women was not, however, simply about high-lighting southern men's bravery; it was also about reclaiming authority in the postwar South. White southern men laid the blame for black men's emancipation at the feet of the North and then used the threat of black-on-white rape as a powerful tool to control the behavior of white women and to terrorize the black population. Thus, the memory of the Civil War glorified the role of white soldiers, occluded the role of blacks, and rendered white southern women victims of northern atrocities and potential victims of black rapists.[22]

Issues of racial and sexual control were, moreover, inextricably entwined with larger military and ideological issues. Military leaders were subject to the cultural politics of memory, and none more so than Robert E. Lee. In 1866 southern historian E. A. Pollard suggested that the "affection and esteem" inspired by Lee was a result of his "epicene nature." This mixture of masculine and feminine qualities may have held special appeal for southern women, particularly those who had confronted his nemesis, Sherman. Moreover, Lee was the only Confederate general whose victories held the promise of southern independence. According to historian Gary Gallagher, "Lee's stunning victories between June 1862 and May 1863 created a mystique that lasted until the final stages of the war." By the turn of the century, southern rhetoric had transformed the general into a symbol of all that was noble about the war.[23]

As a direct antithesis to Lee, Sherman came to represent the lowest level of barbarism. In 1881 ex–Confederate president Jefferson Davis published his *Rise and Fall of the Confederate Government*, a book that John Marszalek describes as a "literary assault on Sherman's method of warfare" that transforms the general into the devil incarnate. Davis accuses Sherman of having only "mediocre" military talent and more aptly describes him as a man driven by savage instincts whose primary goal was to devastate the home front. This demonization of Sherman, combined with southerners' continuing quest to win a moral victory, obscured women's role in shaping Confederate nationalism.[24]

In a world of emancipated blacks, white southern women also played an essential, if passive, role in ensuring racial purity and white supremacy. The misogynistic qualities of chivalry that purported to protect white women from black men's rampant sexuality placed them under intense scrutiny, and it is possible that there were more restraints on elite white women's behavior than in the antebellum period. But although this was a time of cultural trans-formation, it appeared on the surface as cultural persistence.

White southern women were not, however, silent victims of the forces of racial and sexual control; they took an active and vocal role in the creation of historical memory. Their voices took on two diametrically opposed tones. The more familiar is exemplified in a 1911 address to the first college chapter of the United Daughters of the Confederacy. The speaker informed the girls of Winthrop College, South Carolina, that they could "conceive of no nobler and honored name than a Daughter of the Confederacy." Young southern women had a special distinction and a responsibility to remind the world what their fathers had fought for and "to compel for them respect and rever-ence for a noble cause and a worthy fight." She reminded them that "in hon-oring our sires and their patriotism, we honor our selves."[25]

Other southern women were less sentimental, perhaps because they had experienced the war more directly. By the time their memoirs were printed, southern women who had lived through the war had spent years nurturing bit-ter seeds of resentment. Their voices often expressed more rancor and frustra-tion than respect and reverence. The northern view dominated in published works of women's wartime experiences until the early twentieth century, and the first books praising northern women's patriotism did not hesitate to com-pare their virtues with southern female vices. One such volume published in 1867 claimed that history provided few example of more "fiendish" behavior than that of Confederate women. The authors hurled accusations of malevo-lent crimes ranging from displays of "malice" and "petty spite" to demands for the murder of prisoners of war and trophies consisting of "Yankee skulls, scalps, and bones for ornaments." So it is not surprising that when southern women had the opportunity to tell their own stories, any evenhanded portray-als of Yankee soldiers had all but disappeared, and Sherman was fated to live in opprobrium as the scourge of the Confederacy.[26] No one encapsulates this out-look more accurately than Elizabeth Meriwether, who observed:

> In those dark days just after the close of the war hate was a feeling that came into many a southern woman's breast. The southern men were too busy trying to retrieve their fallen fortunes, but the women—they had more time to brood over the wrongs that been done them. . . . To this day I cannot truthfully say I love Yankees, but my dear husband who fought four years in the Confederate army,

seemed to feel no bitterness in his heart, not even in the years following Lee's surrender. Were he living now, more than fifty years after
Appomattox, he would probably be as kindly and as just in his estimate of a northern, as of a southern, soldier. I cannot feel that way—
at any rate, I cannot feel kindly toward Gen. Sherman. He was a
monster and I want the whole world to know it.[27]

Despite the many examples of white southern women's stern resistance in
the face of invasion, postwar rhetoric made Yankee depredations seem even
more outrageous by casting them as attacks on "defenseless" women and children. In the quest to win a moral victory, southerners frequently accused Yankees of violating manly codes by attacking an otherwise peaceful home front.
Sherman and his men were ideal targets for this accusation. Sherman became
the personification of Yankee atrocities, and women were increasingly portrayed as his long-suffering victims. As the perfect foil to Sherman's behavior,
Lee was honored as the epitome of southern chivalry, a valiant and heroic
leader who had surrendered only in the face of overwhelming odds. Thus,
defeat on the battlefield signified Confederate valor, while subjugation of the
home front constituted a display of Yankee moral depravity.[28]

The South constructed memories of war around symbols of Yankee bar-
barity, southern cavaliers, and virtuous ladies, obscuring individual strengths
and frailties and creating an image of a united white Confederacy whose honorable quest to preserve the southern way of life had been thwarted by brute
force.[29] The heroic defense of southern soil was portrayed as a male preroga-
tive, while women were praised for their "feminine" qualities of sentimentality, patience, and endurance. Such rhetoric privileged self-sacrifice over
self-assertion, and as women took on the responsibility for restoring male
honor, they became cultural guardians rather than makers of nations and
nationalisms. The cultural politics of war and memory reflected the interrela-
tionship of race, sex, and the military, linking Sherman and the white women
of the South in an eternal war.[30]

## Notes

Adapted from *When Sherman Marched North from the Sea: Resistance on the Confederate Home Front* by Jacqueline Glass Campbell. Copyright © 2003 by the University
of North Carolina Press. Used by permission of the publisher.

1. Judith Hicks Stiehm, "The Protected, the Protector, the Defender," *Women's Studies International Forum* 5, no. 3/4 (1982): 374; Nancy Huston, "Tales of War and Tears of Women," ibid., 271–82.

2. Mrs. H. J. B., in *When Sherman Came: Southern Women and the "Great March,"* ed. Katherine M. Jones (Indianapolis: Bobbs-Merrill, 1964), 140–48; Sarah Jane Graham Sams to Robert Sams, February 8, 1865, Sams Family Papers, Caroliniana Library, University of South Carolina, Columbia, S.C.

3. Garret S. Byrne diary, February 21, 1865, quoted in Joseph T. Glatthaar, *The March to the Sea and Beyond* (Baton Rouge: Louisiana State University Press, 1985), 72; William Grunert, *History of the One Hundred and Twenty Ninth Regiment Illinois Volunteer Infantry* (Winchester, Ill.: R. B. Dedman, 1866), 181–82; Reid Mitchell, *The Vacant Chair: The Northern Soldier Leaves Home* (New York: Oxford University Press, 1993), 89–113.

4. Edward Behham to "Dear Jenny," February 19, 1865, Edward W. Behham Papers, Special Collections, Perkins Library, Duke University, Durham, N.C.; Reid Mitchell, "'Not the General but the Soldier': The Study of Civil War Soldiers," in *Writing the Civil War: The Quest to Understand*, ed. James M. McPherson and William J. Cooper Jr. (Columbia: University of South Carolina Press, 1998), 91–92; Henry Hitchcock, *Marching with Sherman*, ed. M. A. DeWolfe Howe (Lincoln: University of Nebraska Press, 1995), 224.

5. Both North and South shared an understanding that privileges of race and class afforded certain women protection against physical assault. The point of conflict was the underlying reason for the exercise of this privilege. Although Sherman's march might be considered a form of psychological rape of the southern home front, there was never any widespread rape, murder, or removal of populations, as occurred in the wars against Native Americans in the West or in the civil and global conflicts of the twentieth century. Bertram Wyatt-Brown, *Southern Honor: Ethics and Behavior in the Old South* (New York: Oxford University Press, 1982), 234.

6. Daniel R. Hundley, *Social Relations in Our Southern States* (New York: Henry B. Price, 1860), 73; Captain Eliot Welch to mother, February 14 and 24, 1865, Welch Papers, Special Collections, Perkins Library, Duke University; John C. Bratton to wife, February 17, 1865, Bratton Papers, Southern Historical Collection, University of North Carolina, Chapel Hill, N.C.

7. Civil War historians have long recognized the dynamic nature of soldiers' commitment to war, yet such a nuanced model has never been applied to the women of the Confederacy, the assumption being that women were disillusioned and disaffected by all things military. My argument is that civilians had their own link to cause and comrades and that in the wake of Sherman's march, initial feelings of despondency could be channeled into a demonization of the enemy and a renewed embrace of the Confederate cause. See James M. McPherson, *For Cause and Comrades: Why*

*Men Fought in the Civil War* (New York: Oxford University Press, 1997); Drew Gilpin Faust, *Mothers of Invention: Women of the Slaveholding South in the American Civil War* (Chapel Hill: University of North Carolina Press, 1996); Jacqueline Glass Campbell, *When Sherman Marched North from the Sea: Resistance on the Confederate Home Front* (Chapel Hill: University of North Carolina Press, 2003).

8. Unsigned to My Dear Willie, March 31, 1865, Henry William DeSaussure Papers, Special Collections, Perkins Library, Duke University; Lily Logan to "My Precious Brother," March 2, 1765, in Jones, *When Sherman Came*, 194.

9. Sallie I. Lowndes to Mrs. William Mason Smith, March 18, 1865, in *Mason Smith Family Letters, 1860–1865*, ed. Daniel E. Huger Smith et al. (Columbia: University of South Carolina Press, 1950), 171. As William Blair has argued, enduring and surviving the depredations of an army of invasion might actually stimulate commitment to the cause by "solidifying the portrait of an enemy." See William Blair, *Virginia's Private War: Feeding Body and Soul in the Confederacy, 1861–1865* (New York: Oxford University Press, 1998), 79.

10. C. Vann Woodward, ed., *Mary Chesnut's Civil War* (New Haven, Conn.: Yale University Press, 1981), 800.

11. Earl Schenck Miers, ed., *When the World Ended: The Diary of Emma LeConte* (New York: Oxford University Press, 1957), 95–96; John F. Marszalek, ed., *The Diary of Miss Emma Holmes* (Baton Rouge: Louisiana State University Press, 1979), 436–37 (emphasis in original).

12. Miers, *When the World Ended*, 99.

13. Ibid., 90; Elizabeth Collier diary, July 9, 1865, Southern Historical Collection, University of North Carolina; Woodward, *Mary Chesnut's Civil War*, 716.

14. Marli F. Weiner, ed., *A Heritage of Woe: The Civil War Diary of Grace Brown Elmore, 1861–1868* (Athens: University of Georgia Press, 1997), 176.

15. Drew Gilpin Faust, *Southern Stories: Slaveholders in Peace and War* (Columbia: University of Missouri Press, 1992), 9.

16. Michelle Rosaldo argues that "a woman becomes a woman by following in her mother's footsteps," while "masculinity is never fully possessed, but must be perpetually achieved, asserted and renegotiated"—a theory that meshes perfectly with the gendered discourse of war that offers men the opportunity to display and prove their manhood. See Michelle Rosaldo, "Woman, Culture, and Society: A Theoretical Overview," in *Women, Culture and Society*, ed. Michelle Rosaldo and Louise Lamphere (Stanford, Calif.: Stanford University Press, 1974), 28. See also Michael Roper and John Tosh, eds., *Manful Assertions: Masculinities in Britain since 1800* (London: Routledge Press, 1991), 18; Wyatt-Brown, *Southern Honor*, 35. John Lynn found that war had a similar appeal among aristocratic men in seventeenth-century France, where an honor code dictated that "it was not enough to be brave; one must be seen as being brave by one's peers." See John Lynn, "The Embattled Future of Academic

Military History," *Journal of Military History* 61 (October 1977): 786. James L. Huston, in "Property Rights in Slavery and the Coming of the Civil War," *Journal of Southern History* 65 (May 1999): 266, argues that the significant increase in wage earners by the 1830s modified the republican vision of turning an independent, virtuous population into a "free labor ideology"; thus men were forced to endure a period of "dependency on their road to economic independence." See also Anthony Rotunda, *American Manhood: Transformations in Masculinity from the Revolution to the Modern Era* (New York: Basic Books, 1993), and Gail Bederman, *Manliness and Civilization: A Cultural History of Gender and Race in the United States, 1880–1917* (Chicago: University of Chicago Press, 1995); both authors date this job market crisis as occurring at the end of the nineteenth century.

17. Reid Mitchell, *Civil War Soldiers* (New York: Viking Press, 1988), 161. See also Paul D. Escott, *After Secession: Jefferson Davis and the Failures of Confederate Nationalism* (Baton Rouge: Louisiana State University Press, 1978), 117–18.

18. Nina Silber, *The Romance of Reunion* (Chapel Hill: University of North Carolina Press, 1993), 23–24. On the change from valuing "manly" characteristics of self-control and strength of character to celebrating "masculine" strength and virility, see Rotunda, *American Manhood*, and Bederman, *Manliness and Civilization*. The argument that the ideals of a martial masculinity replaced more genteel Victorian notions is, of course, based on a northern version of gender ideology. See also Joanna Bourke, *Dismembering the Male: Men's Bodies, Britain and the Great War* (Chicago: University of Chicago Press, 1996), 250. Bourke argues that during World War I "the male body was subjected to callous treatment during war and then to the renewed sanitizing of disciplines of peace."

19. General Wade Hampton to President Johnson, 1866, Ulysses R. Brooks Papers, Special Collections, Perkins Library, Duke University; address by Jubal Early on the anniversary of Lee's death, 1872, quoted in Gary W. Gallagher, *The Confederate War: Popular Will, Nationalism and Strategy* (Cambridge, Mass.: Harvard University Press, 1997), 170–71; *Augusta Chronicle and Constitutionalist*, November 1, 1878, clipping in Charles Colcock Jones Jr. Papers, box 4, Special Collections, Perkins Library, Duke University; address at Davidson College by Robert Dabney, quoted in Gaines M. Foster, *Ghosts of the Confederacy* (New York: Oxford University Press, 1987), 29.

20. The reinterpretation of Confederate women's power from courage and defiance to domestic devotion and sacrifice also occurred in northern rhetoric as conciliation transformed the "secesh" woman from "political viper" to "flirtatious belle." See Nina Silber, "The Northern Myth of the Rebel Girl," in *Women of the American South: A Multicultural Reader*, ed. Christie Anne Farnham (New York: New York University Press, 1997), 130. For Silber's larger argument regarding the culture of conciliation, see her *Romance of Reunion*.

21. Studies of reunion and development of the Lost Cause ideology are volumi-nous. See, for example, Silber, *Romance of Reunion*; William R. Taylor, *Cavalier and Yankee: The Old South and American National Character* (1961; reprint, New York: Oxford University Press, 1993); Foster, *Ghosts of the Confederacy*; Charles Reagan Wilson, *Baptized in Blood: The Religion of the Lost Cause, 1865–1920* (Athens: Uni-versity of Georgia Press, 1980).

22. David W. Blight, *Race and Reunion: The Civil War in American Memory* (Cambridge, Mass.: Harvard University Press, 2001); Martha Hodes, "The Sexualiza-tion of Reconstruction Politics: White Women and Black Men in the South after the Civil War," *Journal of the History of Sexuality* 3, no. 3 (1993): 402–17; Jacquelyn Dowd Hall, *Revolt against Chivalry: Jessie Daniel Ames and the Women's Campaign against Lynching*, rev. ed. (New York: Columbia University Press, 1993). Hall argues that "the racism that caused white men to lynch black men cannot be understood apart from the sexism that informed their policing of white women and their exploi-tation of black women" (xx).

23. E. A. Pollard, *Southern History of the War* (New York: Charles B. Richardson, 1866), 608–9; Gallagher, *Confederate War*, 59. Interestingly, Pollard's deconstruction of the nature of military leaders does not appear in later facsimile editions. Thomas L. Connelly places the creation of a "Lee Cult" at the end of the nineteenth century, ignoring its wartime presence in the Confederacy. See Thomas L. Connelly, *The Mar-ble Man: Robert E. Lee and His Image in American Society* (Baton Rouge: Louisiana State University Press, 1978).

24. Jefferson Davis, *The Rise and Fall of the Confederate Government* (New York: D. Appleton, 1881); John F. Marszalek, "Celebrity in Dixie: Sherman Tours the South, 1879," *Georgia Historical Quarterly* 66 (Fall 1982): 368–83; Carol Reardon, "William T. Sherman in Postwar Georgia's Collecting Memory, 1864–1914," in *Wars within a War: Controversy and Conflict over the American Civil War*, ed. Joan Waugh and Gary W. Gallagher (Chapel Hill: University of North Carolina Press, 2009), 223–48.

25. Address by Mrs. August Kohn, reprinted in *The State: Columbia*, April 30, 1911.

26. Linus Pierpont Brockett and Mary C. Vaughan, *Women's Work in the Civil War* (Philadelphia: King and Baird, 1867), 781. See also Jeanie Attie, *Patriotic Toil: Northern Women and the American Civil War* (Ithaca, N.Y.: Cornell University Press, 1998).

27. Elizabeth Avery Meriwether, Recollections, Southern Historical Collection, University of North Carolina.

28. John F Marszalek, *Sherman: A Soldier's Passion for Order* (New York: Free Press, 1993), 333.

29. In the case of Sherman, Merton E. Coulter argues that an unbalanced analy-sis of Sherman's actions as a warrior and as a peacemaker has produced a distorted

picture. See Merton E. Coulter, "Sherman and the South," *North Carolina Historical Review* 8 (January 1931): 41–54.

30. George Rable, *Civil Wars: Women and the Crisis of Southern Nationalism* (Urbana: University of Illinois Press, 1989), 238. Political scientist Cynthia Enloe argues that "nationalism typically has sprung from masculinized memory, masculinized humiliation, and masculinized hope." See Cynthia Enloe, *Bananas, Beaches, and Bases* (Berkeley: University of California Press, 1990), 44.

# 7

# "Johnny I Hardly Knew Ye"

## *The Civil War Navies in Public Memory*

*Matthew Eng*

We are truly at a unique crossroads in American history: the centennial anniversary of the First World War is drawing near, the bicentennial anniversary of the War of 1812 is just past, and the Civil War's sesquicentennial anniversary is upon us—a gold mine for the collection and preservation of history. Memory of the Civil War, many would argue, has always been present. According to historians Alice Fahs and Joan Waugh, the war "has never receded into the remote past in American life."[1] Not since the well-received 125th anniversary has the public fully experienced the weight of the war's impact on American society. Without that collective memory and identity, the current commemoration would crumble.[2] The conflict that separated the country so long ago is set to spark the public's memory of the war again.

For younger generations, information about the war presented during the current commemoration will be brand-new. Accessing the information, however, is easier than ever. There are plenty of events and activities planned to fill any gaps in the historical record, but do they tell the full story? Is something missing? In his 1961 essay *The Legacy of the Civil War*, novelist Robert Penn Warren discusses the complications that arise with the understanding of history over time. "When one is happy in forgetfulness," he writes, "facts get forgotten."[3] Although Warren's words pertain to the war's overall meaning, many historians, educators, and scholars of naval history might agree.

Separate "wars" over the memory of the conflict began immediately after the cannons and muskets were silenced. Certainly, the debate over the war's historical antecedents takes precedence. Others, like embers in a fire, continue to burn low and silent in the American psyche. This is where many naval historians of the Civil War find themselves today—locked in a vacuum of forgotten battles, intrepid commanders, and iron ships. Look at any general history textbook or overview of the Civil War, and you will find a scant number of pages devoted to the navies and their key battles, individuals, or grand strategies. Comb through any monograph published in the last fifty years, and you will likely find the words "Civil War Navy" and "overlooked" placed together.

"Memory," according to John Gillis, "is something to be retrieved." The main difference between memory and identity is that identity is "something that can be lost as well as found."[4] The wartime actions of sailors on the rivers and seas are not altogether lost; they are merely buried beneath the collective memory of "hallowed ground." For others, the Civil War navies represent a portion of history long forgotten. Over time, it became a renewed "lost cause" that is still largely undiscovered. This essay entreats readers to remember the navies' role in the Civil War with a spirit of scientific inquiry. If public memory is any indicator of the preservation of history, the following information on the impact of popular culture and Civil War naval history will excite and enthrall new generations of historians and enthusiasts to remember Uncle Sam's "webbed feet."

One of the problems facing the memory of the Civil War navies is geography. Because naval forces fought primarily on the water, there are no battlefields, at least in the classic sense, for individuals to visit. The public cannot grasp what it cannot see. *Civil War Monitor* blogger Craig Swain echoed these sentiments in a 2011 interview about the nature of memory and the Civil War. According to Swain, "audiences are prewired to a state, often identifying with these homogenous groups that went into battle together." And the majority of monuments visited by the public today are dedicated to states, not organizations. In contrast, navies lack a physical entity that links the war to the common consumer of Civil War history and memory. As Swain notes, it's "rather hard to 'walk' a naval battlefield."[5] In a 2011 article posted to his blog, Swain explains: "One may stand where great actions took place; stand in the footsteps of great leaders, considering their perspective; and even touch buildings and trees that stood at the time of the war. . . . Unlike the landward components of the war, today's visitor has trouble 'immersing' in the naval war."[6] Unlike the armies of the Union and the Confederacy, there was no

"Grand Navy of the Republic" or postwar veterans' organizations for sailors to parade up and down the streets of Richmond and Washington.

Gordon Calhoun, historian at the Hampton Roads Naval Museum, agrees with many of Swain's arguments and cites the "endangered" nature of naval battle sites. He commented in a December 2011 interview that, unlike the armies, the navies existed as a national force. "You have to remember who was driving the history after the war—the states," Calhoun said. "It was the individual units who wrote the public memory of the war in the immediate years following the conflict." And because sailors "tended to be less classically educated and didn't write their stories down," they left fewer "resources for historians today to use." As a result, much of the naval history of the war comes from the officers and the top brass—not the everyday sailor on the blockade. Calhoun believes the general public wants to know about these famous Civil War battles, but unfortunately, many individuals fail to consider the naval side of the war because there were no "battles" in the classic sense of the word. Perhaps the Battle of Hampton Roads is so popular because it has the word "battle" in it.[7]

Part of the difficulty in creating a cohesive set of programs involving the Civil War navies is getting around the idea of them as "overlooked." Some individuals anticipated the sesquicentennial with dread and condemnation before it even began.[8] Indeed, one of the questions from the start was: What does the general public, 150 years after the event, really know or want to know about the Civil War navies? Under the direction of the Naval History and Heritage Command in Washington, D.C., the Civil War Navy Sesquicentennial was organized to analyze the public record and determine the best way to present naval history programs during the commemoration.[9] Where scholarship ultimately fails, modern-day social media and popular culture provide fresh perspectives on a historically misrepresented portion of the war.

How do Americans receive information in general? According to a 2010 CNN report, more Americans get their news from the Internet than from newspapers and radio. Of those using the Internet for news, three-fourths receive informational updates via e-mail or social media sites. The survey, conducted by PEW Internet and the American Life Project, identified Facebook and Twitter as the primary providers of information because they "made news a more participatory experience than ever before." The advent of social media sites and blogs has helped news "become a social experience in fresh ways for consumers."[10]

The fact that many Americans receive their news and knowledge online is invaluable information for Civil War bloggers, because the transfer of historical information is no different. The war is firmly entrenched in this digital landscape. How do the Civil War navies match up to the Civil War armies in the online world? A simple Google search reveals interesting results. Of the approximately 231 million websites devoted to the American Civil War, 28 percent include some information about the Union and Confederate navies. Considering the number of soldiers, units, and battles on land, this is a surprisingly high percentage.[11]

On one educational website devoted to the Civil War, Virginia Tech's "Essential Civil War Curriculum," 5 percent of its topics cover the ships, men, organization, and battles of the Union and Confederate navies. Given that roughly 5 percent of all forces in the Civil War were involved in the Union or Confederate navy, that percentage seems logical. The website boasts over 400 individual topics of "basic knowledge" that any "serious student of [the] Civil War" should know. The "essential" Civil War naval topics range from the Battle of Hampton Roads to the exploits of South Carolina slave pilot Robert Smalls. The site allows individuals to submit new informational topics to be peer-reviewed by a "who's who" of Civil War historians for possible inclusion on the website.[12]

Although history professionals have offered keen advice and insight into the goals and aspirations of the sesquicentennial, the general public and the Civil War "consumer" have the greatest impact on public memory. Living history interpreters are often on the "front line" of the public's interpretation of the war. Based on the success of 125th anniversary commemorations in the 1980s, living history is one of the easiest ways for students and enthusiasts of the Civil War to witness events. It is the first step when merging public history and popular culture. With the sesquicentennial now in full swing, interest is steadily increasing among all age groups around the country.

Unfortunately, many will never be able to see a live reenactment, let alone one in which the navies are represented. Geography comes into play once again. Yet without reenactors and enthusiasts, the public would never be able to fully grasp the complexity and awesome spectacle of the war as presented on the silver screen. Reenactments on television or in films such as *Gettysburg* (1993) and *Gods and Generals* (2003) are now fully ingrained in the nation's notion of the Civil War and popular culture. But film and television are only two of the many ways the general public accesses historical information.

According to scholars William Aspray and Barbara M. Hayes, "everyday life in America is filled with information activity."[13] Most Americans' daily agendas include the enjoyment of the Internet, television, music, or film. An individual is more likely to see or hear about the war through these instruments of popular culture than through more traditional means.

In several instances the ironclad ships and sailors of the Civil War navies have emerged in popular culture. The earliest example was in the 1936 film *Hearts in Bondage*. Film is one of the most recognizable cultural formats by which Americans learn about history, and for its time, this film is well executed. It follows the time-tested principle of a war film: using a tinge of the romantic to chronicle the complicated relationship between an officer and his beloved under the guise of the famous Battle of Hampton Roads. One reviewer on the popular site Flixster noted that the film had taught him "more than any history class ever did about the Civil War."[14] Other recent films, such as the low-budget *Ironclads* (1990) and *Hunley* (1997), were critically panned but serve as important cultural documents. With so many films made about Civil War land battles in the last twenty years, every piece created about the navies—good or bad—provides important insight into the psyche of public memory.

Films about the Civil War navies devolved into absurdity in the 2000s. The most notable examples are the major Hollywood productions *Sahara* (2005) and *Gangs of New York* (2002). *Sahara* takes the very real CSS *Texas* on an unrealistic trek across the Atlantic Ocean to the Niger River. Despite the plot's clichéd treatment of Civil War history and the field of underwater archaeology, many found the film entertaining. Even the most demanding of film critics, Roger Ebert, "treasured the movie's preposterous plot" and asked, "What can you say about a movie based on the premise that a Confederate ironclad ship from the Civil War is buried beneath the sands of the Sahara, having ventured there 150 years ago when the region was obviously damper than it is now?"[15] User reviews on the Internet sites Flixster and Rotten Tomatoes agreed that *Sahara* was at least entertaining.[16]

Martin Scorsese's Oscar-nominated film *Gangs of New York* was well received by both critics and viewers. The visually stunning film follows the fictional exploits of an Irish preacher's son as he embarks on a daring vendetta against the anti-immigrant Five Points leader Bill "The Butcher" Cutting. This 1860s angst culminates in a bare-knuckled gang brawl against the backdrop of the New York City draft riots. Although the film is based on real events that occurred in July 1863, it includes several factual errors, leading the unknowing student of the Civil War to the conclusion that the Union navy was involved in quelling the riot. Gary Gallagher describes the film's historically inaccurate portrayal of the Union navy during the riots: "Naval vessels open fire as well, sending explosive shells into the poor Five Points neighborhood where rival gangs prepare to clash." He goes on to describe the movie event as a "violent harvest."[17] Naval historian Samuel Eliot Morrison called the draft riots "equivalent to a Confederate victory," but the navy was by no means involved.[18]

A discussion of Civil War naval music is even more interesting. In recent years, several artists and musicians have indirectly used iconic Civil War naval events as a backdrop for their musical message. For instance, *Civil War Naval Songs*, released in 2011, is part of an ongoing series of folk albums produced by the Smithsonian Institution. It contains thirteen authentic period pieces that, according to the Folkways website, include "sounds of the cramped quarters of Union and Confederate fighting ships as well merchant craft that sailed in constant peril." The album's artist took pains to craft each of the songs, drawing from Union, Confederate, and British sources. The tracks could be a Civil War naval historian's list of lecture topics, with songs ranging from the upbeat "Monitor & Merrimac" to Dan Milner's somber rendition of "Farragut's Ball." As an added educational component, each copy of the album includes a thirty-six-page booklet on the history of the Civil War navies, as well as a few iconic images from the Smithsonian's collection. The album is an excellent testament to the memory of the war's naval forces, teaching interested listeners about the war through the popular medium of music.[19]

Folk ballads are no longer *en vogue* in popular culture today, but two popular artists are taking the traditional idea of using the music of the Civil War navies to the next level. In *The Monitor*, New Jersey punk rock band Titus Andronicus merges the history of the ironclad *Monitor* into a conceptual rock opera. The album's cover art is a shaded blue image of the *Monitor*'s crew relaxing on the main deck along the James River. The album was released on March 9, 2010, the 148th anniversary of the battle. Select song titles include the Civil War–themed "A More Perfect Union" and the epic fourteen-minute conclusion "The Battle of Hampton Roads." According to Titus Andronicus singer Patrick Sickles, *The Monitor* is "sort of" a concept album. "It doesn't take place in olden times, nor does it necessarily feature any characters that participated in the conflict," Sickles said in an interview with Pitchfork Media. In reality, the record focuses on how "conflicts that led our nation into that great calamity remain unresolved."[20]

Unlike Titus Andronicus's concept album, indie musician Bishop Allen's 2006 song "The Monitor" takes a more literal approach. The lyrics are both informative and inspiring to the memory of the famed vessel. The song's opening words tell the story of the ship's launching in Allen's home borough of Brooklyn:

> Once a great ironworks
> Stood at the end of my street
> And they hauled in The Monitor
> Fit her with armor
> For to save the Union fleet.[21]

The song goes on to retell the story of the *Monitor* and its engagement with the *Merrimack*, or the CSS *Virginia*. The imagery used in the song is impressive, connecting the story of the battle with creative wit and hooks. Although Titus Andronicus's album got more favorable reviews than Bishop Allen's, the latter's words are closer to historical fact, whereas the former cleverly built an album around a façade of memory and meaning.

The popular video-sharing website YouTube incorporates both video and music in an easy-to-use format. According to *Business Insider*, one in five users is uploading a video each month, allowing everyone from amateurs and enthusiasts to the most experienced historians and videographers to tell their stories. YouTube is so popular—with nearly 880 million users worldwide—that video will be 90 percent of all web traffic in the near future, according to content vice president Robert Kyncl.[22] With a little bit of creativity and technological savvy, YouTube users can break the fourth wall of interpretation. Today's computers are tailor-made to create and share videos, and feedback can be instantaneous. Users upload their videos and track their results through user comments. This platform allows users to become active participants in a running dialogue of history and remembrance. Every video can be shared, embedded in a blog, or posted on sites such as Facebook and Twitter. One video can be disseminated to millions with a few simple clicks. In the conflict over the Civil War navies and metrics, YouTube is the newest battleground.

YouTube allows users to bring the story of the Civil War navies to life.

The interpretation of history must be viewed in terms of the collection and presentation of facts. Conversations are created and sustained from the ground up. The greatest videos are the ones with the most creative spin on some of the war's most iconic battles, such as the engagement between ironclads at Hampton Roads. The Mariners' Museum in Newport News, Virginia, held a popular video contest on the 147th anniversary of the famed battle. Users uploaded their videos, telling the story of the engagement between the *Virginia* and the Union fleet quite creatively. Some contestants added their own narration to a rolling slide show of historical images, while others told the story by acting out the parts of the ships involved in the battle. From a history educator's perspective, students learn best when they can incorporate information that is relatable to them. In today's highly mediated society, perhaps there is no better place than the Internet.[23]

One video that encompasses both popular culture and Civil War naval history is the "Anime Boys' Tribute_The Cumberland's Crew." The five-minute video, one of many created by user Lord Drako Arakis, merges American and British history with Japanese animation, or *anime*. The crossover clip, complete with the narrative song styling of "The Cumberland's Crew" by the Cumberland Three, uses popular anime characters from the *Dragonball Z*, *Gundam*, and *Kingdom Hearts* series to tell the story of the sloop of war's destruction by the *Virginia* on March 8, 1862. Gaara, of the popular anime series *Naruto*, portrays Lieutenant George Morris, commanding officer of the USS *Cumberland*. The creator took pains to ensure historical accuracy while paying tribute to the unfortunate crew through an uncharacteristic art form: "Now, let it be known, as with all the historical crossover clips I do, this was created for the sake of art, song, and a way of commemoration. . . . I can assure you that I don't do these period piece crossovers out of spite, or as a light hearted gesture of simple entertainment. I only intend to have those, who understand the anime world, but not much on history, be able to relate better when seeing familiar characters reenacting important historical events."[24] The clip boasts nearly 32,000 views. Placed side by side with popular paintings of the sinking of the *Cumberland*, the anime sketches in the video look nearly identical.

An ongoing narrative consisting of museum collections, histories, public programs, and symposia keeps the memory of the Civil War navies alive, despite their "overlooked" status. The efforts of Civil War sailors continue to impact society today. Five years of conflict at sea included thousands of sailors and hundreds of ships, each with its own story and mark on history. The ebb and flow of awareness surrounding the 50th, 100th, and 125th anniversaries have built up anticipation for the current celebration. As Robert Penn Warren wrote, the Civil War is "our felt history—history lived in the national imagination."[25]

Like all things in the past, some events are remembered better than others. It is not just the message that is important today. How we process and analyze information as users of and participants in popular culture must also be taken into consideration. Accordingly, several foreseeable trends emerge with regard to interpreting and commemorating the Civil War navies. Those who are interested in creating historical conversations within the naval subgenre can use these trends as a road map to the future of the field.

Not all commemorations are created equal. When it comes to topical trends, the great equalizer is the Battle of Hampton Roads. The two-day battle resonated in the minds of Americans far more than any other naval battle during the war. Nearly every facet of Civil War naval history that is talked about, written on, or posted on social media mentions Hampton Roads and the ironclad ships involved in the battle: the USS *Monitor* and CSS *Virginia*. The battle is historical canon in textbooks around the country, from fifth-grade classrooms to the U.S. Naval Academy.

Take a look at any book published about the Civil War navies in the last decade, and you will find that Hampton Roads is prevalent. Maybe you *can* judge a book by its cover—or at least you can judge what is historically popular. The front jackets of Craig Symonds's prize-winning *Lincoln and His Admirals* and Stephen Taffe's follow-up *Commanding Lincoln's Navy* both contain images of the battle, even though each book covers the entire war. From the public's standpoint, President Lincoln's personal involvement with the Union navy boils down to a two-day battle. Other book covers depict the war's most famous vessel. Both Barbara Tomblin's *Bluejackets and Contrabands* and John Quarstein's *Monitor Boys* use James F. Gibson's famous photograph of the *Monitor*'s crew cooking on the main deck along the James River in 1862.

Americans began commemorating the Battle of Hampton Roads almost immediately. The naval battle gave those who were outside the fighting something to connect to. Many saw the battle as an epic contest of will and determination, as well as the embodiment of Victorian principles of heroism. More traditional mediums of popular culture like poetry detail the importance of the battle. Poets Henry Wadsworth Longfellow and Herman

Melville penned epic verses in commemoration of the famous battle immediately after the war. Longfellow's poem, simply titled "The Cumberland," retells the story of the "brave hearts that went down in the seas" at the hands of the *Virginia*'s "fiery breath." Melville's 1866 masterpiece, "A Utilitarian View of the Monitor's Fight," declares the "clangor" of battle "still ringeth round the world," even four years after the contest had ended.[26] New York manufacturer A. Daugherty created playing cards that allowed enthusiasts to reconstruct "the greatest event in naval history" just months after the battle ended in 1862. These are but a few of the earliest examples.

By the early twentieth century, the two ironclad ships were already household names. One of the showcases at the 1907 Jamestown Exposition in Hampton Roads, Virginia, was a circular diorama of the "Battle of the *Merrimac* and the *Monitor*." The façade of the building housing the exhibit looked like a battleship, highlighting the modern steel equivalent of the iron-plated ships. According to one source, the number of tickets sold to the exhibit sometimes exceeded exposition attendance. Sterling silver spoons sold at the exposition commemorated the *Merrimack* (not the *Virginia*) and the *Monitor*. In the hundred years since then, the memory of that battle has stood the test of time.[27]

The recent "Up Pops the Monitor: The Battle of Hampton Roads in Pop Culture" exhibit at the Mariners' Museum was the culmination of nearly 150 years of *Monitor* mania. The nine-month temporary exhibit highlighted the role the USS *Monitor* played in popular culture through advertising, fiction, film, music, art, and gaming. Every item tied to the ship by either name or idea was on display for visitors to learn or reminisce about, including the previously mentioned film *Hearts in Bondage*. The *Monitor* became a celebrated ship and a symbol of the interest of academics and laypeople throughout the last century.[28]

The *Monitor* stood its ground amid the changing perceptions and values of American society. "You really see a shift from the *Monitor* as a patriotic symbol to being a symbol of a powerful, tough, and innovative technology about twenty years after the war," noted Anna Holloway, vice president of collections and programs at the Mariners' Museum. Indeed, the *Monitor* became synonymous with the "ironclad" durability, strength, and patriotism many Americans looked for in household products. The ship's impenetrability became the design principle for the GE Monitor-top refrigerator of the 1920s, as well as the "small, but effective" cure-all pills of Dr. Pierce produced during the 1890s. As Holloway commented, "the *Monitor* became its own salesman."[29]

Every war has a social side. Beyond the machines of war and the vessels that carried them, scholarship continues to detail how sailors dealt with the tedium of the blockade and the horrors of close-quarters combat on western rivers. The men on the ships of the Union and the Confederacy were a "mixed bag" of ethnicities. However, the role of African American sailors has become the most important topic of study in the twenty-first century. Problems of race and reconciliation during the semicentennial and centennial have now been rectified by a bevy of recent commemorative events, including the 2010 Signature Conference of the Virginia Civil War Sesquicentennial Commission at Norfolk State University, titled "Race, Slavery, and the Civil War: The Tough Stuff of American History and Memory."[30]

The social history of African American involvement in the war will take center stage throughout the sesquicentennial. Several books written in the past decade, including Stephen Ramold's *Slaves, Sailors, and Citizens* and Barbara Tomblin's equally important *Bluejackets and Contrabands*, serve as an introduction to what will likely be a great flourishing of scholarship. Nationally recognized organizations are currently working to document and record the names of every Civil War sailor, black and white. Pushing this index forward is a steering committee comprising historians and researchers representing Howard University, the Naval History and Heritage Command, and the National Park Service, among others. According to the National Park Service's Civil War Soldiers and Sailors System (CWSS) website, the online database of African American sailors consists of approximately 8,000 names, out of the more than 18,000 African Americans who served in the Union navy during the war.[31] Thus, there is still some work to be done.

America's social history is bookended by the plight of African Americans, from enslavement to the civil rights movement. The Civil War marked the climax of their struggle for freedom. James McPherson, Pulitzer Prize–winning author of *Battle Cry of Freedom*, presented a paper titled "Slavery, Freedom, and the Union Navy" at the 2010 Virginia Civil War Sesquicentennial Signature Conference and is currently working on a book about African American sailors during the Civil War—a project that will undoubtedly breathe new life into both Civil War and African American history. Even if the Union navy's rank and file were not always progressive thinkers when it came to the abolition of slavery, as one blogger commented, "the demands of war caused them to adapt to the vagaries of war and they were soon singing the praises of the African Americans serving on their vessels."[32]

The naval "melting pot" best represents how the majority of Americans want to remember the Civil War. Despite disagreements over the institution of slavery on both sides, many different races, colors, and creeds marched to the Union flag, and examining the role of the African American sailor is a way for Americans to connect with their history and heritage. "African American sailors were needed," historian Stephen Ramold remarked in a 2004 interview with the *Journal of African American History.* "They were Americans who didn't hesitate to fight for their country." African Americans made the conscious choice to fight for their freedom, regardless of the conditions they faced. Ramold goes on to say that the Union navy "was remarkably modern . . . where everything was not a racial struggle."[33]

In the century before Executive Order 9981 mandated the full racial integration of American armed forces in 1948, white sailors operating around the world fought and died alongside their black brethren. Military equality was borne on the shoulders of these sailors, some of whom are more notable than others in the public consciousness. For example, South Carolinian Robert Smalls, the slave pilot of the *Planter,* fled with his family to Union lines for freedom, becoming "the closest thing to a national black war hero from the Civil War."[34] Several buildings and monuments are named in honor of the slave turned Reconstruction-era politician, including an army logistical support ship (LSV-8) and a Great Lakes training camp for African Americans during the Second World War.[35] Like Cuba Gooding Jr.'s true-life "zero to hero" navy characters in the films *Men of Honor* and *Pearl Harbor,* Smalls's experiences would translate well to stage and screen. Long before the Fifty-Fourth Massachusetts attacked Fort Wagner, African Americans forged the identity of today's navy through their service. Blacks in blue jackets represented the fighting spirit in the cause of freedom. The story of black sailors serves as a constant reminder to Americans how far we have come.

The trends discussed here come together through the platform of social media, which is the future of information dissemination to the masses. Digital technologies broadcast every concept demonstrated, viewed, or discussed to the entire world. Somewhere along the line, information about the Civil War that was once confined to museums, classrooms, and institutions of higher learning moved outside those boundaries and into the digital world. According to technical communications guru Saul Carliner, the era of social

media utilization began in the mid-2000s,[36] and this has become the best ave-
nue to showcase the history of the Union and Confederate navies today. As
an added bonus, anyone can weigh in on the conversation.

Imagine that, twenty years ago, you were interested in the famous Confederate raider CSS *Alabama*, captained by southern maverick Raphael
Semmes. Before the advent of the Internet and social media, your first source
would be the *Official Records of the Union and Confederate Navies*, available at
most university and academic libraries. Otherwise, you could see what your
local library had to offer or buy a historical monograph on the subject from a
bookstore. Artifacts from the *Alabama* are still held at the National Museum
of the United States Navy in Washington, D.C., and at the Alabama Department of Archives and History. The famous Édouard Manet painting depicting the battle off the shores of Cherbourg, France, is held at the Philadelphia
Museum of Art. But you would have to travel to see these artifacts and paintings, assuming they were available for public viewing. You could buy traditional music at a record store, but such albums were rare. Back then, historical
roundtables and living history groups were the easiest way to connect with
others interested in the history of the Confederate raider on a personal basis.

Today, it is as simple as a few clicks of a button. With a computer, anyone
can use Internet search engines to find and download museum podcasts and
images of artifacts or purchase the latest rendition of "Roll, Alabama, Roll!"
from iTunes without leaving the confines of home. Social networking allows
users to comment on YouTube clips about the CSS *Alabama*, as well as connect with and participate in user groups and fan pages dedicated to the ship
on Facebook, Twitter, and LinkedIn. Through social media, military history
and cultural history merge.

Members of Generation X and Y are now having children. Members of
Generation Z, or the Internet Generation, exist in a world where the Internet
has always been readily available. However, we cannot assume that such technology is available to all; the argument for the "digital native" or "digital generation," described by authors John Palfrey and Urs Gasser, is hotly debated
for its lack of sensitivity to those without such access.[37] Those born prior to
1980 now have an opportunity to associate with these emerging
technologies.[38]

To say technological change is "annoying" or "frightening," as Palfrey and
Gasser discuss in *Born Digital*, might be extreme.[39] Change is change, and
nothing else. Whether change is slow or rapid, the pieces of our memory

constantly shift and alter. We are all both vessels of knowledge and emissaries of technology. Disregarding a metaphorical debate over nature versus nurture, however, the fact remains that technology is here to stay. For the sake of future generations, it is more important than ever to utilize digital technology to preserve the history of the Civil War navies.

Civil War Navy Sesquicentennial blogger Sarah Adler weighed in on the need to reach out to the Generation Z in an April 2011 interview. As a student of Civil War history and a member of that generation herself, her insight is invaluable for identifying the foreseeable trends of social media utilization: "Today's youth have grown up with advancing technology that can bring them closer to history in new and increasingly creative ways. Therefore, it is extremely important that the Civil War Navy's commemoration harness this opportunity to educate through technology and get more young people involved."[40] Americans will always have the traditional methods of obtaining information about the Civil War. Newspapers will still print articles, books will be published, scholars will present lectures, enthusiasts will interpret through living history, and museums will continue to educate the public through artifacts. Conversations about the Civil War will undoubtedly continue to flourish in scholarly circles across the country. If anything, the old guard will remain crucial, providing the foundation for our memory of the Civil War navies. As Henry Jenkins suggests, "history teaches us that old media never die"; the only thing that changes is the way we access that content.[41] The myriad new ways the Civil War is being presented to the public today will merely supplement what we already know about the war.

"Commemorative activity," according to John Gillis, "is by definition social and political, for it involves the coordination of individuals and group memories, whose results may appear consensual when they are in fact the product of [a] process of intense contest, struggle, and in some cases, annihilation."[42] When done right, history can continually change in breadth and scope, either mimicking or drastically differing from social or political correctness. Using the Internet does not dumb down the public perception of the Civil War. Instead, it enhances what is already out there. The beauty of history is that it can breathe new life into the minds of Americans, both young and old. The first years of the sesquicentennial have already displayed a seemingly coordinated effort by historians and scholars to avoid the mistakes of their centennial predecessors.

There is no benefit to arguing over which military branch was more important during the war. Referring to naval operations as "overlooked" seems more like a broken record than a missing record of events. There will always be historians and enthusiasts, as well as naysayers and flag wavers. It is more important than ever to commemorate all aspects of the war, on land and at sea, with equal amounts of respect. Taking part in any way, whether by visiting battle sites, creating scholarship, participating in programs, or engaging digitally, aids the collective memory of the war. The more people talk about it, the better chance we have of preserving the overall memory of the conflict, even if opinion and favor tend to sway on political and social pendulums. By definition, popular culture exists to capture a wider audience than specialists could ever imagine. Novelist Barbara Kingsolver said it best in *Animal Dreams*: "It's surprising how much of memory is built around things unnoticed at the time."[43] Perhaps she is right. The memory of the Civil War navies has always been there; we just need to look a little bit harder.

## Notes

1. Alice Fahs and Joan Waugh, *The Memory of the Civil War in American Culture* (Chapel Hill: University of North Carolina Press, 2004), 1.

2. John R. Gillis, "Memory and Identity: The History of a Relationship," in *Commemorations: The Politics of National Identity*, ed. John R. Gillis (Princeton, N.J.: Princeton University Press, 1994), 3.

3. Robert Penn Warren, *The Legacy of the Civil War* (Cambridge, Mass.: Harvard University Press, 1983), 60, quoted in David Blight, *Race and Reunion: The Civil War in American Memory* (Cambridge, Mass.: Belknap Press, 2001), 1.

4. Gillis, "Memory and Identity," 3.

5. Craig Swain, e-mail to the author, April 19, 2011.

6. Craig Swain, "Bolting on the Civil War Navy," *Civil War Monitor* (blog), October 13, 2011, http://civilwarmonitor.com/front-line/bolting-on-the-civil-war-navy (accessed December 12, 2011).

7. Gordon Calhoun, interview by the author, Norfolk, Va., December 7, 2011.

8. Frank Cagle, "Let's Not Let a Celebration of Heritage Get Hijacked," Metro Pulse, http://www.metropulse.com/news/2010/apr/21/lets-not-let-celebration-heritage-get-hijacked/ (accessed December 4, 2011).

9. The Civil War Navy Sesquicentennial began as an official U.S. Navy commemoration in December 2009. Its mission is to disseminate information about the Union and Confederate navies during the war.

10. Doug Gross, "Survey: More Americans Get News from Internet than Newspapers or Radio," CNNTech Online, http://articles.cnn.com/2010-03-01/tech/

social.network.news_1_social-networking-sites-social-media-social-experience?_s=PM:TECH (accessed December 10, 2011). The results are from a survey of 2,259 adults aged eighteen or older.

11. The Google search terms used were "American Civil War Army" and "American Civil War Navy." Of the 231 million websites included in both searches, there were 65.2 million hits for "American Civil War Navy." This does not include websites devoted to specialized topics in Civil War naval history, such as individual ships or battles. The majority of those sites focus on the Battle of Hampton Roads and the ships involved in that conflict—CSS *Virginia* and USS *Monitor.*

12. "Essential Civil War Curriculum," Virginia Center for Civil War Studies at Virginia Tech, http://www.essentialcivilwarcurriculum.com/ (accessed December 2, 2011).

13. William Aspray and Barbara M. Hayes, introduction to *Everyday Information: The Evolution of Information Seeking in America*, ed. William Aspray and Barbara M. Hayes (Cambridge, Mass.: MIT Press, 2011), 2.

14. Bruce B., comment on *Hearts in Bondage*, http://www.flixster.com/movie/hearts-in-bondage/ (accessed December 2, 2011).

15. Roger Ebert, "Review of *Sahara,*" *Chicago Sun Times* Movie Reviews, http://rogerebert.suntimes.com/apps/pbcs.dll/article?AID=/20050407/REVIEWS/50323001 (accessed January 11, 2012).

16. According to Rotten Tomatoes, the "tomatometer" of critics' reviews gave the film a "rotten" 39 percent rating. Audience reviews, however, gave *Sahara* a favorable score of 61 percent, based on 193,867 user ratings. See "*Sahara* (2005)," Rotten Tomatoes, http://www.rottentomatoes.com/m/1144274-sahara/ (accessed January 11, 2012).

17. Gary Gallagher, *Causes Won, Lost, and Forgotten: How Hollywood and Popular Art Shape What We Know about the Civil War* (Chapel Hill: University of North Carolina Press, 2008), 128.

18. Samuel Eliot Morrison, *The Oxford History of the American People*, vol. 2, *1789 through Reconstruction* (New York: Signet, 1972), 451.

19. Smithsonian Institution, "Smithsonian Folkways—Civil War Naval Songs," Smithsonian Folkways, http://www.folkways.si.edu/albumdetails.aspx?itemid=3331 (accessed December 12, 2012).

20. Tom Brelhan, "Titus Andronicus Reveal Civil War–Themed Second Album," Pitchfork Media, http://pitchfork.com/news/37386-titus-andronicus-reveal-civil-war-themed-second-album/ (accessed December 12, 2011).

21. "The Monitor Lyrics," Lyricsmania, http://www.lyricsmania.com/the_monitor_lyrics_bishop_allen.html (accessed December 12, 2011).

22. Jay Yarow and Kamelia Angelova, "1 in 5 YouTube Users Uploads a Video Each Month," *Business Insider*, http://articles.businessinsider.com/2010-09-02/

tech/29957695_1_youtube-users-tubemogul-uploaded (accessed December 10, 2011); "Research Data for Domain: YouTube," Google Ad Planner, https://www .google.com/adplanner/?pli=1#siteSearch?uid=domain%253A%2520youtube .com&geo=US&lp=false (accessed January 12, 2012); Tom Krazit, "@CES: YouTube Thinks Web Video Is Big, Also Pretty Sure Sun Rises in East," Paid Content, http:// paidcontent.org/article/419-ces-youtube-thinks-web-video-is-big-also-pretty-sure-sun-rises-in-east/ (accessed January 12, 2012).

23. Amy Ritchie, "The Mariners' Museum Announces YouTube Meetup and Video Contest," Mariners' Museum, http://www.marinersmuseum.org/visitor-information/mariners-museum-announces-youtube-meetup-and-video-contest (accessed December 12, 2011).

24. Lord Drako Arakis, "Anime Boys' Tribute_The Cumberland's Crew," You-Tube, http://www.youtube.com/all_comments?v=QaKej7TmGhQ (accessed December 13, 2011).

25. Warren, *Legacy of the Civil War*, 4.

26. Hendry Wadsworth Longfellow, "The Monitor," in *Historic Poems and Ballads*, ed. Rupert S. Holland (Philadelphia: George W. Jacobs, 1912), 255–56; Herman Melville, "A Utilitarian View of the Monitor's Fight," in *Select Poems*, ed. Robert Faggen (New York: Penguin Books, 2006), 37.

27. Jon Caron, "Civil War Battle of Hampton Roads, Merrimac vs. Monitor, Silver Souvenir Spoon," Souvenir Spoons, http://www.souvenirspoons. comframesstories/merrimacandmonitor.html (accessed December 13, 2011).

28. "Up Pops the Monitor," Mariners' Museum, http://www.marinersmuseum .org/main/pops-monitor (accessed December 10, 2011).

29. Anna Holloway, interview by the author, Norfolk, Va., April 14, 2011.

30. For more information on the 2010 Virginia Civil War Sesquicentennial Signature Conference, go to "2010 Signature Conference," Virginia Civil War Sesquicentennial Commission, http://www.virginiacivilwar.org/2010conference.php (accessed December 11, 2011).

31. Some sources place the number of African American sailors at nearly 29,000. These numbers are still hotly debated today, primarily due to the Union navy's lack of a standardized classification system during the war.

32. Jimmy Price, "James McPherson—Slavery, Freedom, and the Union Navy," *The Sable Arm* (blog), September 24, 2010, http://sablearm.blogspot.com/2010/09/ james-mcpherson-slavery-freedom-and.html (accessed December 13, 2011).

33. Helen Hannon, "African Americans in the Navy during the Civil War," *Journal of African American History* 89, no. 4 (Autumn 2004): 361.

34. Blight, *Race and Reunion*, 195.

35. For more information on the Great Lakes, Illinois, training camp, go to "African Americans and the U.S. Navy: World War II Activities in the United

States—Great Lakes Naval Training Station, General Views, Naval History and Heritage Command," http://www.history.navy.mil/photos/prs-tpic/af-amer/gt-lakes.htm (accessed December 10, 2011).

36. Saul Carliner, "Computers and Technical Communication in the 21st Century," in *Digital Literacy for Technical Communication: 21st Century Theory and Practice*, ed. Rachel Spilka (New York: Routledge, 2010), 41–42.

37. John Palfrey and Urs Gasser, *Born Digital: Understanding the First Generation of Digital Natives* (Philadelphia: Basic Books, 2008). Henry Jenkins expresses his "discomfort" with the term "digital native" in his popular blog, stating that it "helps us see some aspects of the world clearly while masking others." See Henry Jenkins, "Reconsidering Digital Immigrants," *Confessions of an Aca-Fan* (blog), December 5, 2007, http://www.henryjenkins.org/2007/12/reconsidering_digital_immigran.html (accessed December 5, 2011).

38. "Are You All Digital Natives," Harvard Law, http://cyber.law.harvard.edu/research/youthandmedia/digitalnatives/areallyouthdigitalnatives (accessed December 9, 2011).

39. Palfrey and Gasser, *Born Digital*, 2.

40. Sarah Adler, interview by the author, Norfolk, Va., April 14, 2011.

41. Henry Jenkins, *Convergence Culture: Where Old and New Media Collide* (New York: New York University Press, 2006), 13.

42. Gillis, "Memory and Identity," 5.

43. Barbara Kingsolver, *Animal Dreams: A Novel* (New York: Harper Perennial, 1990), 287.

# Section IV

# The Civil War in Fiction and Film

# 8

# From History to Fiction

## *Abraham Lincoln's Most Famous Murder Trial and the Limits of Dramatic License*

*Daniel W. Stowell*

Filmmakers offer dramatic representations of historical events that shape how Americans perceive the past. As recent movies demonstrate, Abraham Lincoln continues to exert a powerful influence on the American imagination. Although the movies *The Conspirator*, *Abraham Lincoln: Vampire Hunter*, and *Lincoln* take very different approaches to aspects of Lincoln's life and death, *The Conspirator* and *Lincoln* present themselves as stories from the American past. In doing so, they raise important questions: What responsibility do filmmakers have to their audiences? Is it simply to entertain? Or is there a broader duty to the historical record in general or in detail? How do these film representations distort Americans' understanding of the past?

These issues are far from new. By analyzing the documentary evidence from a key trial in which Abraham Lincoln participated, as well as later fictional accounts in which portions of the trial are central, this essay examines the distance between the historian's view of Lincoln as a lawyer and the views of the novelist and the screenwriter. Do these differences matter? When do fictionalized accounts distort historical understanding rather than enhance it?

In May 1858, in a crowded courtroom in central Illinois, Abraham Lincoln defended a young man on trial for his life against a charge of murder. The one-day trial of *People v. Armstrong* would be Lincoln's most famous case. This trial intrigued the public at the time and later biographers and screenwriters largely because Lincoln used an almanac to discredit a key prosecution witness.[1] However, scholars who examine portrayals of Lincoln in film and popular culture, as well as those who study the portrayal of legal topics in film, have rarely compared the historical facts of the trial with these popular presentations.

As with most historical topics, the full story is a bit more complex. The fight that led to the trial occurred outside a Methodist camp meeting in rural Mason County, Illinois, twenty-five miles north of Springfield. Near the whiskey wagons, one mile from the camp meeting, young men gathered to drink, gamble, socialize, and fight. On the evening of August 29, 1857, James Norris and William Duff Armstrong each fought, individually, with James Preston Metzker. The next morning Metzker rode away from the camp meeting and died two days later from injuries received there. The Mason County sheriff promptly arrested both Norris and Armstrong for Metzker's murder.

The Mason County Circuit Court held its second semiannual session for 1857 in late October and early November. The court impaneled a grand jury, and after hearing eleven witnesses against Norris and Armstrong, the grand jury returned a true bill in the indictment for murder. The indictment declared that Norris and Armstrong, "not having the fear of God before their eyes, but being moved and seduced by the instigations of the Devil . . . unlawfully, feloniously, willfully and of their malice aforethought did make an assault" on James Metzker. The indictment claimed that both men had used weapons: Norris a stick of wood about three feet long, and Armstrong a slungshot (a small metal ball, usually made of lead, encased in leather and attached to a strap).[2]

Norris went to trial immediately, and a jury found him guilty of the lesser charge of manslaughter. The judge sentenced Norris to eight years' confinement at hard labor in the state penitentiary—the maximum sentence. Attorneys for Duff Armstrong requested a change of venue because they feared he could not get a fair trial in Mason County. The court granted the request and moved the case against Armstrong to neighboring Cass County.

Sometime before the Cass County Circuit Court met ten days later, Armstrong's mother, Hannah, asked Abraham Lincoln to defend her son. Lincoln had known Hannah and her husband, Jack, since he was a young man. When Lincoln first arrived in New Salem, Illinois, his wrestling match against Jack Armstrong had initiated him into the male culture of the town and won him the respect and loyalty of Armstrong's extended family and friends, known as the "Clary's Grove boys."[3] When the governor of Illinois called for volunteers to drive Sauk and Fox Indians from the northern portion of the state during the Black Hawk War, the men from New Salem elected Lincoln as the captain of their company, and Jack served as one of his sergeants. Hannah sewed leather onto Lincoln's pants to extend their usefulness, and Lincoln sometimes stayed at the Armstrongs' home a few miles from New Salem. Lincoln never forgot their kindness, so when Hannah asked, Lincoln agreed to represent Duff Armstrong and charged nothing for his services.[4]

Lincoln tried to get Armstrong released on bail while the court awaited the arrival of records from Mason County, but the judge rejected Lincoln's plea, and Armstrong remained in jail until the court's next term, six months later. Armstrong's case came up for trial on Friday, May 7, 1858, at the Cass County courthouse in Beardstown, Illinois. Judge James Harriott presided over the trial; state's attorney Hugh Fullerton, assisted by J. Henry Shaw, represented the people of the state of Illinois for the prosecution; and William Walker, Caleb J. Dilworth, and Abraham Lincoln represented the defendant Armstrong.

For decades, participants and scholars have debated the progress and outcome of this trial. Historical detectives interviewed the attorneys, several jurors, the judge, witnesses, court officials, the mother of the defendant, and eventually the defendant himself to obtain their memories of the trial. Predictably, these memories, recorded from seven to thirty-nine years after the event, diverge from and even contradict one another. However, they also provide details about the case and the trial that are unavailable in the sparse official documentation.[5]

What is clear is that Lincoln played a pivotal role in the case and that he had several strategies for victory. His first goal was to obtain the proper type of jury. "Lincoln was smart enough to get a jury of young men," recalled witness William O. Douglas. Younger jurors would be more sympathetic to the passions aroused in young men when they drank too much whiskey. The oldest juror, foreman Milton Logan, was thirty-eight, and the average age of the jurors was twenty-eight.[6]

During the trial itself, Lincoln carefully examined and cross-examined witnesses. Among the prosecution's principal witnesses was Charles Allen, a farm laborer from Menard County. Allen testified that he had seen both Norris and Armstrong strike Metzker in the head. Under cross-examination,

Allen told Lincoln that he had seen the events from thirty yards away by the light of a nearly full moon high in the sky. Lincoln repeatedly questioned Allen on this point, and Allen insisted that the moon was high in the sky and nearly full, lighting the scene of the assault, etching this testimony in the jurors' minds. Lincoln then introduced an almanac for 1857 that showed that at the time of the fight, the moon was low in the sky and within one hour of setting (the moon set at just after midnight on August 29, 1857). According to one of the prosecuting attorneys, the almanac "*floored* the witness" and discredited his testimony in the eyes of the jury. One of the jurors later remembered that "the impression of the almanac evidence led the jury to the idea that if Allen could be so mistaken about the moon, he might have been mistaken about seeing Armstrong hit Metzker with a slung-shot."[7]

Lincoln also questioned witnesses for the defense, including Dr. Charles Parker, who testified that a blow to the back of the head, like the one Norris had inflicted on Metzker, could cause injury to the front of the skull as well. Dr. Parker used a human skull to illustrate his testimony to the jury. Lincoln argued that when Norris hit Metzker in the back of the head, that blow also cracked the front of the skull near the right eye, where Armstrong supposedly struck Metzker. Judge Harriott later recalled that "the Almanace may have cut a figure, but it was Doct Parkers testimony confirming Lincolns theory" that led to Armstrong's acquittal.[8]

In his closing argument before the jury, Lincoln summarized the witnesses' testimony and the scientific evidence presented by Dr. Parker (regarding injuries to the skull) and by the almanac (regarding the moon's location on the night of August 29). Finally, he told the jury how the defendant's parents had been kind to him when he was a young man, friendless and alone. He told the jurors he was defending Armstrong without charging a fee because of his great love and respect for the young man's mother. Co-counsel William Walker observed, "The last 15 minutes of his Speach, was so eloquent, as I Ever heard, and Such the power, & Earnestness with which he Spoke that Jury & all, Sat as if Entranced, & when he was through found relief in a Gush of tears[.] I have never Seen Such mastery Exhibited over the feelings and Emotions of men, as on that occasion." One of the prosecuting attorneys agreed that "Armstrong was not cleared by any want of testimony against him, but by the irresistable appeal of Mr. Lincoln in his favor. He told the jury of his once being a poor, friendless boy, that Armstrong's father took him into his house, fed & clothed him & gave him a home &c. the particulars of which were told so pathetically that the jury forgot the guilt of the boy in their admiration of the father. It was generally admitted that Lincoln's speech and personal appeal to the jury saved Armstrong." He later added that "it was Lincoln's *speech* that saved that criminal from the Gallows, and neither money or fame inspired that speech, but it was incited by gratitude to the young man's father." Nearly forty years after the trial, the accused himself admitted that Lincoln's speech had been critical:

> It seemed to me "Uncle Abe" did his best talking when he told the jury what true friends my father and mother had been to him in the early days, when he was a poor young man at New Salem. He told how he used to go out to Jack Armstrong's and stay for days; how kind mother was to him, and how, many a time, he had rocked me to sleep in the old cradle. He said he was not there pleading for me because he was paid for it; but he was there to help a good woman who had helped him when he needed help. Lawyer Walker made a good speech for me, too, but "Uncle Abe's" beat anything I ever heard.[9]

At the end of the trial, both the prosecuting and the defense attorneys proposed a series of instructions they wanted the judge to give to the jury. Fullerton presented four jury instructions for the prosecution, and Lincoln presented the following two for the defense:

> That if they have any reasonable doubt as to whether Metzker came to his death by the blow on the eye, or by the blow on the back of the head, they are to find the defendant "Not guilty" unless they also believe from the evidence, beyond reasonable doubt, that *Armstrong* and *Norris acted by concert*, against Metzker, and that Norris struck the blow on the back of the head.
> That if they believe from the evidence that Norris killed Metzker, they are to acquit Armstrong, unless they also believe beyond a reasonable doubt that Armstrong acted in concert with Norris in the killing, or purpose to kill or hurt Metzker.[10]

Judge Harriott gave all six proposed instructions to the jury. Caleb J. Dilworth, one of the other defense attorneys, later insisted that "what the case turned upon was the instructions given by the court. There was no question but what the fight with Armstrong and Metzker was an individual affair, and Norris was not present and had nothing to do with it. The assault of Norris was also a separate and distinct affair, and Armstrong was not present and had nothing to do with the other matter. Norris had been convicted of the killing." After receiving the instructions proposed by Lincoln, "of course the jury found for the defendant, as the testimony was clear and conclusive that Armstrong had nothing to do with the assault which Norris made."[11]

Whatever proved to be the decisive factor in the verdict, *People v. Armstrong* reveals lawyer Lincoln at his best. He took advantage of a change of venue for which he could claim no credit but that might have been crucial. He used the structure of the court system to his advantage by selecting a jury of younger men and proposing brilliant jury instructions. He demonstrated his detective skills in the careful examination and cross-examination of witnesses. He employed scientific evidence both to support and to refute testimony. Finally, he marshaled his considerable oratorical skills to appeal to the jurors' emotions and sense of nostalgia. Lincoln's adroit blend of tactics earned his client a rapid acquittal on a charge that could have cost him his life.[12]

Among the thousands of cases that Lincoln handled as an attorney, *People v. Armstrong* came to represent his entire law practice. Although routine debt cases were his most common type of litigation, the dramatic elements of this trial proved to be irresistible to biographers, historians, novelists, and screenwriters. Many emphasized the use of the almanac to discredit the prosecution's witness, and with each retelling, this aspect of the trial assumed more prominence while others were transformed or disappeared entirely.

In 1887 novelist Edward Eggleston used a version of this trial as the dramatic climax of his historical romance *The Graysons: A Story of Illinois.* Born in 1837 in Indiana, Eggleston became a Methodist minister and later an author of religious literature. In the 1870s and 1880s he published a series of historical novels that included vivid descriptions of life in the rural Midwest.[13] Eggleston took the local folklore surrounding the Armstrong case and folded it into his story about the Graysons, a family that shared some similarities with the Armstrongs. Eggleston also took considerable liberties with historical events. In his version, although the fight occurs on the outskirts of a camp meeting in August, the victim George Lockwood is shot with a flintlock pistol and dies immediately. Tom Grayson (a member of the title family) is the only suspect arrested, and he is tried in the fictional county seat of Moscow. Lincoln uses an almanac to prove that at the time of the alleged fight the moon had not yet risen, and his cross-examination of the key prosecution witness, Dave Sovine, reveals not only that Sovine did not see Grayson shoot Lockwood but also that Sovine himself is the murderer. As in the real case, the jury acquits Grayson, and Lincoln refuses to accept a fee from Grayson's mother.[14]

Almost as intriguing as Eggleston's transformation of historical events is his dogged insistence that his version of the story needs no confirmation. He wrote the novel, he declares in the preface, mostly in Italy, "where I could not by any possibility have verified the story . . . from one of Lincoln's old neighbors." To have "investigated the accuracy of my version of the anecdote would have been, indeed, to fly in the face and eyes of providence, for popular tradition is itself an artist rough-hewing a story to the novelist's hands." After writing one more novel, Eggleston turned to history. He became a prominent social historian and, in 1900, served as president of the American Historical Association.[15]

Fifty years after Eggleston used a folk history version of the trial as the climax of his novel, Lamar Trotti crafted the screenplay for a film about Lincoln's early life, using an even more inaccurate version of the case. Trotti, who began work on the screenplay in 1935 and had completed it by 1937, relied heavily on Carl Sandburg's two-volume *Abraham Lincoln: The Prairie Years*, published in 1926.[16] In 1937 producer Darryl F. Zanuck at Twentieth Century–Fox assigned *Young Mr. Lincoln* to director John Ford, who convinced Henry Fonda to play the title role. In many of Ford's films from 1924 to 1962, Lincoln plays a key role as a character or a symbol. One student described Lincoln as "a central obsession with Ford." None of his films deals more extensively with this obsession than *Young Mr. Lincoln*.[17]

Released in June 1939, *Young Mr. Lincoln* offers an overview of Lincoln's life in New Salem and Springfield in the 1830s. Like *The Graysons*, much of the drama in the latter half of the film centers around Lincoln's defense of a client charged with murder. Lincoln wins the acquittal of not one but two defendants by discrediting a prosecution witness using an almanac. Screenwriter Trotti takes even more liberties with historical events than Eggleston did. He shifts the story from the 1850s to the 1830s, when Lincoln was just starting to practice law. In addition to changing the names of nearly all involved parties, Trotti shifts the fight from a camp meeting in August to

Statehood Day (December) in Springfield, and the victim becomes a deputy sheriff. After two brothers, Matt and Adam Clay, are arrested for the murder, Lincoln steps in to avert a lynching by the outraged townspeople. Their mother, though a witness to the fight, refuses to name either of her sons as the guilty party. Unwilling to choose between them, she imperils both.[18] Among the spectators at the trial are Lincoln's future wife Mary Todd and his future political rival Stephen Douglas. "The story, therefore," Trotti wrote to Zanuck, "has some historical basis, although the characters and incidents used, with the exception of Lincoln, Douglas and Mary Todd, are fictional."[19]

In the film version of the trial, Lincoln discredits key prosecution witness J. Palmer Cass (played by character actor Ward Bond) by producing an almanac showing that the moon had already set before the fight occurred, proving that Cass could not have seen it clearly by the light of the moon. As in *The Graysons*, Lincoln reveals that the discredited prosecution witness is himself guilty of the murder by provoking a courtroom confession. Lincoln promptly restores the acquitted sons to their grateful mother.[20]

How should historians view these fictionalized versions of the trial? Did the alteration of historical events in Eggleston's novel and Trotti's screenplay fundamentally change the story? Are some of those changes irrelevant? Does it matter that they took liberties with the details of a trial that took place decades earlier? I submit that it does matter, that such altered representations of historical events distort our understanding of the past and diminish the richness of the history they purport to represent.

Both *The Graysons* and *Young Mr. Lincoln* caricature Lincoln's preparation for the case and his role in the trial by emphasizing the almanac to the exclusion of other defense strategies. Doing so diminishes his legal skills to a one-dimensional stroke of fortune. In addition, both the novel and the film feature a climactic confrontation between Lincoln and the prosecution witness that reveals not only the error of the witness's testimony but also the unexpected truth that the witness himself is the murderer. *Young Mr. Lincoln* departs even further from historical events than *The Graysons* by moving the trial from near the end of Lincoln's legal career to the beginning. Rather than presenting Lincoln as an accomplished lawyer who employs both the law and a variety of evidence to exonerate his client, the inexperienced attorney in *Young Mr. Lincoln* is armed with little more than a sense of justice and keen powers of observation.[21]

It is perhaps appropriate that *Young Mr. Lincoln* premiered in 1939, a few months before *Gone with the Wind* began to teach generations of Americans, white southerners in particular, how to interpret the Civil War and Reconstruction eras. Like the commentary on the Civil War and Reconstruction gleaned from a few scenes in *Gone with the Wind*, the courtroom drama presented in *Young Mr. Lincoln* has defined popular views of Lincoln's skill and reputation as a lawyer.

The release of *Young Mr. Lincoln* even inspired "A Guide to the Study of the Historical Photoplay *Young Mr. Lincoln*," published in 1939 by Educational and Recreational Guides. This guide, recommended by the Secondary Education Committee of the National Education Association, was aimed at high school students. It provided a synopsis of the film and a series of questions, including "How does the photoplay add to your knowledge of Lincoln's life?" and Would Lincoln "accept the ideas of the fascists, their hatred of democracy, their belief that they are 'chosen' races to rule the rest of humanity, their cruelty and disregard of treaties and human rights?" Part of a "rapid quiz" on *Young Mr. Lincoln* included these questions: "Why did Lincoln take the case of the Clays?" and "By what odd point did he win it?" These questions treated the film's presentation of the trial as historical fact. For those who wanted to read more about Lincoln, the guide suggested Sandburg's biography and Eggleston's *The Graysons*, among others.[22]

Why do readers and viewers find such heroic portrayals of Lincoln as an attorney appealing? His image as a flatboatman, a rail-splitter, and a hardworking Common Man has appealed to voters since his election as president in 1860. If manual labor is ennobling, why should he not be a skilled attorney who works hard to prepare for his cases? Audiences seem to want Lincoln to be "better" than that. They want him to possess an unstudied ability to detect lies in witnesses and ask questions that reveal their deceptions; they want him to be extraordinarily perceptive without having to prepare or rely on strategy to defend his client. Thus, at the climax of *Young Mr. Lincoln* he pulls the almanac, representing Truth, "out of his hat like a conjurer."[23]

Merrill D. Peterson's fine study titled *Lincoln in American Memory* barely mentions *The Graysons* and devotes only a paragraph to *Young Mr. Lincoln*. Peterson admits that the onscreen trial "bears a faint resemblance" to the Armstrong trial, without explaining how. He concludes, "without any pretensions to historical accuracy, Ford plays Lincoln for laughs."[24] Although Ford evidently did not care about historical accuracy, his audiences formed a specific view of Lincoln as a lawyer based on his film. Mark S. Reinhart's

*Abraham Lincoln on Screen* devotes two pages of text and three photographs to *Young Mr. Lincoln* and admits that the case at the center of the film is "very loosely based" on Lincoln's defense of Duff Armstrong. Reinhart notes the film's problematic chronology (placing the trial at the beginning of Lincoln's legal career instead of the end), but he finds its canonization of Lincoln its "most historically lacking aspect." Reinhart rightly concludes that the film is "a decidedly unsatisfying Lincoln screen biography" that does not "accurately reflect the Lincoln of history."[25]

Robert A. Rosenstone goes even further in insisting that the historical record has little to do with the making of historical films. "Film must be taken on its own terms as a portrait of the past that has less to do with fact than with intensity and insight, perception and feeling, with showing how events affect individual lives, past and present. To express the meaning of the past, film creates proximate, appropriate characters, situations, images, and metaphors." Though Rosenstone cares little for accuracy, he espouses film as "useful" history.[26] Thus, Robert Redford's distortions of the past in *The Conspirator* are acceptable because they help build a "useful" indictment of President George W. Bush's policies and the use of military tribunals.

More recently, J. E. Smyth rejects the idea that Trotti's screenplay for *Young Mr. Lincoln* is "just another example of Hollywood's manipulation of history in the interest of a trite narrative." Instead, Smyth argues that the screenplay is based on "Trotti's extensive knowledge of and research on Lincoln's life" and that Trotti "worked more as a traditional historian than as a screenwriter" on this project. His screenplay explored "the difference between the real, 'historical' Lincoln and the myth in American consciousness." Smyth admits that historians' misgivings "are valid" but argues that *Young Mr. Lincoln* "did not merely record historical events or document Lincoln's life but assumed the audience's knowledge and moved beyond to a more subtle engagement with the past." The film was "constructed to contrast the many Lincolns known in both history and myth."[27] What this assessment ignores is films' power to create and shape audience's "knowledge" of historical events. Instead of exploring the contradictions between the historical and mythical Lincolns, the fictionalized trial makes Lincoln the lawyer more mythical, giving him an intuitive sense of right divorced from the technical details of the law and an innate ability to divine truth where others cannot detect it.

Americans have long had a love-hate relationship with attorneys. Around the same time he defended Armstrong, Lincoln wrote that "there is a vague popular belief that lawyers are necessarily dishonest. I say vague, because when we consider to what extent confidence and honors are reposed in and conferred upon lawyers by the people, it appears improbable that their impression of dishonesty is very distinct and vivid. Yet the impression is common, almost universal."[28] Later generations likewise did not want Lincoln to be a "typical" lawyer who used the rules of the legal system, strategy, and rhetoric to win acquittal for his clients. In the retellings of the Armstrong trial, Lincoln's client could be innocent, but *someone* had to be guilty of murder—hence the witness-stand confessions of Sovine and Cass.

Scholars whose field of study is the presentation of the law and the courtroom on film have examined *Young Mr. Lincoln*, but their analyses likewise ignore the film's deviation from the historical record. The editors of *Cahiers du Cinéma* read the "text" of the film as a myth designed to defend corporate capitalism and the Republican Party that supported it against the assaults of Franklin D. Roosevelt and the New Deal. Other authors have critiqued the legal aspects of the trial as presented in the film, rather than comparing them to the actual trial of Duff Armstrong.[29]

All presentations of the past, whether a historical monograph, a novel, or a movie, have a point of view, and they all emphasize some aspects of the past over others. Whereas historians are held accountable by their professional peers for their use of sources and their presentation of historical material, novelists and screenwriters are responsible only to their readers and viewers. It is unlikely that historians will have much impact on the way movies present history. Even when filmmakers consult historians, those who write, direct, and produce movies focus more on pleasing the audience than on presenting the past accurately.

Despite their flaws, fictional presentations of historical events present an opportunity to inform in this visual generation. For students who form their perceptions of Abraham Lincoln from *The Conspirator*, *Lincoln*, or even *Abraham Lincoln: Vampire Hunter*, teachers have an opportunity to juxtapose the historical record with popular presentations and ask students to think about what they are watching. A black-and-white film like *Young Mr. Lincoln*, with which most students are unfamiliar, may allow them to think about the presentation more objectively than is possible with modern movies filled with special effects. By comparing the history of the trial, revealed in court documents and the memories of those who were present, with the presentation in

*Young Mr. Lincoln*, students can explore the similarities and differences and reflect on how the film changes the meaning of Lincoln's involvement in the case.

The fictional representation of historical events in novels and movies often distorts public perceptions of the past. Historians and teachers cannot and should not control popular portrayals of history, but they should use them as opportunities to teach students and the general public to think more critically about what they read and see.

## Notes

1. For brief treatments of the trial in major biographies, see Benjamin P. Thomas, *Abraham Lincoln: A Biography* (New York: Knopf, 1952), 159–60; Stephen B. Oates, *With Malice toward None: The Life of Abraham Lincoln* (New York: Harper and Row, 1977), 141–42; David Herbert Donald, *Lincoln* (New York: Simon and Schuster, 1995), 150–51; Michael Burlingame, *Abraham Lincoln: A Life*, 2 vols. (Baltimore: Johns Hopkins University Press, 2008), 1:342–46.

2. Indictment, filed November 5, 1857, *People v. Armstrong* case file, Cass County Circuit Court Records, Cass County Courthouse, Virginia, Ill.

3. The "Clary's Grove boys" were members of the Clary, Armstrong, Watkins, Jones, and related families who lived in the pioneer settlement of Clary's Grove, three miles west of New Salem.

4. Reminiscence of Hannah Armstrong to William H. Herndon, ca. 1866, Herndon-Weik Collection, Library of Congress, Washington, D.C.

5. For the problems inherent in using reminiscences as historical sources, see Daniel W. Stowell, "The Promises and Pitfalls of Reminiscences as Historical Documents: A Case in Point," *Documentary Editing* 27 (Winter 2005): 99–117.

6. Reminiscence of William O. Douglas to J. McCan Davis, ca. 1896, Ida M. Tarbell Collection, Allegheny College, Meadville, Pa.; U.S. Census Office, Seventh Census of the United States (1850), Cass County, Ill., 43; U.S. Census Office, Eighth Census of the United States (1860), Cass County, Ill., 78–279.

7. J. Henry Shaw to William H. Herndon, August 22, 1866, Herndon-Weik Collection; John T. Brady to J. McCan Davis, May 12, 1896, Tarbell Collection.

8. Reminiscence of James Harriott to William H. Herndon, ca. 1866, Herndon-Weik Collection.

9. William Walker to William H. Herndon, June 3, 1865, and J. Henry Shaw to William H. Herndon, August 22 and September 5, 1866, all in Herndon-Weik Collection; reminiscence of William Duff Armstrong to J. McCan Davis, May 1896, *New York Sun* June 7, 1896, 2:3.

10. Jury instructions, May 7, 1858, copy files, Henry Horner Lincoln Collection, Abraham Lincoln Presidential Library and Museum, Springfield, Ill.

11. Caleb J. Dilworth to J. McCan Davis, May 18, 1896, Tarbell Collection.

12. For an authoritative presentation of the documents from the case, see Daniel W. Stowell et al., eds., *The Papers of Abraham Lincoln: Legal Documents and Cases*, 4 vols. (Charlottesville: University of Virginia Press, 2008), 4:1–48. For the presentation of *People v. Armstrong* in studies of Lincoln's law practice, see John J. Duff, *A. Lincoln: Prairie Lawyer* (New York: Bramhall House, 1960), 350–59; John P. Frank, *Lincoln as a Lawyer* (Urbana: University of Illinois Press, 1961), 175–76; Brian R. Dirck, *Lincoln the Lawyer* (Urbana: University of Illinois Press, 2007), 116–19.

13. William Randel, *Edward Eggleston* (New York: Twayne, 1963), 17–18.

14. Edward Eggleston, *The Graysons: A Story of Illinois* (New York: Century Company, 1887), 107–314.

15. Ibid., iii; Randel, *Edward Eggleston*, 141. In his 1935 survey of Lincoln in literature, Roy P. Basler devotes only part of one paragraph to *The Graysons*, largely dismissing it as unrealistic and "oddly romantic." He also notes that in biographies, there is "very little emphasis on the use of the almanac" in the trial. Roy P. Basler, *The Lincoln Legend: A Study in Changing Conceptions* (Boston: Houghton Mifflin, 1935), 45–46.

16. Carl Sandburg, *Abraham Lincoln: The Prairie Years*, 2 vols. (New York: Harcourt, Brace, 1926), 2:53–57. Although Sandburg provides a colorful recounting of the fight and the trial, the general outlines of his presentation are correct. He places the fight at the right place and time, and he credits Armstrong's acquittal to a combination of factors: a young jury, the almanac that discredited Allen, and Lincoln's closing speech recounting the Armstrongs' kindness to him. Mark E. Neely Jr. argues that Sandburg's view of Lincoln's early life "dictated the content" of both *Young Mr. Lincoln* and *Abe Lincoln in Illinois* (1940). Mark E. Neely Jr., "The Young Lincoln," in *Past Imperfect: History According to the Movies*, ed. Mark C. Carnes (New York: Henry Holt, 1995), 124.

The case of *People v. Armstrong* still inspires writers to embellish the details to make them more "dramatic." For a recent example, see John Evangelist Walsh, *Moonlight: Abraham Lincoln and the Almanac Trial* (New York: St. Martin's Press, 2000). For some of the flaws in this presentation, see Daniel W. Stowell, "Moonlight Sheds Little Light," *Journal of the Abraham Lincoln Association* 24 (Winter 2004): 66–74.

17. J. A. Place, "Young Mr. Lincoln, 1939," *Wide Angle* 2 (1978): 28; Tag Gallagher, *John Ford: The Man and His Films* (Berkeley: University of California Press, 1986), 10n.

18. This particular plot twist is based on a trial that Trotti covered while working as a reporter in Georgia. The mother of two young men was the only witness to a murder, and she refused to tell which son was guilty. Both were hanged. Gallagher, *John Ford*, 162n.

19. Lamar Trotti to Darryl F. Zanuck, ca. January 1, 1938, Fox Collection, University of California–Los Angeles, quoted in George F. Custen, *Bio/Pics: How Hollywood Constructed Public History* (New Brunswick, N.J.: Rutgers University Press, 1992), 273, n. 3.

20. Other distortions in *Young Mr. Lincoln* include a jury of older men, a clerk who writes down verbatim testimony, a knife as the murder weapon, Lincoln dressed in a black suit, Mary Todd and Stephen A. Douglas as spectators in the courtroom, and Lincoln's stopping a mob from lynching the accused.

21. For an analysis of the presentation of the law in *Young Mr. Lincoln*, see Norman Rosenberg, "*Young Mr. Lincoln*: The Lawyer as Super-Hero," *Legal Studies Forum* 15, no. 3 (1991): 215–31; Virginia Wright Wexman, "'Right and Wrong; That's [Not] All There Is to It!': *Young Mr. Lincoln* and American Law," *Cinema Journal* 44 (Spring 2005): 20–34.

22. Max J. Herzberg, "A Guide to the Study of the Historical Photoplay *Young Mr. Lincoln*," *Photoplay Studies* 5 (1939): 8–11.

23. Editors of *Cahiers du Cinéma*, "John Ford's *Young Mr. Lincoln*: A Collective Text by the Editors of *Cahiers du Cinéma*," *Screen: The Journal of the Society for Education in Film and Television* 13 (Autumn 1972): 35. J. A. Place adds that "Lincoln is a mythological figure because of a special state of being, not a state of becoming." Rather than showing years of hard work spent learning the law, *Young Mr. Lincoln* implies that Lincoln knows the law intuitively: "He does not *learn*—that which he learns does him little good. But what he *knows* on intuition saves his clients." Place, "Young Mr. Lincoln," 30–31.

George F. Custen suggests that a series of screen biographies with "Young" in the title denotes that "fame is often largely a genetic predisposition, present from a very early age." Thus "young" Abraham Lincoln already possesses the judgment and abilities he will employ as a mature president of a divided nation. Custen, *Bio/Pics*, 51.

24. Merrill D. Peterson, *Lincoln in American Memory* (New York: Oxford University Press, 1994), 137, 344–45.

25. Mark S. Reinhart, *Abraham Lincoln on Screen: Fictional and Documentary Portrayals on Film and Television*, 2nd ed. (Jefferson, N.C.: McFarland, 2009), 219–22.

26. Robert A. Rosenstone, ed., *Revisioning History: Film and the Construction of a New Past* (Princeton, N.J.: Princeton University Press, 1995), 7. See also Robert A. Rosenstone, "History in Images/History in Words: Reflections on the Possibility of Really Putting History onto Film," in *Visions of the Past: The Challenge of Film to Our Idea of History* (Cambridge, Mass.: Harvard University Press, 1995), 19–44; Robert A. Rosenstone, *History on Film/Film on History* (New York: Longman/Pearson, 2006).

27. J. E. Smyth, *Reconstructing American Historical Cinema: From* Cimarron *to* Citizen Kane (Lexington: University Press of Kentucky, 2006), 176, 185–86.

28. Speech on the Practice of Law, ca. 1859, Abraham Lincoln Papers, Library of Congress, Washington, D.C.

29. Editors of *Cahiers du Cinéma*, "John Ford's *Young Mr. Lincoln*," 5–44; Paul Bergman and Michael Asimow, *Reel Justice: The Courtroom Goes to the Movies* (Kansas City, Mo.: Andrews and McMeel, 1996), 147–52. See also Michael Böhnke, "Myth and Law in the Films of John Ford," *Journal of Law and Society* 28 (March 2001): 50–57.

# 9

# The War in Film

## *The Depiction of Combat in* Glory

*Paul Haspel*

Edward Zwick's film *Glory* (1990) dramatizes the story of the Fifty-Fourth Massachusetts Infantry Regiment, the first African American regiment raised in the North during the Civil War, and its commander, Colonel Robert Gould Shaw. Any Civil War combat film will be judged, to some extent, by the verisimilitude of its battlefield sequences, and according to Martin Blatt, one element of the film that has received particular praise is "the authenticity with which *Glory* depicts battle scenes." In an effort to build on the best traditions of Civil War cinema, Zwick viewed two classics of the genre—John Huston's *The Red Badge of Courage* (1951) and Robert Enrico's *Au Coeur de la Vie* (*In the Midst of Life*, 1963)—in preparation for directing *Glory.* Accordingly, the film's dramatizations of three battles—Antietam, James Island, and Fort Wagner—differ significantly from one another in tone and style. Moreover, the film reconciles two differing schools of thought on the dramatization of war in the cinema—a tendency to show war as a meaningless hell, and a countervailing trend to present war as a difficult event that somehow allows a greater good to be achieved—contributing to its success as a work of art. Taken together, the sequences suggest that warfare without a higher purpose is simple butchery, whereas war with a clear ethical goal that goes beyond questions of national self-interest can be legitimate.[1]

Shaw's own testimony, as recorded in his wartime letters, reveals that Antietam, the first battle depicted in *Glory*, made a deep impression on him. On September 21, 1862, then-Captain Shaw of the Second Massachusetts

Regiment wrote to his father about the carnage he had witnessed four days earlier in western Maryland: "Beyond the cornfield was a large, open field, and such a mass of dead and wounded men, mostly Rebels, as were lying there, I never saw before; it was a terrible sight, and our men had to be very careful to avoid treading on them; many were mangled and torn to pieces by artillery. . . . Every battle makes me wish more and more that the war was over. It seems almost as if nothing could justify a battle like that of the 17th, and the horrors inseparable from it."[2]

*Glory*'s Antietam sequence effectively reproduces the factors that filled Shaw with horror. After a prologue that shows African American refugee families traveling through the countryside, Captain Shaw (played by Matthew Broderick) is heard in a voice-over expressing the hope that Union victory will create a new set of conditions in which "all [Americans] can speak." Shaw's reflections gain additional power from James Horner's evocative score, with the angelic vocals of the Boys Choir of Harlem indicating the moral righteousness of the Union cause. Robert Carr claims that "in this opening moment, the film is . . . predicated on a lie and a caesura," as conveyed by "the lushly sentimental voice of [Shaw as] our central narrator." In fact, however, the opening works to remind the audience of the moral issues at stake in the Civil War and puts the issues of African American freedom and human rights out front—in stark contrast to most earlier Civil War movies. From the beginning, the viewer is prompted to think about freedom and slavery as crucial issues in the war. The film is *not* predicated on a lie. Rather, *Glory* is what Ray Kinnard calls a "welcome and extremely forceful counterbalance to previous cinematic insensitivities," refuting the old lies of Lost Cause apologists who downplayed slavery as a cause of the war while emphasizing southern gallantry.[3]

Immediately after Shaw's voice-over ruminations, the caption "Antietam Creek, Maryland—September 17, 1862" appears on the screen. We see Shaw leading his Union soldiers forward in the assault, as other Union regimental officers do likewise. The accuracy and precision of the formations reflect the fact that reenactors well versed in Civil War history, rather than ordinary extras, were carrying out the maneuvers. Early in the production of *Glory* (a project with limited funding), Zwick and producer Freddie Fields took a film crew and obtained footage from a 1988 reenactment of the Battle of Gettysburg. Zwick and Fields not only observed but also participated in the 12,000-strong reenactment. As Zwick declared, "We were out there for three days, wearing Union uniforms and carrying film cans. It was 100 degrees with 99% humidity." This uncomfortable scenario may have helped the filmmakers identify with the Unionist heroes of their movie as they relived at least a small part of the Civil War soldier's experience. Shots from the Gettysburg reenactment were combined with scenes filmed in McDonough, Georgia, where art directors and set decorators worked to re-create the Antietam battlefield, including a mock-up of the Dunker church around which the first part of the battle raged.[4]

In the early part of *Glory*'s Antietam sequence, everything seems orderly, with soldiers marching in straight and sensible lines. Jim Cullen observes that "director of photography Freddie Francis bathes his images in a warm light that exudes ripeness and accessibility, particularly in the panoramic long shots of the Antietam sequence, where a hundred years' worth of black and white photographs seem magically transformed into color." This statement, however, applies only to the early part of the sequence. As Union artillerists open fire, the sun is obscured by the smoke of battle, and the hitherto bright colors turn dull. Confederate soldiers, lined up behind a rail fence, commence firing, and Shaw calls out, "Steady, boys!" A series of quick edits and cuts conveys the speed with which things are moving.[5]

One reviewer for the *New York Times* complained that "during the first charge at Antietam, which opens the film, the boys' faces are prettily smudged, as if by a volunteer make-up artist. One seems to be looking at a tasteful re-enactment." More valid, however, is the perspective of Philip Beidler—a combat veteran as well as a literary and cultural scholar. In a comparison of the battlefield realism in *Glory* and in Ronald Maxwell's *Gettysburg* (1993), Beidler says of the Antietam sequence: "55 seconds of Matthew Broderick as the young Captain Robert Gould Shaw at Antietam somehow supply the thing that is missing in four hours of *Gettysburg*. [It is]. . . the unique capacity of film to combine spectacle with horrific concentration of focus."[6]

Toward that end, Zwick conveys the violence of war quickly and uncompromisingly. One of Shaw's fellow captains turns back toward his men and calls out, "For God's sake, come on!" As he turns to face the enemy, a shell fragment strikes him and blows his head apart in plain view of Shaw, who is spattered by the blood. Zwick orchestrated this shot—one of the few moments of explicit battlefield gore in the film—with a specific audience response in mind. As he remarks in the director's commentary that accompanies the latest DVD release of *Glory*, "One moment such as that . . . would put it in the audience's mind and obviate the need to do anything more. You would be so dreading that kind of thing happening that I wouldn't need to hold their hands over a flame." In contrast to the casual, can-you-top-this gore so common in modern cinema, this shot, like the sequence as a whole, represents a uniquely "creditable attempt at . . . realistic representation of Civil War combat and combat injury." It is filmic violence with a moral purpose and an ethical basis.[7]

Quick cuts combined with someone shouting, "We must fall back!" convey the idea that all order, all sense of organization, has been lost among the attacking Union soldiers. Barbara Correll suggests that this part of the Antietam sequence "present[s] a kind of demented formalism, with officers urging men forward when there was no direction to be discerned." At the beginning of the sequence, establishing shots clearly differentiated which troops were where, with Confederates at screen left and Unionists at screen right. As the sequence continues, however, the viewer, watching the battle from the point of view of Shaw and the other Union soldiers, has no idea where the enemy is. In this context, it is understandable that Shaw seems paralyzed by the sheer horror of warfare—unable to go forward or back.[8]

Amid the stillness in the aftermath of the Antietam battle action, we hear a voice say, "You all right there, Captain?" As the wounded Shaw looks up, the audience looks up with him into the face of Rawlins (played by Morgan Freeman), a gravedigger for the Union army. Immediately afterward, in what Patricia Turner calls a "marvelous exception" to the film's tendency to portray events through Shaw's eyes, "the camera shifts . . . to the view of Rawlins . . . as he peers down on the wounded white character who looks like little more than a boy." The shift in camera angle and point of view prefigures that, for both Shaw and the recruits of the Fifty-Fourth, Rawlins will be someone to look up to.[9]

Shaw nods in silent indication that he is all right, and Rawlins resumes the grim task of walking among the fallen soldiers on the Antietam battlefield and differentiating the living from the dead. Shaw wanders away from the spot where Rawlins found him and sees, in the distance, artillery action taking place on another part of the field. Here, the filmmakers seem to be illustrating one of the strange and unique aspects of Antietam: due to the poor organizational and tactical command of Union general George B. McClellan, the Battle of Antietam was, in effect, three battles that took place around Sharpsburg, Maryland, on the same day. As Peter Burchard puts it, "First it had been Hooker, then Mansfield, now Sumner and so on down the line, making the day a series of battles instead of one crushing blow that could have shattered Lee's line."[10]

As Zwick describes it in his director's commentary on the DVD, this was originally "one of the early shots in the scene, just to show the scale of battle, and as I cut the movie together I realized it served even better for him to see that what he had been through was only the beginning of something rather than the end." Consequently, Captain Shaw, who participated in the first part of the engagement at the north end of the battlefield, seems to be looking over at the second phase of the day's action—the fighting around a sunken farm road that came to be known as "Bloody Lane."

The next scene shows Captain Shaw in a field hospital being treated for a minor neck wound, which he described in a letter to his father written four days after Antietam: "I was struck once by a spent ball in the neck, which bruised, but didn't break the skin." In the hospital scene, a man is vainly begging Union field surgeons not to amputate his leg. At the same time, an orderly tending to Shaw's neck wound speaks of rumors that "Lincoln's gonna issue an Emancipation Proclamation—gonna free the slaves." "What?" Shaw asks. The orderly, not taking much note of Shaw's response, goes on: "Well, maybe not the ones in the border states, or somethin'—I dunno—but he's gonna free some of 'em, anyway. . . . Said he would have done it sooner, only he was waitin' on a big victory—which is I guess what this is." Shaw looks with sadness at the screened-off operating theater where the soldier's leg is being amputated; he seems very conscious of the incongruity between the other man's immense suffering and his own minor wound. Cullen suggests that the scenes of the amputation "not only record the hideousness of combat's aftermath, but in their juxtaposition with the dialogue also suggest an allegory of emancipation as a necessary but torturous struggle in which the infection of slavery is removed from the body politic."[11]

The orderly's sardonic words to Shaw emphasize the massive human cost of Antietam—still the bloodiest day in all of American history. Although Antietam was a strategic victory for the Union, it was a tactical draw. In the wake of such massive human casualties, it is understandable that the orderly, a firsthand witness of the carnage at Sharpsburg, might have had considerable trouble accepting President Lincoln's description of Antietam as a victory.

Shaw is subsequently shown at a party in Boston, his neck wrapped in white cloth to conceal his wound. The combination of slow-motion footage of the partygoers and the sound track's elegiac choral music emphasizes the distance between Shaw and these civilians who have never experienced the horrors of war. Not until his friend Thomas Searles (played by Andre Braugher), a free, upper-class African American, calls his name does Shaw join the party. Even then, the sound of a window being slammed shut sounds like a gunshot, startling Shaw and causing him to almost spill his glass of punch. The viewer at once senses that although Shaw survived the carnage at Antietam, he was traumatized by it. As Beidler puts it, "The rest of the movie will be a study of character indelibly shaped by a memory of these images of horror at Antietam."[12]

Shaw's combat experience at Antietam gives him insight into the awful realities of battle—an insight not shared by the enlisted men of the Fifty-Fourth (with the exception of Rawlins). This difference is emphasized when, after Shaw has accepted Massachusetts governor John Andrew's offer of command of the brand-new regiment, the soldiers of the Fifty-Fourth are issued their .577-caliber Enfield rifles. The young recruits, who have never experienced combat or seen its bloody human cost, begin to play with their rifles—pretending to shoot one another and falling down "dead." Shaw looks horrified. The sounds of real battle are heard on the film's soundtrack; the visuals of the men's make-believe warfare are counterpointed by the sounds of men actually being killed and wounded. We hear the voice of that unnamed Union officer at Antietam who called out, "For God's sake, come on!"—just before his head was blown apart.

Subsequent scenes set forth what David Blight calls "a Civil War platoon drama that follows certain predictable formulas." According to Thomas Cripps, the conventions of the platoon drama require that "the group must be a microcosm of an American life in need of cohesive unity." In other words, the platoon drama typically presents a group of soldiers whose diversity in terms of race, religion, socioeconomic class, region, and the like reflects the diversity of the society for which they are fighting. These soldiers must learn to overcome their differences and work together in order for their side to achieve victory. Zwick and screenwriter Kevin Jarre were well aware of the war-film traditions they were exploiting. As Zwick told interviewer David Heuring, "There were certain conventions of 1940s and 1950s film that *Glory* partook of, and I think that although we wanted to subvert them a little, we wanted to honor them also." These well-worn cinematic conventions, which might have seemed clichéd if the soldiers had been white, somehow gained renewed freshness and energy when applied to the African American experience in the Civil War.[13]

Under the harsh circumstances of the regiment's Readville, Massachusetts, training camp, we see a complex and multilayered interaction among four soldiers who have been assigned to share a tent—in contrast to real life, where the soldiers were quartered in barracks rather than tents. Rawlins, the gravedigger Shaw met at Antietam, serves as a guide for the other three soldiers in his tent, just as he does for Shaw. Rawlins's military training only builds on the qualities of wisdom and leadership he already possesses, as demonstrated in a later scene in South Carolina when he is promoted to sergeant major, the highest rank available to an African American soldier at that time.[14]

Thomas Searles, with his excellent education and high social position, initially identifies with the white officers such as Shaw and Major Cabot Forbes (played by Cary Elwes). He tends to look down on his fellow enlisted men, describing them in a condescending manner as "charming—extraordinary conversationalists, every one." He must learn that his background does not count for much as an enlisted infantryman. He can no longer mix with the white officers who were his social peers in civilian life—that would be "fraternizing"—and he must buckle down and acquire the skills of a good soldier. Shaw describes Thomas as "not a very good soldier," and Sergeant Mulcahy, the Irish American noncommissioned officer assigned to train the recruits, says that Thomas needs to "grow up some more." Over the course of the film, Thomas learns to identify with his fellow African American soldiers rather than dwelling on class issues. When the black soldiers learn that they are being paid less than white soldiers and start to tear up their pay vouchers in protest, Thomas joins in the cry of "Tear it up!"

Jupiter Sharts (played by Jihmi Kennedy), an escaped slave from South Carolina, is a kind and pleasant man, dedicated to the Union cause and freedom. His illiteracy (he does not even know right from left) and his speech impediment speak to how the slave system has held back countless people of intelligence, talent, and goodwill. A crack shot, he must learn that in combat, the ability to reload quickly is at least as important as shooting accurately—a lesson imparted by Shaw when he interrupts a training sequence, orders Jupiter to reload, shouts at him, and fires a pistol repeatedly into the air as the unhappy private tries to reload his Enfield rifle. Throughout the rest of the film, Shaw seems to regret his earlier harshness toward Jupiter. When the regiment's uniforms arrive, Shaw hands one to Jupiter personally, and just before the Fort Wagner charge, when then-Corporal Sharts salutes Shaw and says, "We ready, Colonel," Shaw clasps the corporal's shoulder and smiles.

Trip (played by Denzel Washington), like Jupiter, has escaped from slavery, and his scarred back speaks to the physical and psychic wounds inflicted by the slave experience. He must learn to channel his anger and hostility and direct those feelings in an appropriate direction. Trip insults all his fellow soldiers, calling Thomas "Snowflake," referring to Jupiter as "field hand," and asking Rawlins, "Is you a old man or a old woman? I forget." Actor Washington said of his character, "He's a product of racism who's *become* a racist. He hates all white people, Confederates most of all." Additionally, Trip, who has fought slaveholders with pride and defiance all his life but has never experienced combat, must learn that it will take more than anger and determination to overcome the tough and battle-hardened soldiers of the Confederacy.[15]

Trip also fails to take seriously the concept of military discipline, leaving the camp without authorization and trying unsuccessfully to persuade Jupiter to go with him. Trip pretends that his motivation for going AWOL is "biscuits and gravy," but he is in fact trying to find himself a decent pair of shoes, as the Fifty-Fourth Massachusetts has been denied even the most basic supplies. When Trip is caught he is sentenced to be flogged for desertion—a scene that is powerful in dramatic terms but contrary to the actual history of the times. As U.S. Army historian Russell F. Weigley points out, "To accommodate and attract recruits, the volunteer regiments relaxed the harsh disciplinary punishments of the Regular Army. Flogging was abolished in 1861, much to the satisfaction of humanitarians who had long campaigned against it." Thus, it is inconceivable that a proper and procedure-minded officer like Shaw would have ordered a flogging in 1863. Nevertheless, the scene projects an enormous amount of dramatic power, recalling all the cruelty and horror of the slave system. Trip throws off his ragged shirt to reveal a back scarred by many whippings, and he stares into Shaw's face while he is flogged—never screaming or crying out, with only a single tear trickling down his face to reveal his pain.[16]

While the film veers from historical accuracy in that scene, it seems dedicated to achieving a higher level of truth by tearing down accumulated levels of myth. That goal may be indicated indirectly by a scene in which Shaw, on horseback, is shown practicing for saber combat by slashing at watermelons that have been placed atop wooden stakes. Historian James McPherson clarifies what this scene means in symbolic terms: "Shaw . . . gallops his horse along a path flanked by stakes, each with a watermelon (in February in Massachusetts?) jammed on its top. Shaw slashes right and left with his sword slicing and smashing every watermelon. The point becomes clear when we recall the identification of watermelons with the darky stereotype. If the image of smashed watermelons in *Glory* can replace that of moonlight and magnolias in *Gone with the Wind* as America's cinematic version of the Civil War, it will be a great gain for truth."[17]

This watermelon-slashing scene, which takes place immediately after Shaw's harsh treatment of Jupiter, provides insight into the growing conflict between Shaw and Forbes. The latter does not share Shaw's experience of the horrors of combat and therefore does not understand the reasons for Shaw's strict discipline. Forbes starts a conversation by saying, "If you wouldn't mind getting down from your horse," thereby seeking to restore their prewar equality as old friends, and then asks Shaw, "Why do you treat the men this way?" In response to Shaw's insistence that he is "getting these men ready for battle," Forbes leans in close and sarcastically asks, "Who do you think you are—acting the high-up Colonel? You seem to forget I know you." Shaw is resolute, telling Forbes, "If you don't believe in what we're doing here, maybe you shouldn't be part of it." Forbes, who knows that Shaw has had a tough time procuring even the most basic military supplies for the men, insists that "marching is probably all they'll ever get to do." Shaw's reply shows that he has a better understanding of the big picture: "It is my job to get these men ready—and I will. They have risked their lives to be here; they have given up their freedom. I owe them as much as they have given; I owe them *my* freedom—my life, if necessary. Maybe so do you, Cabot. I think you do." Forbes's response is a sarcastic low bow; clearly, he is unconvinced.

This conflict between Shaw and Forbes comes to a head in the scene in which Trip is flogged for desertion. When Forbes hears Sergeant Mulcahy say, "The prisoner is to be flogged before the entire regiment," a horrified Forbes protests: "Robert! Not with a whip—not on them!" Shaw reprimands Forbes, "Never question my authority in front of others." In reply, Forbes adopts a slave dialect, effectively accusing Shaw of acting like a southern slaveholder: "Well, I is sorry, massa. You be the boss man now, and all us chilluns must learn to obey." Diana Culbertson describes the paradoxes inherent in this singularly painful scene, suggesting that Trip's "capture forces Shaw to replicate the master-slave relationship he abhorred, against which both of them were fighting. The military structure required the same level of violence that characterized . . . the whole slavery system. . . . Its bitter irony climaxes when the lashes fall across old wounds originally inflicted when Trip was whipped as a slave." Shaw orders Forbes to stand at attention and witness the agonizing punishment.[18]

When Shaw subsequently learns from Rawlins that Trip was only looking for a decent pair of shoes, and then visits the infirmary and sees Trip's bloody feet, it gives him the resolve he needs to strong-arm a recalcitrant quartermaster sergeant into providing shoes for the men. The film thus indicates that when Shaw and Rawlins (and, by implication, whites and blacks) communicate and work together, the unit (like the Union) will be able to accomplish its goals.

The battle-guided leadership of Shaw and Rawlins and the tough training provided at Readville help the regiment perform well in its first test of actual combat at James Island, South Carolina, on July 16, 1863. As with the Antietam sequence, a subtitle announces the location and date of the battle, as if to indicate that although some elements of the film are fictional (e.g., the characters Rawlins, Searles, Sharts, and Trip), this scene is dramatizing a real battle that took place on a particular day. The Fifty-Fourth forms ranks as the Confederate cavalry charges. Ordered to fire by battalion, the Fifty-Fourth repels the Rebel cavalry and cheers. Trip and Rawlins, however, remain watchful, and Rawlins's shout of "Here they come!" reveals that the cavalry was just a screen for a large group of Confederate infantrymen.

As hand-to-hand combat ensues between the Fifty-Fourth Massachusetts and their Rebel adversaries, details of the fight validate Shaw's tough training methods. Jupiter, scolded earlier for being unable to reload quickly, does so in haste as a Rebel charges him, completing the process just in time to shoot down his enemy. Thomas, who had not seemed to be a very effective soldier up to this point, is wounded but stays in the fight. Trip, seeing his fellow Union soldiers fall, now knows that neither the presence of the Fifty-Fourth nor the righteousness of their cause guarantees that only Rebels will die. Trip fights well and proficiently but finds himself facing death at the hands of a Confederate; only a quick bayonet thrust by the wounded Thomas (who had been subjected to some particularly harsh bayonet training by Sergeant Mulcahy) saves Trip. Their brave fighting, combined with effective troop dispositions and maneuvers, forces the Rebels to retreat, and members of the Fifty-Fourth cheer.

In the wake of the regiment's victory, a conversation between Thomas and his commanding officers demonstrates the extent to which he has come to identify with his fellow soldiers and believe in their cause. Greeted by Shaw, Thomas says, "How do, Colonel," abandoning his customarily elaborate diction and speaking as the other enlisted men might. Shaw pretends to be jealous that Thomas will be "back in Boston before me—sitting by the fire, reading Hawthorne." But Thomas says, "I'm not going back." Forbes, in a well-meaning but somewhat paternalistic tone, tells him, "Thomas. Listen to me. You were shot. You have to go back." In response, Thomas makes Shaw promise that he can stay. Sergeant Mulcahy's previous recommendation that Thomas "grow up some more" has been fulfilled. Thomas *has* grown up— into a strong and committed soldier.

After James Island, the men of the Fifty-Fourth—like Shaw after Antietam—know that they are equal to the task of battle and all its associated horrors. Captain Luis Emilio, an officer and later historian of the Fifty-Fourth, recorded the men's pride once they had proved themselves in combat: "It was a supreme moment for the Fifty-Fourth, then under fire as a regiment for the first time. The sight of wounded comrades had been a trial; and the screaming shot and shell flying overhead, cutting the branches of trees to the right, had a deadly sound. But the dark line stood stanch [*sic*], holding the front at the most vital point."[19]

In the same vein, Corporal James Henry Gooding wrote of the regiment's cool behavior under fire: "The men of the 54th behaved gallantly on the occasion—so the Generals say. It is not for us to blow our horn; but when a regiment of white men gave us three cheers as we were passing them, it shows that we did our duty as men should." A white soldier of the Tenth Connecticut, which the Fifty-Fourth Massachusetts rescued at James Island, wrote in a letter, "But for the bravery of three companies of the Massachusetts Fifty-Fourth (colored), our whole regiment would have been captured. . . . They fought like heroes." Such historical expressions of appreciation by white Union soldiers may have inspired a later scene in *Glory*: As the soldiers of the regiment march through a group of Union columns on their way to lead the assault on Fort Wagner, a white soldier who had insulted them earlier calls out, "Give 'em hell, 54th!" And all the white soldiers in the column echo that cry of encouragement.[20]

The night before the Fort Wagner battle, the men of the Fifty-Fourth sing and give testimony, providing the viewer with a sense of how these combat veterans have bonded. Trip, orphaned by the slave system, tells his fellow soldiers, "Y'all's the onliest family I got. And—I loves the 54th. Ain't much of matter what happens tomorrow—we men, ain't we?" The men respond with affirmation. Clearly, the shared experience of battle has forged a strong sense of unit cohesion.

The Fort Wagner sequence, which McPherson praises as "the most realistic combat footage in any Civil War movie I have seen," begins with a daytime charge. Shells fired from the Confederate battery explode on the beach where the Fifty-Fourth is charging, sending up clouds of smoke and sand. As in the Antietam sequence, the viewer gets a feel for how difficult it is to make sense of what is going on during battle. Yet the organization of the Fort Wagner sequence sets it in opposition to the Antietam sequence. As the Fifty-Fourth Massachusetts attacks the fort, the viewer's sense of direction is not lost, and the battle does not resemble the pure chaos of Antietam; subsequent shots in the Fort Wagner sequence reinforce the establishing shot, emphasizing that the soldiers maintain formation even as shells burst among them, inflicting death and injury. The regiment hunkers down next to a wall of the fort, and Shaw covers his head as he did at Antietam. This time, however, he is not paralyzed by the experience of battle. Rather, he crawls along a ridge, giving orders and orchestrating the upcoming attack: "Company commanders: We will wait here and advance under cover of darkness. Sergeant Rawlins, pass the word along: Forward on my command!"[21]

Once night has fallen, the viewer sees the soldiers' dire situation: they have charged through the fort's outer defenses, crossed a moat, and made their way through a barrier of pointed stakes to a hold a precarious position next to a rampart of the fort. Red and blue filters emphasize how the battle lights up the night sky, while at the same time reminding the audience of the American values for which the soldiers are fighting. The Confederates shoot their rifles almost straight down at the men, throw homemade hand grenades, and even tilt a cannon at a precarious angle to fire at the soldiers of the Fifty-Fourth. One last time, Shaw shields his head; then he pulls his pistols and begins running up the rampart, shouting, "Come on, 54th!" A Rebel volley cuts him down and, as Michael C. C. Adams describes it, the camera "lingers agonizingly on Shaw's monumental effort to force his dying body upward" before a second volley sends him plummeting down the hill to lie dead at the feet of his men. This is a great and moving cinematic moment, even if, in fact, Shaw actually made it to the top of the rampart and fell forward among the Confederates.[22]

Mark Golub, analyzing *Glory* in the context of what he calls the "Hollywood redemption narrative," describes Shaw's death as it is dramatized in the film: "His death is preceded by an introspective lull in the fighting, as the 54th crouches behind a bunker, thus highlighting the voluntaristic element of Shaw's death: he decides it is time, he stands and advances, knowing he will die, and when he is shot in the chest he falls backward, arms extended as Christ's on the cross."[23]

Trip, who had earlier refused the honor of carrying the regimental flag—calling it "your flag" in a conversation with Shaw—now takes up the flag and calls out "Come on!" inspiring the soldiers of the Fifty-Fourth to charge. He is shot repeatedly but holds the flag high and looks resolutely at his enemies, proud and defiant to the end. It is, for many viewers, this courageous soldier's most heroic moment.

The Union soldiers fight bravely, moving forward through the fort. In contrast to the confusion and chaos of the Antietam sequence, the trajectory of the soldiers' movements is consistently clear from the establishing shot on, with the Unionists charging from left to right. Heike Bungert, comparing the Fort Wagner and Antietam sequences, states, "Although showing injuries and death, the scene of fighting at night is so obscured that one misses much of the actual suffering." In contrast to the explicit onscreen violence of the Antietam sequence, most of the violence in the Fort Wagner sequence occurs at the edge of or just outside the frame. To some extent, the violence of war is given order and even aesthetic beauty. Correll comments that "at Fort Wagner the men flow through the distractions of the shelling, as casualties—dropping off as the movement surges forward—are synchronized with the music." Perhaps this is why Robert Burgoyne accuses the film of "suggest[ing] . . . that racial difference is dissolved in warfare, valorizing war as the defining moment when racial and national self-realization coalesce."[24]

Director Zwick explained how he wanted to make each of the battle sequences different:

We wanted each of the battles to have a separate look. If the first one [Antietam] was somehow objectified, the skirmish [James Island] was much more subjective, and scary and confused. But the final battle [Fort Wagner] needed to be somehow elevated. The attempt was to make visual that accomplishment of myth—the myth that was accomplished by virtue of this battle. In history, this battle took on a life beyond itself, in memory and in importance to the culture. Somehow, without romanticizing it, keeping it scary and violent, we had to give it an elevated style.[25]

*New Yorker* film reviewer Pauline Kael sensed Zwick's burden as he tried to satisfy the emotional and storytelling needs of the different battle sequences: "In the early scenes at Antietam, when body parts erupt and hover in the air, the randomness of the carnage seems appropriate." But by the time of the Fort Wagner sequence, "if the movie is to live up to the feelings it stirs in us, we need to see the bravery of the troops as they steadily move toward the concentrated power of Fort Wagner, the dead piling up on the slopes of the bastion and on its walls." Responding to this challenge, Zwick effectively uses the tools of cinema to depict battle in different ways, depending on context, and to present an ethically consistent argument about the moral issues underlying combat in general and the American Civil War in particular.[26]

Zwick's film received a great deal of popular acclaim. *Boston Globe* film critic Jay Carr, for example, called *Glory* "the most overdue war movie ever made, filled with terrible beauty, richness, and grandeur." Tom O'Brien of *Commonweal* declared it "the first American movie to brush greatness since *The Godfather*."[27]

Professional historians, meanwhile, differed in their assessment of *Glory.* James McPherson called the film "the most powerful and historically accurate movie about that war ever made." Eric Foner, in contrast, noted that "there were many historical inaccuracies in it" and declined to give the film his "Good Housekeeping Seal of Approval."[28]

Joining Foner in lamenting the film's departures from historical reality was Carl Cruz, a descendant of Sergeant William H. Carney (the Fifty-Fourth Massachusetts flag-bearer who survived wounds received at Fort Wagner to become the first African American awarded the Congressional Medal of Honor). Cruz complained that while the film foregrounds the real Colonel Shaw, it ignores the real-life soldiers of the Fifty-Fourth in favor of fictional characters: "I told them [the film crew] what I knew [about Sergeant Carney] over the telephone," he said, "but they never followed through."[29]

Douglas Brode offers an interesting alternative, describing the film that *Glory* could have been: "A true 'black film' about the Fifty-Fourth" would have emphasized the individual soldiers, "either with one African-American character (perhaps Denzel [Washington]'s) employed as the film's focus or from a standpoint shared by all four key black characters equally, ensemble style, as was the case with [William Wellman's 1949 World War II film] *Battleground*." Similarly, David Nicholson, a former editor of *Black Film Review*, wrote that "the real reason for the reservations I have about the film . . . is that I want 'Glory' to be more than it is, want it to be the story of black heroism and determination, of the black struggle to be allowed to be wholly American. . . . 'Glory' gives us a sense of this, perhaps more than we have ever seen before on the screen, but the whole story is so much more than that."[30]

Still, even those who criticized the historically inaccurate aspects of the film have generally acknowledged *Glory* as "at least an initial attempt to confront some central questions of African American history." According to William S. McFeely, "The film, despite . . . scholarly criticisms, is surely a celebration of involvement and valor. . . . The important thing about the movie is that a great many Americans, both black and white, saw [*Glory's* African American protagonists] going off to fight a war that would end slavery."[31]

I agree with Morris Dickstein's suggestion that, in *Glory*, "a relatively minor incident in the military history of the Civil War . . . was reconstituted into myth." And the requirements of myth are different from those of documentary. As Thomas Cripps puts it, "A tolerable credibility requires only that the details *ring* true rather than speak truth: the trigger housings and the flash pans of the muskets, the badges on the kepis, the mundane details of . . . Carolina campfires allow us to believe that the accompanying story seems true enough to carry the freight of its meaning."[32]

At the time of its release, *Glory* succeeded in awakening interest in the Civil War, and in African American participation in that war, within the larger culture. Zwick's goals for *Glory* included "redressing historical misperception, providing positive role models and doing whatever it can to contribute to healing the commonality of purpose between people." The director of Boston's Museum of Afro-American History, discussing *Glory's* New England benefit premiere in the context of the Charles Stuart murder case that had divided the city along racial lines, said, "I'm hoping that this [film] helps the process of healing." Similarly, at the time of *Glory's* Washington, D.C., release, drug-prevention educator David Miller of Shaw Junior High School (named for Colonel Shaw) commended the film as a valuable educational tool: "These kids need to be fed the image of these courageous black soldiers. If we could teach a generation of students to see how they need to stand together and help each other, we could eliminate the drug problem."[33]

Years after the film's initial release, educators continue to turn to *Glory* to awaken students' interest in this important period of history. A 1994 teachers' resource book recommended *Glory* as the definitive Civil War film for classroom use, "especially in light of the reemergence of the virtues of military prowess in the wake of the 'techno-war' in the Persian Gulf." Indeed, some educators have suggested that critics' focus on *Glory*'s historical inaccuracies may be misplaced. As Harvey H. Jackson states, "The very inaccuracies and interpretations which trouble literalists" regarding historical dramas can help all of us "gain some insight into the era in which the films were made. . . . What society accepts as history reveals as much about the society as it does about the past, and there are few places where a society's historical perspective is more clearly revealed than in its response to films." Consequently, a film's historical inaccuracies can lead to fruitful discussion. James Percoco, a teacher in northern Virginia, points out, "I am compelled to tell students that if the film is shown in a vacuum we come away with the perception that the assault on Fort Wagner was the only engagement in which the 54th fought." In fact, Fort Wagner was not even the largest or bloodiest of the regiment's battles; that distinction is held by the 1864 Battle of Olustee, Florida.[34]

In the context of Civil War cinema, *Glory* was truly revolutionary. Bruce Chadwick accurately states that it "shattered the great Civil War movie taboo—it told a story of African Americans." A number of Civil War films have come out since *Glory*—Ronald Maxwell's *Gettysburg* (1993) and *Gods and Generals* (2003), Ang Lee's *Ride with the Devil* (1998), Anthony Minghella's *Cold Mountain* (2003). And although these films have achieved varying degrees of critical acclaim and commercial success, none has matched the long-term impact of *Glory*, perhaps because none of them engages the issues of slavery and racism as directly or as artfully as *Glory* does.[35]

Part of the success of *Glory* is attributable to the manner in which its well-staged battle scenes relate, in terms of both form and content, to the film's themes. At the time of its release, Richard A. Blake pointed out a paradox the filmmakers faced: "*Glory* . . . carries the twin burden of showing that black soldiers, and by analogy, black people, are equal to whites and that war is futile." *Glory* overcomes this contradiction by using the stylistic differences in its three battle scenes to suggest that, in the absence of a higher moral cause, war is nothing but butchery, whereas if one is fighting for a cause that involves human rights, war can serve a higher good. Robert Burgoyne argues that "the links the film establishes among patriotism, militarism, and nationalism, its endorsement of a 'mystic nationhood' revealed only on the battlefield, reinforce the dominant fiction" of American life "at the site of its greatest potential harm, where it can have the most consequences." Yet *Glory* certainly cannot be accused of romanticizing or glorifying war the way Sylvester Stallone's *Rambo* movies do. Rather, *Glory* points out, in a responsible manner, that all wars are bloody exercises in death, maiming, and pain, while suggesting that some causes are worth fighting for.[36]

## Notes

This essay originally appeared, in a somewhat different form, as "Antietam, James Island, and Fort Wagner: The Battle Sequences in Edward Zwick's *Glory*," *Studies in Popular Culture* 30, no. 1 (Fall 2007).

1. Martin H. Blatt, "*Glory*: Hollywood History, Popular Culture, and the Fifty-Fourth Massachusetts Regiment," in *Hope and Glory: Essays on the Legacy of the Fifty-Fourth Massachusetts Regiment*, ed. Martin H. Blatt, Thomas J. Brown, and Donald Yacovone (Amherst: University of Massachusetts Press, 2001), 226; John Simon, "Swords and Bullets," *National Review*, March 19, 1990, 58.

2. Russell Duncan, ed., *Blue-Eyed Child of Fortune: The Civil War Letters of Robert Gould Shaw* (Athens: University of Georgia Press, 1992), 240, 242.

3. Robert Carr, "From *Glory* to *Menace II Society*: African American Subalternity and the Ungovernability of the Democratic Impulse under Super-Capitalist Orders," in *The Latin American Subaltern Studies Reader*, ed. Ileana Rodriguez (Durham, N.C.: Duke University Press, 2001), 230; Ray Kinnard, *The Blue and the Gray on the Silver Screen* (Secaucus, N.J.: Birch Lane Press, 1996), 270.

4. Glenn Collins, "'Glory' Resurrects Its Black Heroes," *New York Times*, March 26, 1989, 16; David Heuring, "*Glory*—The Rockets' Red Glare," *American Cinematographer*, November 1990, 59; C. Peter Jorgensen, "The Making of 'Glory,'" *Civil War Times Illustrated*, November/December 1989, 59.

5. Jim Cullen, *The Civil War in Popular Culture: A Reusable Past* (Washington, D.C.: Smithsonian Institution Press, 1995), 159.

6. Vincent Canby, "Black Combat Bravery in the Civil War," *New York Times*, December 14, 1989, 15; Philip Beidler, "Ted Turner et al. at Gettysburg; or, Reenactors in the Attic," *Virginia Quarterly Review* 75, no. 3 (Summer 1999): 501.

7. Beidler, "Ted Turner," 500.

8. Barbara Correll, "Rem(a)inders of G(l)ory: Monuments and Bodies in *Glory* and *In the Year of the Pig*," *Cultural Critique* 36 (Spring 1995): 151.

9. Patricia A. Turner, *Ceramic Uncles and Celluloid Mammies: Black Images and Their Influence on Culture* (New York: Anchor Books, 1994), 172.

10. Peter Burchard, *One Gallant Rush: Robert Gould Shaw and His Brave Black Regiment* (New York: St. Martin's Press, 1990), 64.

11. Duncan, *Blue-Eyed Child*, 241; Cullen, *Civil War in Popular Culture*, 159.

12. Beidler, "Ted Turner," 501.

13. David W. Blight, "The Meaning or the Fight: Frederick Douglass and the Memory of the Fifty-Fourth Massachusetts," *Massachusetts Review* 36 (Spring 1995): 143; Thomas Cripps, "Frederick Douglass: The Absent Presence in *Glory*," *Massachusetts Review* 36 (Spring 1995): 156; Heuring, "*Glory*—The Rockets' Red Glare," 62.

14. Russell Duncan, *Where Death and Glory Meet: Colonel Robert Gould Shaw and the 54th Massachusetts Infantry* (Athens: University of Georgia Press, 1999), 71.

15. Glenn Collins, "Denzel Washington Takes a Defiant Break from Clean-cut Roles," *New York Times*, December 28, 1989, C13.

16. Russell F. Weigley, *History of the United States Army* (New York: Macmillan, 1967), 231.

17. James M. McPherson, *Drawn with the Sword: Reflections on the American Civil War* (New York: Oxford University Press, 1996), 109.

18. Diana Culbertson, "'Ain't Nobody Clean': The Liturgy of Violence in 'Glory,'" *Religion & Literature* 25, no. 2 (Summer 1993): 35–52.

19. Luis Emilio, *A Brave Black Regiment: History of the Fifty-Fourth Regiment of Massachusetts Volunteer Infantry, 1863–1865* (New York: Arno Press, 1969), 61.

20. Virginia Matzke Adams, ed., *On the Altar of Freedom: A Black Soldier's Civil War Letters from the Front* (Amherst: University of Massachusetts Press, 1991), 38; Joseph T. Glatthaar, *Forged in Battle: The Civil War Alliance of Black Soldiers and White Officers* (New York: Free Press, 1990), 136.

21. McPherson, *Drawn with the Sword*, 23.

22. Michael C. C. Adams, "Seeking Glory: Our Continuing Involvement with the 54th Massachusetts," *Studies in Popular Culture* 14, no. 2 (1992): 12, 18.

23. Mark Golub, "History Died for Our Sins: Guilt and Responsibility in Hollywood Redemption Histories," *Journal of American Culture* 21, no. 3 (1998): 36.

24. Heike Bungert, "*Glory* and the Experience of African-American Soldiers in the Civil War: An Attempt at Historical Film Analysis," *Amerikastudien/American Studies* 40, no. 2 (1995): 279; Correll, "Rem(a)inders of G(l)ory," 151; Robert Burgoyne, "Race and Nation in *Glory*," *Quarterly Review of Film & Video* 16, no. 2 (1997): 136.

25. Heuring, "*Glory*—The Rockets' Red Glare," 61.

26. Pauline Kael, "The Current Cinema: The 54th," *New Yorker*, February 5, 1990, 111.

27. Jay Carr, "'Glory': War Film Filled with a Terrible Beauty," *Boston Globe*, January 12, 1990, 36; Tom O'Brien, "At War with Ourselves," *Commonweal*, February 9, 1990, 84.

28. James M. McPherson, "The 'Glory' Story," *New Republic*, January 8–15, 1990, 22; Eric Foner, "A Conversation between Eric Foner and John Sayles," in *Past Imperfect: History According to the Movies* (New York: Henry Holt, 1995), 17.

29. Desiree French, "The Soldiers Untouched by 'Glory,'" *Boston Globe*, January 11, 1990, 77.

30. Douglas Brode, *Denzel Washington: His Films and Career* (Secaucus, N.J.: Birch Lane Press, 1997), 88; David Nicholson, "What Price 'Glory'? The Movie May Be Stunning, but It's Surpassed by the Past," *Washington Post*, January 21, 1990, G7.

31. Blight, "The Meaning or the Fight," 143; William S. McFeely, "In the Presence of Art," *Massachusetts Review* 36 (Spring 1995): 165–66.

32. Morris Dickstein, "Going to the Movies: War!" *Partisan Review* 57, no. 4 (1990): 612; Thomas Cripps, "*Glory* as a Meditation on the Saint-Gaudens Monument," in Blatt et al., *Hope and Glory*, 239.

33. Armond White, "Fighting Black," *Film Comment*, January/February 1990, 24; Carol Flake, "In Troubled Times, 'Glory' Pulls People Together," *Boston Globe*, January 13, 1990, 9, 13; Thomas Bell, "D.C. Teachers Praise 'Glory's' Message," *Washington Post*, January 18, 1990, DC1.

34. Wendy S. Wilson and Gerald H. Herman, *American History on the Screen: A Teacher's Resource Book on Film and Video* (Portland, Maine: J. Weston Walch, 1994), 24; Harvey H. Jackson, "Can Movies Teach History?" *OAH Newsletter* 18, no. 4 (November 1990): 4; James A. Percoco, *A Passion for the Past: Creative Teaching of U.S. History* (Portsmouth, N.H.: Heinemann, 1998), 84.

35. Bruce Chadwick, *The Reel Civil War: Mythmaking in American Film* (New York: Alfred A. Knopf, 2001), 280.

36. Richard A. Blake, "The Tide of Pomp: Images of War in a Season of Peace," *America*, January 27, 1990, 64; Robert Burgoyne, *Film Nation: Hollywood Looks at U.S. History* (Minneapolis: University of Minnesota Press, 1997), 36.

# Section V

# The Civil War as Entertainment

# 10

# The War in Cardboard and Ink

## Fifty Years of Civil War Board Games

*Alfred Wallace*

Michael C. C. Adams begins *Echoes of War* by listing some of the ways Americans enjoy military history: museums, reenactments, popular history books, television programs, movies. The popularity of these military entertainments is apparent from sales figures. For instance, *Saving Private Ryan* earned $224.7 million in gross ticket sales just a few years before Adams's book was published, leading a large pack of blockbuster war movies.[1]

A year after *Echoes of War* was published in 2002, the first *Call of Duty* game was released. Even the game's creators probably could not have imagined that its descendant, 2011's *Call of Duty: Modern Warfare 3*, would gross more than $1 billion in just over two weeks. That figure is far larger than the total domestic gross of *Gettysburg* (1993), *Saving Private Ryan* (1998), *Pearl Harbor* (2001), *Cold Mountain* (2003), *Gods and Generals* (2003), *Valkyrie* (2008), and *Inglourious Basterds* (2009) combined. Games have taken their place alongside—or perhaps even ahead of—Adams's list of popular military culture.[2]

At the time, *Modern Warfare 3* was merely the most recent in a century-long history of games of war. Before war games made their way to television screens, they were played on the floor and on the tabletop. The history of war games is a rich one, revealing changes influenced by both technology and taste. This essay focuses on one corner of the war-game world: tabletop games depicting (some would prefer "simulating") the American Civil War on a strategic scale—that is, the entire war. This consists of some twenty games, produced from the war's centennial in 1961 up to 2010. Until the late 1990s, these games (not surprisingly) tended to focus on battles and leaders while largely ignoring of the causes of the war and its nonmilitary features. In recent years, however, these games have become more sophisticated, with slavery and emancipation and political and social events becoming much more prominent. This is one area of the Civil War in popular culture that has become deeper and more complex over its lifetime. This essay examines the evolution of that complexity.

Games depicting war in highly abstract ways—like chess—have existed for millennia in many cultures, but the genesis of modern commercial war games is much more recent. Table exercises for military purposes date to the early modern period, but these never evolved into a civilian pastime. War gaming as a civilian hobby began in the early twentieth century. H. G. Wells took advantage of the new availability of mass-produced toy soldiers—and his own fertile imagination—to concoct a set of rules, called *Little Wars*, by which these toy soldiers played out imaginary battles. These rules were designed with boys (and "that more intelligent sort of girl") in mind "from twelve years of age to one hundred and fifty."[3] The successors of *Little Wars*, from more complex games for toy soldiers to *Call of Duty*, have attracted much the same audience: men and teenage boys.

Miniatures games have retained a certain appeal over the years, but war games became more mainstream in the United States when the popularity of board games enjoyed a resurgence in the 1950s. The games under discussion here were born out of this efflorescence. During the era of their greatest popularity, these games could be found at Sears and other major U.S. retailers and sold more than 100,000 copies each. Such numbers may seem quaint today, but at the time, these games represented a distinct subculture of popular military history.[4]

Martin van Creveld devotes some space in *The Culture of War* to this kind of military consumer culture, but he declares that the board war game was "brought down" by computer games in the 1990s. This view is largely shared by Rex A. Martin, once a significant figure in the war-game publishing industry himself, who wrote his PhD dissertation on the "rise and fall" of the war-gaming subculture. Although war gaming may not be as popular as it once was, it certainly survives and is producing many games—including those covering the Civil War.[5]

A great many games have been produced over the years that have martial themes but would not be considered war games. Devising a precise definition of "war game" has confounded the war-gaming community. A war game is more than merely "a game about war"; it has grander ambitions. The criteria by which H. G. Wells judged his own game are still hallmarks of war games in any medium. First, a war game must be "realistic," in that it attempts to model a particular (though perhaps not historical) conflict. This eliminates highly abstract games such as chess. The game must also reward strategic play. This eliminates highly luck-based games and role-playing games. Finally, a war game is meant to be fun—a concept that is sometimes lost in huge rule books. Hereafter, all references to "war games" are to tabletop games rather than games involving miniature soldiers or video games.[6]

War games have their own vocabulary. Games are said to be designed by a designer. War games cover wars, campaigns, or battles—combat at one scale or another. Games are played on a map, which might be realistic or very abstract. Typically, maps are printed on one or more sheets of paper, usually measuring twenty-two by thirty-four inches. *War between the States* has three such maps; other games on other conflicts have as many as nine. Maps are divided into areas; in most games these are regular hexagons, but games with irregular areas or "point-to-point" maps with nodes and paths have become more popular in recent years. Military forces are represented most commonly by small pieces of cardboard called "counters," usually measuring a half-inch square. These forces are allowed to move a certain number of spaces per turn; it "costs" more to move through difficult terrain such as woods or mountains than through clear terrain. There are usually different kinds of counters; for example, in games on the Civil War there are usually counters representing commanders, who are given numerical scores for their competence in one or more areas. Forts, naval forces, and informational markers round out the usual set of game pieces.[7]

Combat on these maps can be handled in many ways. One typical method is to count up the combat strength (number and quality of units and leaders) of both sides and compute the ratio between the attacker and the defender, which can be found on a chart of such ratios. The attacker then rolls a die, and the number rolled is cross-referenced with the previously determined ratio to produce a certain result—one side or the other losing so many units, retreating, and so forth. In virtually all war games, combat eventually comes down to a roll of the die or some other chance element. Victory is generally obtained by accumulating "victory points," which are awarded for such things as taking territory and winning battles. After a certain number of turns, the side with the most victory points wins the game. Alternatively, accomplishing a particular goal may end the game immediately. In *A House Divided*, for instance, the Confederate player wins immediately if he or she captures Washington, D.C.[8]

*Battle-Cry* and *Civil War* came out in 1961, during the Civil War centennial. *Battle-Cry*, produced by Milton Bradley, was almost certainly the best-selling game on the Civil War and was available in many mainstream stores during the war's centennial and the nation's bicentennial. (Sales figures for games, from both small publishers and large, are difficult to come by. Production runs for contemporary games are in the low thousands.) *Civil War* was produced by Avalon Hill, which created the war-gaming genre, but largely through its other products.[9] These two games are primitive by later standards, reflecting the war only obliquely. In *Battle-Cry* the war is fought largely over railroads, which dominate the map and make long-distance marches very easy. *Civil War* has significantly more terrain, but the battles and strategies resemble those of the Civil War only accidentally, due to rules borrowed from an entirely abstract game, *Nieuchess*. The real historical lesson from *Battle-Cry* comes in the form of a thirty-one-page booklet, a vastly boiled-down version of one of the landmarks of centennial-era popular history, *The American Heritage Picture History of the Civil War*. The various campaigns and battles mentioned in the booklet are followed by superscript red numbers, each of which matches a red number printed on the game board. This was likely done to help maintain the illusion of re-creating the Civil War. Despite their relative lack of realism, these games evoke the war for many players.

A gap of more than a decade separated the centennial games from their successors. From 1974 to 1983, the high-water mark of war gaming's popularity, five games appeared covering the entire Civil War. Some of these are still highly regarded; two (the most and least complex) have been reprinted in the twenty-first century, testifying to their staying power. All of them conform to traditional war-game standards, with cardboard counters and paper maps. The first was *The American Civil War*, published by Simulations Publications Inc. (SPI), whose neglect of race set a standard. This game was designed for the company's bimonthly magazine called *Strategy & Tactics*, which included a game with each issue. Each game was fairly simple, with a single standard-sized map and rarely more than 200 counters.

The three most important games from this period are *War between the*

*States, A House Divided,* and *The Civil War.* The first is a so-called monster game, with three maps and thousands of counters. The rule book is twenty pages long—with three and a half pages of errata—and full games can take days to complete. *The Civil War,* published by Victory Games, is another highly complex game, boasting forty-four pages of rules and covering the entire theater of war into the New Mexico Territory. Amid this complexity, *A House Divided* stands out for its simplicity. In its original incarnation, the game had four pages of rules, making it accessible to a much wider audience. Detail suffered, of course. The game entirely lacks leaders and ignores the war at sea, features that gamers had come to expect. This game proved popular, however, and was republished twice with revisions (and added complexity) in 1989 and 2001.[10]

The next decade, a kind of middle period, saw a parade of mostly lackluster and unsuccessful games. The major players from the earlier era—Avalon Hill (and its subsidiary Victory Games) and SPI (which went bankrupt in 1982)—did not release any Civil War games during this time, leaving the field open to new companies. Fresno Gaming Association's *The Civil War* was another attempt at a monster game, but the rules are so poor that the game is virtually unplayable. Most of this period's games, produced by very small publishers, did not find a wide audience. The best-regarded game from this time is *The War for the Union* by Clash of Arms. One of the more physically attractive games in this study, it is also notable for being one of the most Lost Cause–oriented games. It is difficult to say what inspired the designer, Rob Beyma, to devise a game with a superior-by-birth Confederate soldier and other Lost Cause tropes. This was not a particularly pro–Lost Cause period, and the mood of gamers was difficult to discern in the pre-Internet age. Likely, it was just the product of the designer's idiosyncratic beliefs.

Also appearing in the 1990s were a pair of games from Columbia Games: *Bobby Lee* and *Sam Grant* cover the eastern and western theaters of war, respectively, and can be joined together. Columbia's games are notable for their "fog of war." Instead of cardboard counters or toy soldiers, units are represented by stickers placed on wooden blocks, with the sticker facing the owner and the blank side facing the opponent. The units' identities are revealed only for battles, and it takes a fine memory to keep track of them all.[11]

The Internet era for war gamers might be dated to 1996, when Consimworld opened as a popular forum for war gamers, designers, and publishers.

Avalon Hill, the most venerable game publisher, was sold to Hasbro Inc. in 1998; most of Avalon's product line was killed off, including all of its Civil War titles. It was also during this period that games began to deal with off-the-battlefield events. The particular issues of race and emancipation are discussed in detail later, but the movement was widespread.

Companies have also found ways to profitably sell games in smaller quantities, albeit with reduced production values. For instance, *The Lost Cause*, a solitaire game, is sold directly from its tiny publisher, and its cards are printed on business card stock rather than the glossy playing cards used by larger companies.[12] Such measures have allowed smaller companies to do better than in times past. And thanks to the Internet, some games that are out of print remain available through websites such as ebay.com or direct sales through board-game forums.

All war games, of whatever period, require research and serious design choices that address H. G. Wells's three criteria: realism, strategic play, and fun. This requires the designer to act as a historian and consider some of the perennial questions: Why did the South lose the Civil War? What effect did the Emancipation Proclamation and race have on the war? What was the likelihood of foreign intervention? How did politics influence military leadership? This essay deals with the first two questions.

One common explanation of the South's loss of the war is the Lost Cause theory—that the gallant Confederacy was doomed from the beginning in a fight against the overwhelming, industrialized North. Although the Lost Cause interpretation has steadily lost ground among historians, it remains a common trope of popular culture. What has increasingly engaged historians is the role of race in the war—most notably, emancipation, the role of black troops, and slavery as the ultimate cause of the war. Only relatively recently, however, has race become part of the popular memory of the war—at least among white Americans (who constitute the overwhelming majority of war gamers). Has this waning and waxing of interpretations been present in war games, and if so, how?

In *The Myth of the Eastern Front*, Ronald Smelser and Edward J. Davies III look at war games as ways for "romancers" of the Nazi Wehrmacht on the Eastern Front to live out their fantasies. Based on a combination of subject matter, titles, and cover art, a surprising number of games were seemingly crafted for believers in a "clean Wehrmacht." Much as that myth was a politically expedient whitewashing of World War II history, the Lost Cause gained popularity as an explanation for the Confederacy's loss of the Civil War. The Confederacy lost the war not because it could not win enough battles but because it was doomed from the beginning, and its gallant soldiers bore up as best they could against the mighty Yankee machine. Gary Gallagher has spent much of his career documenting the enduring popularity of the Lost Cause, and one might expect the Lost Cause to be prominent in war games, given its prominence in other areas of memory such as movies, novels, commercial art, and reenactment.[13]

Games are a very visual medium, and one's first impression is the box cover. Excellent art cannot save the reputation of a bad game, but a great game can be hurt in the market by poor art and graphic design. With art being so important, the choices made when selecting and creating it are worthy of attention. Gallagher has looked at art—both still pictures and movies—as vectors of the various "causes" he traces. Historical art prints—which often serve as cover images for games—have long tilted heavily toward Confederate themes—2.5 to 1 in recent years, by Gallagher's calculation.[14]

War-game covers are much more balanced. Typical is the art for *C.S.A.*, which is evenhanded despite its name.[15] Underneath the title stand two officers back-to-back: a Confederate officer before a battle flag, and a Union major general backed by a U.S. flag. They are cut off at the waist, and beneath them is a tableau of two lines of infantry and artillery facing each other at point-blank range. Most games' cover art is similarly evenhanded. *War for the Union* uses an American flag as a backdrop, but furled U.S. and Confederate battle flags behind a cannon form a secondary image. It also depicts an assault—as does SPI's *American Civil War* (1983), *A House Divided* (1981), *For the People* (1998 and 2006 editions), and many others. Only *A House Divided: The Brothers War* features only Confederate images—that of Robert E. Lee. Lee is the most famous general of the war—thanks in no small part to postwar exponents of the Lost Cause who promoted Lee as a paragon of Christian, southern, and martial virtue—so his popularity on game covers is not surprising. (Columbia's *Bobby Lee* features a painting of the general, but it is balanced by its matching game, *Sam Grant*.) Xeno's *The Civil War* features Dale Gallon's *Hancock's Ride*, depicting a notable exchange just before Pickett's Charge at Gettysburg; it and Victory Games' *The Civil War*—which uses Gilbert Gaul's *The Skirmish Line*—are the only two Union-only covers.

A comparison between game art and historical art prints is striking. The market for art prints is strongly Confederate in character, but game publishers don't perceive their audience that way. Although, per the findings of Smelser and Davies, publishers often trade on "clean Wehrmacht" tropes on game covers, Lost Cause imagery is largely absent.

The Lost Cause appears in other guises, however. One notable game with a Lost Cause element is *War for the Union*—despite its title and cover art. The game features nine pages of historical commentary (providing a brief history of the conflict) and Rob Beyma's notes justifying his design choices. It is not a pure Lost Cause document, however; slavery is cited as the "main cause" of "the Civil War (War Between the States, War for Southern Independence—you pick)," but the commentary notes that the South would have abandoned slavery even in the war's absence. In a sidebar on Civil War generalship, after brief discussions of the (vast) merits of Robert E. Lee, Thomas J. "Stonewall" Jackson, and J. E. B. Stuart, Beyma closes: "The South had other brilliant leaders, such as James Longstreet, A. P. Hill, and Joe Johnston. It also had audacious and fiery cavalry leaders like John Hunt Morgan, Nathan B. Forrest, and John Singleton Mosby. All these glittering stars, however, were extinguished by the superior numbers of the Blue tide." In game terms, the strongest evidence of the Lost Cause is how soldiers are mustered in: they have three levels of quality—militia, volunteer, and veteran. Battle experience allows soldiers to advance up the ladder. But southern soldiers, who enter the game as volunteers, are naturally better than northern ones, who enter the game as militia. It can take half a "campaign" for Union troop quality to match that of the Confederates. That said, it is certainly possible for the Confederacy to win this game. *War for the Union* also contains a number of optional rules that players can use to "spice up a game, or simply see how the war might have turned out if things had been different." Such optional rules are common to many games, reflecting the popularity of "what if" hypotheticals in popular history. The most notable pro-Confederate option gives the southern player one state—Kentucky, Missouri, Maryland, or West Virginia—along with its manpower and industrial capacity (in the case of Missouri [St. Louis] or Maryland [Baltimore]).[16]

One might expect a game actually titled *The Lost Cause* to be rooted in the mythology. In this solitaire game, the player—representing the Confederacy—attempts to hold back advancing columns of Union armies striking at Richmond, Atlanta, and Vicksburg, all while maintaining home-front morale and trying to coax the European powers to intervene. The war is "winnable," in the argot of the hobby, but doing so is very difficult. The rules give six levels of defeat and two of victory—giving some indication of what the Confederacy is up against. The true goal is to play the game repeatedly and try to score higher every time and eventually win the war, if the fates (in the shape of dice and cards) allow. The historical and designer's notes accompanying the game shed little light on the designer's intent.[17]

These games back the Lost Cause in one important respect: none of them addresses any of the issues that started the war, including slavery. Because these are games meant to depict the war, anything that occurred before the firing on Fort Sumter is outside their temporal purview. That, however, reinforces the view that the Civil War was just another contest between two nations (or a nation and a quasi-nation) and that only battles and leaders were important; ideology and motivation lay outside. (This is discussed in more detail later.)

Overtly, however, the Lost Cause finds few outlets in these games. Most of the packaging goes to great lengths to be evenhanded, and all the games assume that the Confederacy has a fair chance to win the war. It is worth remembering that games are supposed to be fun—and if the Union won every time, that would hardly qualify as fun for competitive gamers. The attitude that the Confederacy was doomed from the outset is acceptable only in a game with one player who is challenged only to better his or her previous score.

The Lost Cause is most apparent in these games' silence on race and slavery as causes of the war. Indeed, one of the most important results of the war—the abolition of slavery—is absent from nearly all games that appeared before the Internet era. The earliest, most abstract games that came out during the Civil War centennial lack any reference to race; this is hardly surprising, given their publication date and the fairly primitive way they approach history of all kinds. When games started taking their mission more seriously, however, race was not a cause they immediately took up. SPI's *The American Civil War* (1974) was the first serious attempt to simulate the entire conflict. The game accompanied a lengthy historical article in SPI's *Strategy & Tactics*. The article's author, Albert A. Nofi, specifically disclaims the Lost Cause (citing Rollin Osterweis's *The Myth of the Lost Cause* in his bibliography), roots the secondary causes of the war (religious and economic differences) in slavery, and then largely ignores race, discussing the Emancipation Proclamation as a document that "greatly improved America's relations with Britain and helped assuage the feelings of Northern abolitionists, while at the same time trying to conciliate some slaveowners." Its effects on slavery and slaves go unnoticed. Nofi does state, however, that it had "a marked effect on the course of the war," but he cites the firing of Union general George B. McClellan as the only example.[18]

This is more attention than emancipation gets in the game, which was designed by SPI founder James F. Dunnigan. His designer's notes reveal that his inspiration for *The American Civil War* was an earlier game on the Second World War. Dunnigan changed that design to add the "flavor" of the conflict, "examining in detail some of the truths, as well as many of the myths which make up the commonly accepted perception about what the American Civil War was all about." He then lists a number of these truths and describes how he included them in the game. The first is the southern war economy, "one of the most ignored aspects" of the war. But this focuses only on southern industrialization rather than agricultural mobilization—which was also vital to the war effort and was made possible by slaves. Emancipation is utterly ignored, even when using the optional rules for foreign intervention.[19]

Four years later, in 1978, SPI published its huge *War between the States*. Emancipation does make an appearance in this game—in one paragraph of the rules: "Whenever he has more political points than his opponent, the Union player may issue an Emancipation Proclamation. He simply gazes beatifically toward the ceiling and says 'I free the slaves.' There are two results to such an event: 1) the Confederate player gains five political points and 2) any foreign intervention is eliminated if in effect, and is forbidden in the future." When *War between the States* was revised and reissued in 2004, this rule—minus the sarcastic "gazing beatifically"—remained. Political points are the currency of victory in the game; if a player has built up a sufficient surplus of political points over his opponent, he can roll the dice and hope the result grants him victory over his opponent. It can also bring on foreign intervention if the Union is doing especially poorly, but that is very unlikely. Emancipation, then, makes an unlikely result impossible, but it materially helps the Confederacy win the game. It is often wisest for the Union player not to emancipate the slaves, unless by some chance foreign intervention has come into play.[20]

Until the late 1990s, games either ignored race and emancipation, like *The American Civil War*, or made only passing reference to it, like *War between the States*. This includes *The Civil War*, published in 1993 by Victory Games. Many still consider this game to be the ultimate depiction of the war. It has myriad generals, a detailed naval system, and even Indian wars. It has a weighty rule book with a thirty-two-item bibliography. Playing it takes a long weekend, but at no point does race or slavery make an appearance—not in terms of raising manpower, affecting southern economics, or other effects on the war on the ground.[21]

How this came to pass can only be speculated. War games have always focused on combat, which leads to a bias against anything unrelated to combat—although this bias can be broken. It is also difficult to imagine that race and slavery would be missing as game elements if there were more black war gamers. Again, war gaming wants for an anthropologist, but the overwhelming anecdotal evidence suggests that war gamers of color (other than those of Asian descent) are extremely rare, as are women. Why few women or people of color play war games has been the subject of speculation within the hobby. The discussions typically bring more heat than light. To date, no one has offered a satisfactory explanation.[22]

*For the People* (1998) would change the way game designers approached race and the Civil War. It was part of a revolution in games called "card-driven strategy games" (or CDGs, for short). Games had utilized cards for some time, of course, but designer Mark Herman used them in a new way. Players are dealt a hand of six or seven cards, each of which has an event and a number (representing "operations"). Players play one card per turn, using it either for an event or for its operations points, which can move their forces or enact other changes on the board. These events cards depict many actual social and economic events that went unnoticed in previous games. Events are important in the game, as they affect each side's "strategic will"—the reduction of which is how the game is won. Winning and losing battles affects strategic will, but so does something like a timely editorial from Horace Greeley (in the game's most recent edition). For example, if the northern Democratic Party adopts a peace platform in 1864, that lowers the Union's strategic will by five points (equivalent to losing a major battle). A bad patch of cabinet intrigue lowers Union strategic will by three points. Some events are more curious: a revival can sweep through Confederate army camps, which improves an army's morale but diminishes strategic will at the national level. Most notably, however, race is a factor in the game.[23]

The "Contraband of War" card represents Union general Benjamin Butler's declaration that any slave who escaped to his lines would not be sent back to his or her owner but would be kept as seized property useful to the enemy. This card requires the Confederate player to reduce some of his manpower—presumably sending men back to work on the plantations. The "Glory Hallelujah" card gives the Union a considerable boost in manpower, representing the raising of black troops—which can be done in either the Union or the Confederacy. Most important, however, is the "Emancipation Proclamation" card. The Union player can play the card only if he has won a significant battle during that turn (representing Antietam in real life). When the card is played, the Union player loses five points for strategic will (representing Democratic opposition, presumably) but gains no direct benefit. What emancipation does is hurt the Confederacy. The Confederate player loses a certain number of troops but also a whopping ten points in strategic will (equivalent to losing Tennessee)—and every year thereafter he loses another five points for "war guilt." Confederate war guilt was something of a passé concept even when *For the People* came out, but it makes emancipation a powerful tool in the Union's hands—and even reflects the proclamation's ambiguous effects on the war.

*For the People* was a great success for Avalon Hill, but not enough to save the company, which went bankrupt shortly thereafter and was bought by Hasbro. Mark Herman recovered the rights to his game, however, and helped bring out a new edition from GMT Games Inc. The current version is more complicated than its predecessor and features many more cards. In the new version, the "Frederick Douglass" card raises 30,000 black troops in the North.

Every mainstream game on the Civil War that has come out since *For the People* has included emancipation. Race has entered the gaming world and shows little sign of leaving. But how emancipation and race are incorporated into games differs from one game to another. The most notable example is *Battle Cry of Freedom*—a game designed by Civil War PhD David Smith. This game, played entirely with cards, includes many nonmilitary events such as southern bread riots, infighting between state governors, and the British labor movement's support for the Union. The heart of the game is a system of "command points" (CPs), a catch-all representation of each side's ability to wage war. Emancipation is a two-step process: playing the "Preliminary Emancipation Proclamation" card lowers the Union's CPs (again, representing dissent), but issuing the "Final Proclamation" raises the Union's CPs and lowers the Confederacy's. Once the final proclamation is made, a third card, "Men of Color: To Arms! To Arms!" mobilizes freed slaves, again raising the Union's CPs and lowering the Confederacy's. A fourth card,

"African-American Soldiers Prove Their Valor," does the same thing again. *Battle Cry of Freedom* gives emancipation the greatest role in any Civil War game to date.[24]

This essay has sampled only twenty games released over the past fifty years. Their development has not been linear. The biggest, *War between the States* (1978), was one of the earliest games on the war. The most complex, Victory Games' *The Civil War*, is now in its thirtieth year. Game designers have become more aware of how social, economic, and political events influenced the war. *For the People* and *Battle Cry of Freedom* have relatively short rules, compared with the games published during the height of war games' popularity, but they include far more of the war than do most of their competitors.

As a form of memory, these games have a unique place alongside movies, documentaries, reenactments, and museums. Unlike most other aspects of the popular culture of the Civil War, these games require interactivity, competitiveness, and a significant outlay of time (all these games take longer to play than any movie). The complexity of their rules represents another major investment. Players are actively involved, and a good game imparts an illusion that history is unfolding before their very eyes. How these games reflect the Lost Cause mythology or emancipation is significant, as the games are meant to be realistic, as well as fun and strategically challenging. These games will likely never be as popular as *Call of Duty* or Gettysburg National Military Park, but they reflect how an inventive subculture of history enthusiasts has shaped the Civil War into the ultimate interactive medium.

## Notes

1. Michael C. C. Adams, *The Echoes of War: A Thousand Years of Military History in Popular Culture* (Lexington: University Press of Kentucky, 2002), ix. All data on movie earnings are from the Internet Movie Database, http://imdb.com (accessed December 10, 2011).

2. Nick Bilton, "Modern Warfare 3 Passes $1 Billion in Sales in 16 Days," *New York Times*, December 12, 2011.

3. See H. G. Wells, *Little Wars* (New York: Macmillan, 1970), 8–38, on the development of the rules.

4. For the early history of the hobby, see Rex A. Martin, "Cardboard Warriors: The Rise and Fall of an American Wargaming Subculture, 1958–1998" (PhD diss., Pennsylvania State University, 2001), 202–10.

5. Martin van Creveld, *The Culture of War* (New York: Ballantine, 2008), 325–27; Martin, "Cardboard Warriors."

6. Ronald Smelser and Edward J. Davies III, *The Myth of the Eastern Front: The Nazi-Soviet War in American Popular Culture* (Cambridge, N.Y.: Cambridge University Press, 2008). This definition, like any other, allows for a number of edge cases, but the overwhelming majority of hobbyist war gamers would likely consider any game covered by these criteria a war game.

7. *Battle Cry of Freedom* (Bakersfield, Calif.: Decision Games, 2003); *War between the States* (New York: Simulations Publications Inc. [SPI], 1978); *The Civil War: The War that Pitted Brother against Brother* (Fresno, Calif.: Fresno Gaming Associates [FGA], 1991).

8. A dated but still useful introduction to war games is James Dunnigan, *The Complete Wargames Handbook: How to Play, Design and Find Them* (New York: Quill, 1992). Dunnigan, one of the major figures in the hobby, founded SPI and designed the first "serious" war game on the Civil War before becoming a military affairs pundit. A sample game, illustrating many of these concepts, is *Battle for Moscow*, http://grognard.com/bfm/game.html (accessed December 20, 2011).

9. *Battle-Cry* (Springfield, Mass.: Milton Bradley, 1961, 1976); *Civil War* (Baltimore: Avalon Hill Game Company, 1961).

10. *War between the States* (SPI); *A House Divided* (Bloomington, Ill.: Game Designer's Workshop [GDW], 1981); *The Civil War* (Baltimore: Victory Games [VG], 1983).

11. *The Civil War* (FGA); *The War for the Union* (King of Prussia, Pa.: Clash of Arms Games [COA], 1992); *Bobby Lee* and *Sam Grant* (Blaine, Wash.: Columbia Games, 1993). For a review of FGA's *The Civil War*, see http://richardhberg.tripod.com/brog3.html (accessed December 20, 2011).

12. *The Lost Cause* (n.p.: Victory Point Games, 2010), http://www.victorypointgames.com.

13. Smelser and Davies, *Myth of the Eastern Front*, 187–200; Gary Gallagher, *Causes Won, Lost, and Forgotten: How Hollywood and Popular Art Shape What We Know about the Civil War* (Chapel Hill: University of North Carolina Press, 2008).

14. Gallagher, *Causes Won, Lost, and Forgotten*, 138.

15. *C.S.A.* (Toronto: Fiery Dragon Productions, 2007).

16. *War for the Union* (COA). The quotes are from the enclosed booklet titled "Scenarios, Optional Rules, Historical Commentary, and Designer's Notes," 10.

17. *The Lost Cause* (Victory Point Games).

18. Albert A. Nofi, "The American Civil War: 1861–1865," *Strategy & Tactics*, March/April 1974, 5–22.

19. *The American Civil War* (1974), rules.

20. *War between the States* (1978), rule 25.5.

21. *The Civil War* (Victory Games).

22. For discussions of African Americans and women in war gaming, see http://boardgamegeek.com/thread/636274/do-you-know-any-black-wargamers and http://boardgamegeek.com/thread/788243/interesting-speech-against-bigotry.

23. All examples in this and succeeding paragraphs come from the cards included in *For the People* (Baltimore: Avalon Hill Game Company, 1998), except for Horace Greeley, which is from the 2006 GMT reissue.

24. *Battle Cry of Freedom* (Decision Games).

# 11

# "Oh, I'm a Good Ol' Rebel"

## *Reenactment, Racism, and the Lost Cause*

*Christopher Bates*

Captain Vern Padgett is a Confederate Civil War reenactor—a member of the Richmond Howitzers. Though a California native, he is one of the more die-hard Confederate reenactors—not in terms of his devotion to an accurate impression but in his commitment to what he perceives as the southern cause. His e-mail messages often have titles like this: "Rebuttal to ravings of misinformed Yankee propagandists." He thinks nothing of lecturing his fellow reenactors on the "facts the historians leave out," with the goal of correcting what he calls "Northern platitudes."[1]

Padgett is best known—both inside and outside reenactment circles—for his advocacy of the notion that the Confederate army included significant numbers of African American soldiers.[2] The fact that academic historians categorically reject—and even deride—this idea only encourages Padgett. He has a lengthy and highly polished lecture on the subject that he has delivered at dozens of Civil War roundtables and other Civil War–related gatherings. His presentation makes use of all the hard evidence he has been able to gather—a few photographs, a handful of quotations and diary excerpts, and several other odds and ends. The centerpiece of his argument, however, is creative mathematics. Working backward from a single piece of information—that a dozen African Americans qualified for veterans' pensions in Tennessee in 1905—he "calculates" how many black soldiers actually served in the Confederate army. By his figuring, Tennessee had about 10 percent of the South's population in 1905, so those 12 pensioners actually represent 120 soldiers if extrapolated across the entire South. Next, he calculates that because only 20 percent of Civil War soldiers lived until 1905, those 120 survivors represent 600 soldiers. Padgett continues through several more iterations using this mathematical sleight of hand and ultimately concludes that the Confederate army had as many as 200,000 black soldiers. This is a staggering number, given that, at its height, the entire Confederate army numbered perhaps 1 million soldiers. When pressed to explain why a group that—in his analysis—constituted as much as 15 or 20 percent of the Confederate army has left so little evidence of its existence behind, Padgett falls back on the other main theme of his lecture: that professional historians can't be trusted and are inclined to hide information that doesn't fit their preconceived notions.[3]

Don Worth is also a Confederate reenactor—primarily as a member of the Third Georgia. "I am an absolute nut about the Civil War," he explains. "I have no idea why."[4] Worth, a retired computer systems administrator, has been reenacting for nearly two decades. His interest in the Civil War dates back much further, however, to when he was a youngster during the Civil War centennial of 1961 to 1965. He explains how he was first drawn to the Civil War:

> My grandfather gave me the *Life* magazines in the early 1960s and the *American Heritage Book of the Civil War.* I had to do a Civil War project for school—sixth grade?—and I remember cutting out pictures from the magazines for the report and looking up what I then considered obscure generals in the encyclopedia. At the same time, because of the centennial there were lots of other Civil War–related things around. For example, I had the Marx Blue and Gray plastic soldiers play set. . . . *The Gray Ghost* was on TV and I had seen the movie *Friendly Persuasion* and loved it. One of my friends had the Avalon Hill Game *Gettysburg* and I had to get that too. I ended up buying their Chancellorsville game too. And I had stacks and stacks of the Whitman Confederate play money. When I visited Knott's Berry Farm, I bought replicas of *Harper's Weekly* from the Civil War era too.[5]

Worth believes that in the 1950s and 1960s, children's exposure to the past was more extensive than it is today. Toy stores, for example, were filled with items inspired by historical events and individuals. Besides its Blue and Gray line, Marx sold toy soldiers from the Mexican-American War, the War of 1812, the Revolutionary War, and the Indian Wars. There were Red Ryder BB Guns, Lincoln Logs, Davy Crockett coonskin caps, and miniature Sherman tanks. History was also a mainstay of television programming. "Disney immersed us in every historical character he could lay his hands on—*Davy Crockett, Johnny Tremain, The Swamp Fox*," Worth remembers. Still, it was the Civil War that captured his heart:

> I remember being very impressed with John Mosby—the main character of *The Gray Ghost* TV series. I remember being much more interested in the Confederates—those dashing cavaliers! I suspect I was mostly a product of my times—the centennial washed over all of us like a giant wave. Perhaps it was partly that we were living in the era of the Cold War—with the constant threat of annihilation, and it was pleasant to cast oneself back to an earlier, simpler time. . . . The stories that came from the war seemed full of passion and heroism and noble deeds. I couldn't get nearly as excited about the Revolutionary War—even with movies like *Johnny Tremain*—or other wars.[6]

As he entered young adulthood, Worth's passion for the Civil War waned. He attended college during the height of the antiwar movement; this was followed by marriage and the start of his career, and his attention was directed elsewhere. In the late 1980s, however, his interest reblossomed. He's not sure why, although he says some personal problems—and the desire to escape, on occasion—played a role. This time in his life coincided with a dramatic increase in attention to the Civil War, thanks in part to the movies *Glory* (1989) and *Gettysburg* (1993), as well as Ken Burns's PBS series *The Civil War* (1990). Today, the Civil War is once again a major part of Don Worth's life. Besides reenacting, he has created extensive Civil War–related websites, compiled a large collection of Gettysburg photographs, visited dozens of battlefields, taken courses on the war, and attended several Civil War conferences.

On those occasions when Padgett and Worth attend reenactments as Confederates, they find themselves with a lot of company. Roughly two-thirds of reenactors play Confederate soldiers or civilians as their primary roles. If those individuals who sometimes trade in northern blues for southern grays—"galvanizers," in reenactor parlance—are included, then the percentage of reenactors who at least occasionally do southern impressions jumps to about 85 percent.[7] In many places, the imbalance between the two sides is so overwhelming that new reenactors are required to portray Union soldiers for several months to a year, just to ensure that there are enough Federals to actually stage a battle. Although it may not be surprising that this is the case in the South, the imbalance between Union and Confederacy also exists beyond the Mason-Dixon line. Of the fifty states, only Massachusetts has more Union reenactors than Confederates, in large part due to the many African American units based there.[8] Among the 10,000 or so individuals who participate in foreign Civil War reenactment groups—primarily in Australia, France, Germany, Italy, and the United Kingdom—the same imbalance exists.

These numbers—with Confederate outnumbering Federal reenactors by about 2 to 1—are essentially the inverse of the actual Civil War. During the war itself, the Union army comprised roughly 2.4 million men, which means it enjoyed a manpower advantage of about 2.5 to 1.[9] This was primarily because states in the North and the West had far more people than those in the South. It was also due to the fact that—regardless of what Vern Padgett says—the Union government could draw on its working classes to build its army, whereas the South's 4 million slaves were largely unavailable to the Confederate army.[10] These facts were true in the 1860s, and they remain true for Civil War reenactment today. That is, the states of the North and the West—not to mention the nations of Europe and Oceania—still have far more people than the South does. It is also the case that the reenacted Confederate army cannot draw on African Americans.[11] Thus, it is intriguing that the majority of reenactors are Confederates. The South did, after all, lose the war.

Most outsiders who have analyzed this conundrum have reached a fairly straightforward answer: southern racism. The presumption is that the reenactment community—or at least the Confederate segment of that community—is made up of backward-looking, ultraconservative, reactionary white southerners who are threatened by the changes that have taken place since the civil rights movement. The views of political scientist James O. Farmer are characteristic of this perspective. In a 2005 essay he concludes, "It is not surprising that the era of affirmative action has seen a corresponding growth in the reenactment hobby, for it offers both an escape from that world, however brief, and a symbolic defiance of it." Participation in reenactment offers "the "tradition loving white Southerner" a chance to "send his message to the NAACP."[12]

A more careful analysis, however, makes it clear that this interpretation is a gross oversimplification at best and wholly inaccurate at worst. If one met Don Worth and Vern Padgett at a Civil War reenactment, it would be difficult to detect much of a difference between the two. However, as the preceding twin narratives make clear, there *is* a great deal of difference. Indeed, there is a broad spectrum of Confederate reenactment, with Worth at one end and Padgett at the other. And both ends of this spectrum are far better understood not as a product of modern-day racism but in the context of the southern "Lost Cause" interpretation of the Civil War—a blend of romance and politics that still has enormous resonance today. The perception of Confederate reenactors as backward-looking racists is primarily the result of factors beyond their control. Since the 1950s, *actual* backward-looking racists—the Ku Klux Klan, the League of the South, Dixie Republic, some neo-Nazi groups—have made extensive use of the Confederacy and its symbols, particularly the Confederate battle flag and the common soldier of the Confederate army. The South in general, and any person who utilizes or affiliates with these symbols in particular, has suffered by association. The average Confederate reenactor is hardly a tree-hugging, Prius-driving, ACLU card–carrying, left-wing radical, but even if he were, it would make little difference.

In the past half century, scholars of various stripes have taken a great deal of interest in the symbolic meaning of the South in American culture. That meaning has grown and evolved over time, such that the region now has many and varied significances—both positive and negative. "The South today," as historian Tara McPherson observes, "is as much a fiction, a story we tell and are told, as it is a fixed geographic space below the Mason-Dixon line."[13] A full survey of this subject is beyond the scope of this essay; a brief overview must suffice.

The South's geography, economy, culture, and religious traditions have been distinctly different from those of the North for more than 400 years, but it was not until the 1850s that southern writers began to strive in earnest to articulate a distinctly southern identity. The novels of John Pendleton Kennedy, the poetry of William Grayson, and the scholarship of William Fitzhugh all sought to emphasize the positive qualities of the South (usually by contrasting them with the negative qualities of the industrial North). A number of northerners aided their cause—among them Ohioan David Christy with his book *Cotton Is King* (1855), New York printmakers Nathaniel Currier and James Merritt Ives, and Pennsylvania composer Stephen Foster, responsible for the popular songs "My Old Kentucky Home," "Oh! Susanna," and "Old Folks at Home."

During the Civil War and Reconstruction, the South took a literal and metaphorical beating, and it is from this context that the Lost Cause interpretation of the war emerged from the pens of writers such as Jubal Early, John Esten Cooke, Thomas Nelson Page, and Edward A. Pollard. The bedrock of the Lost Cause was romantic imagery—gentlemanly Robert E. Lee, daring Stonewall Jackson, magnolias and cotton fields, the idyllic life of the plantations. These appealing notions were the anchor for a series of ideas about the war—that the Confederacy never really had a chance of winning but almost did anyway, that the South's purpose was to fight not for slavery but for states' rights, and so forth. The purpose of the Lost Cause was twofold: to redeem the tarnished image of the South and make a case to northerners for the southern states' full reinstatement into the Union (under white leadership), and to help the defeated Confederates come to grips with their loss of the war.[14]

The architects of the Lost Cause were remarkably successful in their task. The interpretation, not surprisingly, quickly gained traction among white southerners. Perhaps more important, it also gained wide acceptance among white northerners. Scholars Karen L. Cox, Nina Silber, and Robert Wiebe, among others, have observed that a South that symbolized an older, simpler America and a life of leisure, individualism, honor, and romance was very reassuring at a time when the world was modernizing, industrializing, and speeding up.[15] Entrepreneurs in all parts of the country seized on this opportunity, creating what McPherson characterizes as a "vast nostalgia industry."[16] Southerners developed a bustling tourist industry, showcasing their region at a number of high-profile events, including the New Orleans Universal Exposition and World's Fair of 1884, the Atlanta Cotton States and International Exposition of 1895, and the South Carolina Inter-State and West Indian Exposition of 1901. Northern novelists such as Owen Wister, John William DeForest, Frank R. Stockton, Sarah Orne Jewett, and Thomas Bailey Aldrich made frequent use of romantic southern settings and symbols, while *Harper's Monthly*, *Atlantic Monthly*, *Cosmopolitan*, *Lippincott's*, and *Munsey's* regularly published extensive southern travelogues.

By the early decades of the twentieth century, as Gaines M. Foster has observed, the Lost Cause had served its purposes—the South had been rein-tegrated into the United States, and the Civil War generation had either passed from the scene or coped with defeat.[17] Nonetheless, the mythology of the Lost Cause remained salient and even continued to grow. Madison Ave-nue advertising agencies fashioned product names and mascots that refer-enced the antebellum South—Aunt Jemima, Uncle Ben, and Dixie cups.[18] Tin Pan Alley composers, many of whom had never visited the region, pro-duced tune after tune that celebrated southern heritage: "Swanee" (1919), "Carolina in the Morning" (1922), "Way Down Yonder in New Orleans" (1922), and "Sweet Georgia Brown" (1925).[19] Filmmakers had a particularly profound impact, and the "Old South" genre was a Hollywood mainstay for many years. Examples include *The Fighting Coward* (1924), *The River of Romance* (1929), *Hearts in Dixie* (1929), *Mississippi* (1935), *So Red the Rose* (1935), *Way Down South* (1939), *Song of the South* (1946), *The Mississippi Gambler* (1953), *Band of Angels* (1957), and—most famously—*The Birth of a Nation* (1915) and *Gone with the Wind* (1939).[20] Historians, both within the academy and without, also played a role in sustaining a positive image of the South and of the Confederate war effort, among them Douglass Southall Freeman, Ulrich B. Phillips, Shelby Foote, and Bruce Catton.[21]

Though a generally favorable conception of the South and the Confed-eracy remained transcendent until the 1960s, the first signs of a negative counterimage began to appear in the 1920s. Southern writers—William Faulkner, Tennessee Williams, Lillian Hellman—set their novels in a South that had its charms but was deeply flawed.[22] At the same time, news events—the resurgence of the Ku Klux Klan, labor violence, the Scopes trial of 1925, outbreaks of hookworm and pellagra, the Dust Bowl of the 1930s—had some scholars and observers speaking of a "benighted" South. This trend reached its apex in the 1950s and 1960s, as Americans across the nation watched peace-ful civil rights protesters face off against white southerners, many of whom were very angry and violent. For the first time since Reconstruction, the South's image among citizens outside the region was arguably more negative than positive. In particular, the symbols of the Confederacy—utilized exten-sively by opponents of the civil rights movement—took on connotations of racism and oppression that the Lost Cause interpretation had successfully countermanded for more than half a century.

The blow to the South's image was immediately evident in newspapers. By 1951, the *Chicago Tribune* was editorializing against "Bigotry and

Ignorance in [the] Deep South."[23] In 1956 the *Los Angeles Times* characterized southerners as "the prejudiced, the ignorant, and the arrogant."[24] The next year, when nine black students attempted to enroll at Little Rock Central High School in Arkansas and were rebuffed by Governor Orval Faubus, the *Washington Post* spoke of the "nation's disgust."[25] In 1961 the *New York Times* lamented that New Orleans, previously known for its "spirit of tolerance," had become a focal point for "racial hate." Four years later the paper decried "a conspiracy against the law and for the suppression of Negroes."[26] A 1957 poll conducted by George Gallup is particularly instructive: 74 percent of northerners said they would never consider living in the South; among the reasons they cited were the following:

> Southerners are fine people, but they're a little behind the times.
> I think they're kinda slow.
> They're fine, if they'd only stop fighting the Civil War.
> They're lazy, shiftless and ignorant.
> They carry their racial prejudice too far.[27]

Similarly, in a 1970 study northern college students were asked to pick the word they felt best described southerners. The most popular responses included three positive descriptors—friendly, hospitable, and polite—and ten negative ones—lazy, shiftless, unambitious, backward, ignorant, low class, uneducated, intolerant, bigoted, and segregationist.[28]

The change in popular perceptions of the South also became apparent in the world of cinema. Although positive filmic portrayals of the region did not disappear after the 1960s—think *Coal Miner's Daughter* (1980), *Driving Miss Daisy* (1989), *Steel Magnolias* (1989), and *Fried Green Tomatoes* (1991), as well as the television programs *The Golden Girls* (1985), *Designing Women* (1986), and *Evening Shade* (1990)—the "Old South" genre was dead.[29] Further, movies that used the South as a setting for plots centered on racism, ignorance, and other forms of deviance became quite common. Examples include *To Kill a Mockingbird* (1962), *In the Heat of the Night* (1967), *Easy Rider* (1969), *The Texas Chain Saw Massacre* (1974), *The Color Purple* (1985), and *Mississippi Burning* (1988). Perhaps the most memorable specimen of this genre is the 1972 film *Deliverance*, which follows four Atlanta businessmen on a camping trip through the rural South as they are terrorized and raped by a group of backwoods southerners.[30]

Evolving attitudes about the South also resulted in a pair of notable rhetorical developments in American English. First, as sociologist John Shelton Reed has demonstrated, the term *Dixie*—which carries pleasing connotations of the moonlight and magnolias of the antebellum South—fell out of favor, supplanted by the more generic *South*.[31] At the same time, there was a change in the meaning of the term *redneck*. In the nineteenth century, the term simply referred to poor, uneducated southerners who had to work in the fields and thus ended up with sunburned necks.[32] It slowly grew more negative over time and then took a dramatic downward turn in the 1960s. By the end of that decade, rednecks were no longer just poor and stupid; they were also toothless, inbred, and racist. And they were no longer found only in rural areas; they lived all across the South.[33]

The connection between the redneck stereotype and the Confederacy was evident in an April 1965 article in *Time* magazine entitled "The Various Shady Lives of the Ku Klux Klan." It featured a picture of Ku Klux Klan imperial wizard Robert Shelton in front of a Confederate flag, along with this explanation: "No longer a monolithic organization, the Klan today consists of several ragtag independent groups, the best known of which is the United Klans of America, Knights of the Ku Klux Klan, Inc., headquartered in Tuscaloosa, Ala. with an ex–tire salesman named Robert Shelton as its Imperial Wizard. Estimates of Klan strength range from 10,000 to 40,000 members, many of whom for some peculiar reason seem to be rural service-station attendants. Most members, in any case, are deluded rednecks whose only skill is sharpshooting."[34] The Confederate soldier cannot be separated from his flag or his nation, so when the Confederacy and its battle flag were appropriated and transformed by anti–civil rights activists, the Confederate soldier was taken along for the ride. Johnny Reb and the Confederate flag became the embodiment of defiance of the federal government, racism, and a host of other unflattering characteristics ascribed to southerners. As historian James C. Cobb observes, "[When] the Civil Rights Movement unfolded, 'Dixie' soon evoked a vision not of happy darkies on the plantation but of decidedly unhappy rednecks waving the Confederate flag and spewing contempt for national authority."[35]

Such an extended discourse on the evolution of the southern image may seem to be a sidebar to a discussion of reenactors. But it is critical to understand that the sharpening of the redneck stereotype and its pairing with the

Confederate flag and Confederate soldier happened rather quickly and at a critical time not only in the nation's history but also in the lives of most re-enactors. Many of today's reenactors—including Don Worth and Vern Padgett—were drawn to the Civil War as children by an understanding of the South that was heroic and dramatic and that largely ignored issues of race. They are arguably the last generation of Americans who can legitimately claim to have embraced the Confederacy absent the racial overtones that are now associated with the southern soldier and battle flag. By contrast, Americans under the age of fifty, academics, political liberals, people of color, and Hollywood filmmakers are all overwhelmingly likely to be steeped in the negative understanding of the region and its symbols that emerged from the civil rights era. Consequently, Civil War reenactors are almost always presented in a negative fashion by outsiders—as embodying one or more elements of the modern southern redneck stereotype, particularly racism.

To start, scholars have generally been quite critical of reenactment. Elizabeth Young, a professor of English at Mount Holyoke, did one of the first scholarly analyses of reenactment. She reveals her suspicion that many reenactors are closeted homosexuals and asserts that "the collective impact of an admiring reanimation of the Confederacy is the renewal of racism."[36] Similarly, historian Jim Cullen concedes that reenactments make him uneasy "because it is a way that white Americans assure themselves they have a past, too"; folklorist Tom Dunning describes the hobby as a pastime for "individuals threatened by a changing multi-cultural United States"; and sociologist Edward Sebesta asserts that "Confederate reenacting is a form of anti-government militia training."[37] Sebesta is the coeditor of *Neo-Confederacy: A Critical Introduction* and is one of several scholars—Brian Britt and Lain Hart are others—who draw a connection between Civil War reenactment and the exceedingly reactionary, right-wing, neo-Confederate movement.[38]

Documentarians who have examined reenactment are among the community's worst enemies. Particularly troublesome, from the reenactors' standpoint, is Glenn Kirschbaum's 2001 reenactment documentary *The Unfinished Civil War*, which aired repeatedly on the History Channel. The producers received extensive support from members of the reenactment community, including hundreds of hours of interviews. When the program finally aired, the reenactors were shocked and horrified to hear the narrator make liberal use of terms such as "wild-eyed wackos" and "flag-waving racists." Perhaps worst of all, the program featured lengthy clips of interviews with former Ku Klux Klan grand wizard David Duke, implying a relationship between reenactment and the KKK. "Now the public sees that and thinks (re-enactors are) the Ku Klux Klan in hiding," complained Confederate reenactor Greg Walz.[39] "Every time that film airs it does more and more damage to our hobby," lamented Union reenactor Paul Calloway. "It promotes the perception that we're all a bunch of wild-eyed wackos."[40] "It was embarrassing," opined Atlanta-based Confederate Mike Ventura. "A lot of our friends know this is our hobby but didn't know what we did. This portrayed us as a bunch of idiotic racists."[41] Many reenactors were so angry that they mounted a petition drive—unsuccessful—to have the program permanently removed from the History Channel's library.[42]

The print media have also helped to stigmatize reenactors. Most notable is *Confederates in the Attic*, a 1998 best seller by former *New York Times* reporter Tony Horwitz. His book explores many different iterations of the Civil War as expressed in the modern-day South—from the exceedingly troublesome (an unapologetic white supremacist and anti-Semite named Walt) to the quaint (the *Gone with the Wind* museum and the oldest living Confederate widow).[43] One of the central characters of the book—he appears on the cover, in fact—is Robert Lee Hodge, a Confederate reenactor devoted to capturing the past as accurately as possible (usually through long, punishing marches with inadequate food and shelter). Although Horwitz makes it very clear that he is presenting a wide spectrum of beliefs, the juxtaposition of Hodge with people like Walt largely affirms the conception of Civil War reenactors as unredeemed racists. Consider, for example, these reader reviews posted on the website of bookseller Amazon.com:

> Required reading for neo-Confederates and those who want to understand them. The material on the "hard-core" Civil War reenactor fringe is at once both fascinating and pathetic.

> I have concluded that hardcore reenactors and others who worship the battle flag are suffering from an acute case of inferiority. Why don't white southerners take pride in the great writers from that region or music and folk art admired around the world? The first presidents were all Virginians, and half of the 13 original states were

southern. Why can't southerners take pride in these things instead of living up to the stereotypes of racism and ignorance imposed on them by others?

I personally know one of the men that Horwitz interviewed and commented about. Horwitz did a great disservice to this individual in completely misrepresenting him and his motives and activities in the hobby. Instead of presenting him as the calm, thoughtful, introspective individual I know him to be, Horwitz presented him as a rabid extremist.[44]

Social activists, too, have weighed in against reenactment. Tim Wise, who advertises himself as an "antiracist essayist, author, and educator" and "one of the most brilliant, articulate and courageous critics of white privilege in the nation," decries reenactments as "racist bunk."[45] The NAACP has waded into the debate, expressing general opposition to reenactments across the country. This position received particular attention in 2003 when the Reverend James Piper, head of the NAACP's Beauregard-Vernon chapter, demanded that a planned reenactment in western Louisiana be canceled. He asserted that reenactments "disrupt harmony" and "disrupt social and civil peace" and explained that he would not "sit still for something that represents racism."[46]

The entertainment media have been particularly effective at marginalizing reenactors as kooks and racists. To start, the list of modern crime dramas that have had at least one "reenactment episode" includes *CSI*, *Without a Trace*, *NCIS*, *The District*, *Psych*, and *Bones*.[47] Confederate reenactors make excellent suspects, especially when they are presented as social outcasts who are odd, maladjusted, and well armed. A pair of examples will suffice to illustrate the general tenor of these programs. In the *CSI* episode "Way to Go," Confederate reenactor Caleb Carson is a social pariah who wears a tight corset at all times to make his waist narrower and thus conform to nineteenth-century standards.[48] While attending a reenactment, he becomes enraged at a Union soldier who dares to use a cell phone during a battle and challenges him to a duel. Unbeknownst to the poor Union reenactor, Carson has live ammunition in his Civil War–era revolver. A misfire kills Caleb and saves the hapless Union infantryman's life.

In the *Without a Trace* episode "Cloudy with a Chance of Gettysburg," the viewer first sees a flashback of young Kirby Morris, who is humiliated by having his pants torn off in front of his entire high school while receiving a prize for his historical essays. This causes him to become psychotic, and given his love of history, he gravitates toward Civil War reenactment. In the present, we learn that he is competing with a George Pickett impersonator for the affections of a young Confederate nurse. When "Pickett" turns up missing, Morris is the key suspect, although the ultimate culprit proves to be a Robert E. Lee impersonator. At the conclusion of the episode, the police detectives comment on the strangeness of the reenactment community. One remarks, "This [case] was an odd one," and the other agrees that it was "like being in a Salvador Dali painting."

While crime dramas tend to focus on the notion that reenactors—particularly Confederate reenactors—are maladjusted outcasts, comedies tend to emphasize that they are drunkards, fools, and bigots. The movie *Borat: Cultural Learnings of America for Make Benefit Glorious Nation of Kazakhstan* falls into this category, as do the television programs *Family Guy*, *30 Rock*, *South Park*, *The Simpsons*, *Everybody Loves Raymond*, *The Jeff Foxworthy Show*, *The Jeff Dunham Show*, *SpongeBob SquarePants*, and *Mr. Show*.[49] In *Borat*, the foreign-born title character attends a reenactment as a southerner, convincing his comrades in arms to pray that they will win the war or at least avoid being sodomized by the victorious Union armies. Consistent with the general approach of the movie, the purpose of the ruse is to cause discomfort and thus to hint at the reenactors' homophobia.

In the *Family Guy* episode "To Love and Die in Dixie," main characters Brian and Peter Griffin attend a Civil War reenactment where a drunken Ulysses S. Grant is knocked to the ground by Robert E. Lee. Lee declares a Confederate victory, and Peter objects, insisting that the North won the Civil War. A riot nearly ensues until Brian distracts the reenactors by shouting, "Hey, look over there! It's a newly married interracial gay couple burning the American flag!" In *The Jeff Dunham Show* episode "Civil War Games," a black puppet named Sweet Daddy Dee warns Confederate reenactors not to try to sell him into slavery. In the *SpongeBob SquarePants* episode "The Battle of Bikini Bottom"—yes, even children's cartoons have taken their potshots—reenactors fight a battle that will decide whether it is necessary to wash one's hands after using the bathroom. Naturally, the Confederates are the dirty, anti–hand-washing faction.

Generally speaking, these various groups of social elites—academics, documentarians, journalists, entertainers—have done a very effective job of stigmatizing Civil War reenactors. Recently, the news site CNN.com ran a story on a Civil War reenactment that generated more than 600 responses. The comments included the following, and many others like them:

> If it was up to these losers, slavery would still be legal and women wouldn't have rights. It's almost been 150 years since the war ended and yet they still fantasize about these "glory days." BOTTOM LINE: YOU LOST! Take that stupid flag down and actually try to help the nation PROGRESS, not REGRESS.

> What's more redneck: Civil War Reenactments or NASCAR?

> These people are scary. No doubt about it.

> It is a redneck hobby. We should be grateful that they are providing these "history lessons" and not breeding.

> It's still a redneck sport in my opinion. When you talk about honoring Confederates who fought and died for slavery, and wanting to mainly pretend to be the Confederate (the bad guy btw), then it's stupid. It's like reenacting the holocaust and wanting to be the Nazis. Granted I've never been to one, but based on what I read, including this article, there just seems to be no moral at these reenactments, no message on why the confederates lost the importance of the union prevailing.[50]

Reenactors are predominantly white and considerably older and more conservative than the general populace. It is not unreasonable to suggest that their views on race lag a bit behind the prevailing opinion on, say, a college campus. And there are undoubtedly a handful of reenactors who would be more at home at a cross burning than a battle re-creation. But if we are to understand reenactment—or, more specifically, Confederate reenactment—primarily as an expression of white southern racism, we are left with a number of troublesome questions: What about the northerners and westerners who prefer the Confederacy? What about men like Don Worth, who were drawn to the Confederacy as children, well before they had an awareness of race? Do the thousands of foreign Confederate reenactors oppose a civil rights movement that took place in another country? What about the several hundred black men who reenact as Confederates—are they racists? Further, if the goal is to advocate white supremacy, why not join an overtly white supremacist group like the Ku Klux Klan or the League of the South? Why bother with the hot wool uniforms and the antique weapons?

As we consider these questions, it is hard to avoid the conclusion that racism, by itself, is not a satisfactory explanation for the popularity of Confederate reenactment. To gain a better understanding of their motives, it seems reasonable to ask reenactors why they prefer the gray. A good starting place is Robert Lee Hodge, who explains:

My father is from Alabama and my mother's folks are from Tennessee, so even though I am from Ohio, I had a kinship with the South early on. Named after Lee and born on the same day as Jackson's birthday, I tend to lean the gray way. My folks were not rabid neo-Confeds, but my dad used to tease my mom for being a Yankee. . . .

For me it is easy to get wrapped up in the Confederacy; all I had to do was read. The other huge aspect is the visuals. To me, at least, my image of Johnnies looks more connected with the land—homespun, if you will. Civilian soldiers in often earth-colored uniforms, bedrolls, big slouch hats, bloused trousers, etc. fighting against the massive federal government soldiers in their dark blue (almost black) uniforms gives me the feeling of David fighting Goliath. The image of southern soldiers is attractive. As a child, I wanted to be a part of it.[51]

In other interviews conducted for this essay, I got similar answers dozens of times. For example, Duke Harless, who portrays a soldier from the Third Georgia Infantry, asks:

Is it because we can be more colorful and dashing as Confederates? Is it because if we do Union Infantry we are limited in dress to dark blue coat, light blue pants, and a kepi? Is not a trusty Springfield musket enough? Do we have to have sabers, pistols, and shotguns? Do we just like being underdogs, defying the "oppressive government"? Are we worried about our great-great-granddaddy doing monkey flips in his grave if we wore Union blue? Maybe the Union coat of blue and the trappings of an infantryman don't seem to have as much panache as the gaudy vests, feather and animal-part hats, and the arsenal hanging from the belts of a Reb cavalryman.[52]

John Quimby, who does both Rebel and Union impressions, ties the appeal of the Confederate soldier even more explicitly to the Lost Cause interpretation of the war: "We've all consumed the tales of the desperate southern warrior, down to his last patched pair of trousers and barefoot in the mud. This symbolic image was promoted in the postwar era—a time when southerners were struggling with their own self-image. The barefoot Rebel is a heroic icon of the Lost Cause."[53]

As already noted, the Lost Cause interpretation of the war blends heroic storybook elements (e.g., the gallant Robert E. Lee) with a political message (e.g., the insignificance of slavery). Virtually all Confederate reenactors—and most Federals, too—embrace the heroic part of the Lost Cause (recall, for example, Don Worth's childhood fascination with John Singleton Mosby). This is the single most important factor behind the appeal of the Confederacy and the southern soldier. In addition, some Confederate reenactors perceive a parallel between the Reconstruction-era South and today's South. That is, they believe the South needs to be "redeemed" again—not in terms of white political control but in terms of Americans' perception of the region. It is primarily this group of reenactors—Vern Padgett among them—that has revived the political dimension of the Lost Cause interpretation after it lay dormant for more than half a century.

Historian Alan Nolan has identified a number of common motifs in the writings of the Lost Cause. An examination of the most important of these motifs and their place in the reenactment community illustrates the extent to which most reenactors tend to retain the heroic elements of the interpretation, while the political elements find a narrower, though still palpable, expression.[54]

### *Heroic Motif: Lee and Jackson*

Robert E. Lee and Stonewall Jackson are the great heroic figures of the Lost Cause, along with a handful of other Confederates—J. E. B. Stuart, George Pickett, and Nathan Bedford Forrest. The Lost Cause also has its villains; most prominent is Confederate general James Longstreet (who is blamed for the defeat at Gettysburg and committed the sin of becoming a Republican after the war), along with the men who led the North to victory: Ulysses S. Grant and William T. Sherman.

The preeminence of Lee and Jackson is not evident at the reenactments themselves. Portraying specific individuals, particularly high-ranking officers, is not common, so one generally finds a Lee or a Jackson only at very large reenactments of battles at which they were actually present. However, their popularity among reenactors is evident in other ways. The *Camp Chase Gazette*, which styles itself the "voice of Civil War reenacting," has a broader reach than any other reenactment publication.[55] It editors try to provide balanced coverage, but they must also cater to their subscribers. Further, they have little control over the content that is not generated by the magazine's staff—this includes letters to the editor, advertisements, and the "Observation Post," a collection of news items and announcements provided entirely by readers.

An examination of the content of the *Camp Chase Gazette* over the past fifteen years (1998–2012) speaks to the predominance of Lost Cause heroes in the reenactment community.[56] Robert E. Lee was the subject of an article, announcement, letter, or advertisement sixty-seven times in that span, or roughly once every other issue. That number is quite high, given that the magazine's advertisements tend to focus on battle reenactments rather than specific individuals (in contrast to other publications, such as the *Civil War Times Illustrated*, which showcase a lot of Confederate-themed artwork).[57] After Lee, four of the six next most commonly mentioned figures were Lost Cause heroes of various sorts, with only Abraham Lincoln and George Armstrong Custer (a dashing figure in the Lost Cause mold) breaking up the southern monopoly. Ulysses S. Grant ranked ninth, and other important Union generals were lucky if their names appeared in the pages of the magazine once a year. Hapless George Gordon Meade, the triumphant commander at Gettysburg, was *never* mentioned in that fifteen-year span, which is particularly interesting, given the popularity of that battle.

The esteem in which Lee and Jackson are held also comes through in the interviews conducted for this essay. More than 30 percent of reenactors identified either Lee or Jackson as the Civil War figure they admired most. The sentiments of reenactor Mark Silber are representative: "I am a northerner by birth and residence, but I admire Robert E. Lee as one of the greatest and finest Americans to walk on this earth. He is a man of honor, courage, and duty. Robert E. Lee has earned the love of millions of his fellow southerners and other Americans over the decades."[58] Other Lost Cause heroes, including Stuart (cited by 8 percent of interviewees) and Pickett (6 percent), are also more widely admired than northerners Grant (5 percent) and Sherman (4 percent) and the unfortunate Longstreet (1 percent).

### Heroic Motif: The Preeminence of Virginia

An adjunct to the veneration of Lee and Jackson is the Lost Cause ideology's focus on the military theater of Virginia and the two armies that fought there: the Army of Northern Virginia and the Army of the Potomac. To use a term employed by historian Gary Gallagher, Lost Cause writers present Virginia as the "cockpit" of the Civil War.[59] They claim that Richmond was always the main focus of the Union army and that the most significant fighting occurred around the Confederate capital. This area, of course, was where Lee and Jackson scored all their dramatic victories.

There are several ways in which the preeminence of the Virginia theater is reflected in reenactment. The first is the location of each year's grand anniversary reenactment. The Civil War was four years long, so in four out of every five years, there is an "important" anniversary—one divisible by five—for an entire year's worth of Civil War battles. For example, 2012 was the 150th anniversary of the battles fought in 1862—Second Bull Run, Antietam, Fort Donelson, Shiloh, and Murfreesboro, among others. In each of these anniversary years, one reenactment gets the broadest attention and the highest attendance. And invariably, that reenactment is a re-creation of a battle between the Army of the Potomac and the Army of Northern Virginia. For 1861 (1996, 2001, 2006, 2011), the grand reenactment was First Bull Run; for 1862 (1997, 2002, 2007, 2012), Antietam; for 1863 (1998, 2003, 2008, 2013), Gettysburg; and for 1864 (1999, 2004, 2009, 2014), the Wilderness. For each of these years, there are alternative non-Virginia options that might be more justifiable in terms of importance to the Civil War—Fort Sumter for 1861, Shiloh for 1862, Vicksburg for 1863, and Atlanta for 1864. Some dedicated reenactors gamely attempt to stage events at these locations, but the Virginia battles invariably draw many more attendees.[60]

The centrality of Virginia is also reflected in reenactors' choice of units to portray. Of the 3.4 million men who fought in the Civil War, roughly 600,000 (17 percent) served in one of the armies in the Virginia theater for at least part of the war.[61] Of the 211 reenactment groups that are currently active, 137 (nearly 65 percent) portray units that were part of either the Army of Northern Virginia or the Army of the Potomac. In other words, the average reenactor is four times more likely to be in one of the great armies of the Virginia theater than was the average Civil War soldier.

Finally, items appearing in the pages of the *Camp Chase Gazette* also speak to the prominence of the Virginia theater. Based on the number of mentions in the magazine between 1998 and 2012, the two main Virginia armies—Army of Northern Virginia and Army of the Potomac—ranked first and third, with the Army of Northern Virginia far and away the most popular. The Army of Tennessee, though not the "cockpit" of the war, also has an honored place in Lost Cause mythology and served as the home base for Nathan Bedford Forrest and his exploits; it ranked second in terms of mentions in the *Camp Chase Gazette*. The most important Union armies after the Army of the Potomac—including the Army of the Tennessee, which Grant commanded for the better part of two years, as well as the Armies of the Cumberland, Ohio, James, Mississippi, Shenandoah, and Gulf—combined for forty-three mentions over the past fifteen years, fewer than the Army of Northern Virginia by itself (mentioned fifty times).

Civil War battles tell a similar story. Gettysburg, though a southern defeat, is the central battle of the Lost Cause mythology. It is the "high-water mark," the moment when the Confederacy ostensibly came closest to victory, according to postwar southern thinking. It has found its way into the pages of the *Camp Chase Gazette* 295 times in the last fifteen years, or nearly two times per issue. This is more than the next two most popular battles combined. The second entry on the list—the Bull Runs (which are often discussed in combination in the magazine and so are combined here)—is also a Lost Cause favorite. From there, the list is less obviously skewed in favor of Lost Cause battles—Chickamauga, Shiloh, Vicksburg, and Chattanooga were all in the West, while Chancellorsville, a key Lost Cause battle, ranks rather low. These anomalies can be explained by two factors: first, there is a small but die-hard contingent of reenactors that tries each year to use the pages of the *Gazette* to rally support for western reenactments (without success, as noted earlier); second, large reenactments of Chancellorsville are rare, for a pair of reasons. Most important, the anniversary of that battle (May 1863) is only two months before that of Gettysburg (July 1863). Any reenactor who is interested in spending the time and money to travel to a large-scale reenactment is going to wait for Gettysburg. Less significant is that Chancellorsville's role in Lost Cause mythology has more to do with what happened after the battle—the accidental shooting and death of Stonewall Jackson—and less to do with the battle itself (though it was unquestionably a great victory for the Confederacy).

### *Heroic Motif: The Idealized Confederate Soldier*

The Lost Cause interpretation also has a central place of honor for the common soldier of the Confederacy. He was, as Nolan explains, portrayed as "heroic, indefatigable, gallant, and law-abiding."[62] It is not difficult to find similar sentiments among reenactors. When asked why he chooses to reenact a southerner, David Upton of the Third Tennessee says: "I think of Confederate soldiers as being a bit more admirable than their Union counterparts. First of all, their sacrifice was greater, given the suffering that they had to endure due to lack of food, supplies, and so forth. Second, they were fighting to protect their homes, and I can identify with that."[63] An Ohio reenactor echoes these sentiments: "A rebel has got that stigma to it, you're the outcast, you're the black sheep. Kind of like the dark side!"[64]

There is another, more subtle way in which the idealized notion of the Confederate soldier is evident in Civil War reenactment. A common perception in the reenactment community is that men who portray Confederates are more likely to be blue collar than their Union counterparts. Joseph Bolivard of the Ninth New York observes: "The people who [are] middle class will have a tendency to join a Union group. This may show in the education profile as to the amount of education one has as to which side he joins. . . . I would say Union reenactors have a higher income than Confederate soldiers."[65] David Pleger of the Second Vermont shares this perception: "Confederate reenactors are more likely to be truck drivers or construction workers. Union reenactors are more likely to be doctors, lawyers, or teachers."[66] What is interesting about this widely held perception is that it is false. Among the individuals interviewed for this essay, there were dozens of Confederates in white-collar professions and dozens of Federals in blue-collar professions. In a study of income patterns among reenactors, Mark L. Shanks found no particular disparity between the two groups. The average income of the 380 Confederates he surveyed was $61,900; for the 349 Union reenactors that responded, the average income was $63,800. In other words, the average Confederate reenactor and the average Union reenactor are both comfortably middle class.[67]

Lost Cause authors always portray the experience of southern soldiers as vastly more challenging than that of Union soldiers. Due to shortages of men and materials, Confederate soldiers were regularly forced to march and fight hard, often without adequate food or supplies. Meanwhile, Union soldiers were thought to have a much more comfortable existence due to their over-whelmingly superior numbers and almost endless amounts of food and sup-plies. To some extent, these perceptions are based in truth, but there were many cases in which Confederate soldiers were well supplied and Union sol-diers were forced to fight with less than adequate provisions. In any case, it seems reasonable to suggest that the Lost Cause's presentation of Confeder-ates as hardworking, hard-marching, ragtag military men has translated into the perception that Confederate reenactors are also ragtag blue-collar types.

### Political Motif: Slavery

The most important political issue addressed by the Lost Cause, at least for modern Americans, is southern slavery and its role in provoking the Civil War. The Lost Cause writers, for their part, have advanced a number of asser-tions about slavery: that the South did not go to war to protect its "peculiar institution," that slavery would have disappeared eventually, and that the slaves were generally happy with their lot in life.

There are, broadly speaking, three different approaches to the issue of slavery on display in the reenactment community. The first is to confront the issue head-on. Don Worth, for example, says: "As with most wars, what the individuals thought they were fighting for didn't have much to do with what STARTED the war—it was the politicians that started the war. And their beef was over representation in congress (and with the election of a President who the south felt would not be sympathetic to their interests). The defining char-acteristic of that representation was whether a state was slave or free. To me, that makes the war (primarily) about slavery."[68] According to Greg Roma-neck, who does both Confederate and Union impressions, "A reenactor who does not understand the effects of race and slavery on that time period is not coming to grips with one of, if not the most important, factors which resulted in the carnage of 1861–65."[69] Confederate reenactor Levi Miller puts things even more succinctly: "I'm real glad that I was born into the US of A where racial equality is actively promoted, and where on weekends I can freely play the role of a nineteenth century armed secessionist."[70]

A second approach to slavery—the most common one in the reenact-ment community—is to downplay the importance of the issue. This is, pre-sumably, the most effective way to make the Civil War a "usable past." Approximately 50 percent of reenactors argue that the Civil War was caused by an issue or issues other than slavery.[71] The "peculiar institution" is rarely presented at reenactments, as it tends to be uncomfortable for both those playing the role and those witnessing the performance. The *Camp Chase Gazette* has referenced slavery only twenty-six times in the past fifteen years.

The third approach to slavery is the "black Confederate" argument. It is presumably a sign of progress that the myth of "happy slaves," portrayed in movies and books before the 1960s, is dead. Not even the most die-hard Confederate reenactor would argue this position today. Only slightly better, though just as ahistorical, is the notion that Vern Padgett advocates: that tens of thousands or hundreds of thousands of slaves took up arms for the Confederacy. The implication is obvious: if slaves were willing to fight for the Confederacy, then their lives were not so bad and their masters were not as evil or wrongheaded as they might seem. While it is unquestionably offensive to downplay the horrors of slavery, it is worth noting that the primary goals of this argument are not racist in nature—that is, the purpose is not to assert white supremacy or black inferiority but to express disdain for academic elites and their views on the war and to apologize for and "redeem" the South.

Indeed, whatever their position on the question of slavery—which is, after all, a nineteenth-century issue—reenactors are all but unanimous in their abhorrence of racism. Because they know that the media and the general public are suspicious of their hobby, they usually show great sensitivity to this issue, even the Vern Padgetts of the world. Though it tends to avoid the touchy subject of slavery, the *Camp Chase Gazette* regularly tackles racial issues. For example, a 2001 article entitled "Racism: An Issue for Living Historians" exhorts reenactors to remember that perspectives on race have changed in the last 140 years and asks them to be careful not to incorporate the attitudes and language of the past into their impressions.[72]

Confederate reenactors tend to be particularly careful when it comes to this issue. For example, Temple University history professor and Union reenactor Gregory Urwin served as a consultant on a short film. In one scene, three Confederate reenactors were asked to use a rather serious racial slur. Regardless of how much the director pleaded, they simply would not use the word, which eventually had to be looped in during postproduction.[73] There are also a number of stories of Confederate reenactors publicly confronting racists at reenactment events. For example, at a September 2006 reenactment in Gettysburg, twenty Klansmen made an appearance. The first group to stand in their way and to insist that they take their Confederate flags and leave was the Thirty-Seventh Texas Infantry.[74]

Beyond dramatic incidents such as these, Confederate reenactors commonly issue careful disclaimers about their racial predilections whenever they feel it is necessary. This one appears in Jonah Begone's article "Advancing the Southern Cause": "The traditional Southern point of view . . . is one of political and social conservatism. I am for a restrained federal government, more political power given to the states, Second Amendment rights (good luck reenacting without them), an awareness and respect for heritage . . . and the maintenance of the usual social customs and traditions. Racism, obviously, is not one of the customs I would endorse."[75] Nearly every southern reenactment group that has a website includes a similar disclaimer. For example, www.9thvirginia.com advises visitors and recruits: "We portray a Confederate cavalry regiment as it would have looked in 1863. We are not a 'reb' unit, we do not tolerate extremists or racism." Likewise, www.texas-brigade.org announces that the unit's members "denounce racism, racial supremacists, hate groups and other groups or individuals that misuse or desecrate the symbols of the United States of America and/or the former Confederate States of America; and [it] has no modern political agenda or status."

Similarly, as the Sons of Confederate Veterans (SCV) and other organizations have grown more friendly to white supremacy in the last decade, many members of the reenactment community have urged them to change their ways or, failing that, for reenactors to separate from such groups. Confederate reenactor Walter C. Hilderman III, who hosts a website dedicated to this issue, writes:

> [If] SCV reenactors bring their in-your-face attitudes and new found political activism into the hobby, Confederate reenacting will come to be viewed by the public, liberal activists and the authorities with the same suspicion that the entire SCV has generated in recent years. . . . Civil War reenacting has become a popular American teaching and learning experience, complete with big budgets, vendors, permits, first responders, and inevitably, insurance policies. Reenactments, large and small, require public acceptance and support. Without the public's trust in our reasons for being Confederate reenactors, our hobby and our mission of teaching American history through reenacting will end.[76]

And finally, to give Robert Lee Hodge the last word on the issue: "I don't give a shit if my sister marries a black guy. Unless he's a farb."[77]

The above discussion illustrates two important points. The first is the enduring power of the Lost Cause, a 150-year-old interpretation of the Civil War that still has enough salience to resonate with Americans, particularly those who grew up prior to the 1960s. There is no question that the Lost Cause is a better explanation of the enduring popularity of the Confederate soldier than is the notion that Confederate reenactment is a socially acceptable way to express racist sentiments.

The second point is that we must be careful about painting groups such as Civil War reenactors—what W. James Booth has called "communities of memory"—with too broad a brush.[78] There is no reason to assume that all members of a group this large have the same or even similar viewpoints. There are substantive differences between Don Worth and Vern Padgett, and if the label "racist" is to be applied—which is a matter of opinion—it is far more apropos for the latter than the former. Of particular concern is the tendency for some observers to deploy the term *neo-Confederate* in discussing Confederate reenactment. The Southern Poverty Law Center is the foremost authority on white supremacist groups in the United States, and it offers this definition:

> The term neo-Confederacy is used to describe twentieth and twenty-first century revivals of pro-Confederate sentiment in the United States. Strongly nativist and advocating measures to end immigration, neo-Confederacy claims to pursue Christianity and heritage and other supposedly fundamental values that modern Americans are seen to have abandoned.
>
> Neo-Confederacy also incorporates advocacy of traditional gender roles, is hostile towards democracy, strongly opposes homosexuality, and exhibits an understanding of race that favors segregation and suggests white supremacy. In many cases, neo-Confederates are openly secessionist.[79]

There is simply no evidence for the existence of these views among the vast majority of Confederate reenactors, and to argue or imply otherwise is a gross distortion.

In addition to these two points, this essay suggests an obvious question:

Should the Confederacy and its symbols still be automatically associated with racism? As long as the Confederate flag and the Confederate soldier come under attack, the Vern Padgetts of the world will continue to dig in their heels and will undoubtedly continue to embrace and promote ahistorical understandings of the Civil War. Historian Peter S. Carmichael, in an essay penned in 2011, observes, "The extreme categorizing behind this discourse has created impenetrable walls between those on both sides who, in their separate worlds, demonize the other without having to engage in meaningful dialogue."[80] It is hard to argue that maintaining such a wall—between North and South, white and black, liberal and conservative, academic and popular historians—is productive.

This question was also raised at a September 2012 panel on the preliminary Emancipation Proclamation. It was fielded by historian Christy Coleman, who is African American and must address three different constituencies—northerners, southerners, and African Americans—as director of the American Civil War Center at Richmond's Tredgar Iron Works. Her answer may point the way forward on this issue:

> So my point is, when it comes to the Confederate, the Confederate heritage person, . . . you will often see, especially if you drive—the further south you drive—occasionally you'll see the little bumper stickers that say heritage, not hate. For those individuals that's exactly what it is, they're just honoring what their ancestors thought was right. And for me, as an African-American woman who grew up in Virginia hearing all this foolishness, to me it is, okay, I'm willing to acknowledge that, but please don't dismiss the role and the function of our folks.[81]

Very well put.

## Notes

The title of this essay is from a post–Civil War song that expresses the iconoclasm of many southerners in the late nineteenth century. The entire first verse reads: Oh, I'm a good ol' rebel, yes, that's just what I am / And for this, their "land of freedom," I do not care a damn! / I'm proud I fought against 'em; I only wish we'd won, / And I don't want their pardon for anything I done!

1. E-mails by Vern Padgett, May 2, 2001, August 23, 2002, and July 5, 2001.

2. The "black Confederate" argument has become popular among some southern partisans in the last fifteen to twenty years and has been the subject of a number of books and articles. See, for example, Charles Barrow Kelly, J. H. Segars, and R. B. Rosenburg, eds., *Black Confederates* (Gretna, La.: Pelican Publishing, 2001), and Arthur W. Bergeron et al., *Black Southerners in Gray* (Redondo Beach, Calif.: Rank and File Publications, 1997).

3. I personally witnessed Padgett's lecture at the San Gabriel Civil War Round Table on July 14, 2002.

4. From Worth's personal homepage, http://worth.bol.ucla.edu/ (accessed November 26, 2012).

5. Interview with Don Worth, July 4, 2008.

6. Ibid.

7. Because there are no central organizations with which reenactors register, it is difficult to estimate these numbers accurately. This number is based on interviews done for this essay, articles submitted to *Camp Chase Gazette*, and membership rolls from several local organizations around the country.

8. Not surprisingly, many of these African American units portray the Fifty-Fourth Massachusetts Infantry Regiment, the subject of the film *Glory.*

9. The size of the Confederate and Union armies is reported differently in different sources. The *Official Records* puts the size of the Union army at nearly 3 million, but this number is not reliable because it does not account for soldiers who enlisted more than once. Most other sources give numbers within 100,000 of those presented here.

10. In desperation, due to severe manpower shortages and a crumbling war effort, the South finally made arrangements to begin conscripting slaves in December 1864. However, before these units could be assembled and trained, the war came to a close.

11. There are a few exceptions, most notably the reenacted Thirty-Seventh Texas, which is made up almost exclusively of African Americans.

12. James O. Farmer, "Playing Rebels: Reenactment as Nostalgia and Defense of the Confederacy in the Battle of Aiken," *Southern Cultures* 11, no. 1 (Spring 2005): 71–72.

13. Tara McPherson, *Reconstructing Dixie: Race, Gender, and Nostalgia in the Imagined South* (Durham, N.C.: Duke University Press Books, 2003), xiii. Other key books on this subject include Jack Temple Kirby, *Media-Made Dixie: The South in the American Imagination* (Athens: University of Georgia Press, 1986); Peter Applebome, *Dixie Rising* (New York: Times Books, 1996); and Rebecca Bridges Watts, *Contemporary Southern Identity: Community through Controversy* (Jackson: University Press of Mississippi, 2008).

14. For an overview of the Lost Cause, see Gary W. Gallagher, *Lee and His Generals in War and Memory* (Baton Rouge: Louisiana State University Press, 1998); Thomas L. Connelly and Barbara Bellows, *God and General Longstreet: The Lost Cause and the Southern Mind* (Baton Rouge: Louisiana State University Press, 1982); Gaines M. Foster, *Ghosts of the Confederacy: Defeat, the Lost Cause, and the Emergence of the New South* (New York: Oxford University Press, 1987); and Gary Gallagher and Alan T. Nolan, *The Myth of the Lost Cause and Civil War History* (Bloomington: Indiana University Press, 2000).

15. See Karen L. Cox, *Dreaming of Dixie: How the South Was Created in American Popular Culture* (Chapel Hill: University of North Carolina Press, 2011); Nina Silber, *The Romance of Reunion: Northerners and the South, 1865–1900* (Chapel Hill: University of North Carolina Press, 1993); and Robert H. Wiebe, *The Search for Order, 1877–1920* (New York: Hill and Wang, 1966).

16. McPherson, *Reconstructing Dixie*, 3.

17. Foster, *Ghosts of the Confederacy*, 3–8.

18. For an extended discussion of this subject, see Anthony J. Stanonis, ed., *Dixie Emporium: Tourism, Foodways, and Consumer Culture in the American South* (Athens: University of Georgia Press, 2008), and Grace Elizabeth Hale, *Making Whiteness: The Culture of Segregation in the South, 1890–1940* (New York: Pantheon, 1998).

19. There are relatively few overviews of the South's portrayal in popular music, as most studies focus on specific eras or genres. The best available general treatment is Mark Kemp, *Dixie Lullaby: A Story of Music, Race, and New Beginnings in a New South* (New York: Free Press, 2004).

20. The portrayal of the South in film has received extensive attention. See Karl G. Heidler, ed., *Images of the South: Constructing a Regional Culture on Film and Video* (Athens: University of Georgia Press, 1993); Warren French, ed., *The South and Film* (Jackson: University Press of Mississippi, 1981); Deborah E. Barker and Kathryn McKee, eds., *American Cinema and the Southern Imaginary* (Athens: University of Georgia Press, 2011); Allison Graham, *Framing the South: Hollywood, Television, and Race during the Civil Rights Struggle* (Baltimore: Johns Hopkins University Press, 2001); and Bruce Chadwick, *The Reel Civil War: Mythmaking in American Film* (New York: Vintage Books, 2002).

21. Examples with a decidedly Lost Cause influence include Douglass Southall Freeman, *R. E. Lee, A Biography* (New York: Scribner, 1934–1935); Ulrich B. Phillips, *American Negro Slavery: A Survey of the Supply, Employment and Control of Negro Labor as Determined by the Plantation Regime* (Baton Rouge: Louisiana State University Press, 1918); Shelby Foote, *Civil War: A Narrative* (New York: Random House, 1958–1974); and Bruce Catton, *The American Heritage Picture History of the Civil War* (New York: American Heritage, 1960). Foote and Catton are both critical of

some elements of Lost Cause thinking but thoroughly embrace others, particularly those that mesh well with their taste for dramatic narrative.

22. For a discussion of this point, see Mark Royden Winchell, *Reinventing the South: Versions of a Literary Region* (Columbia: University of Missouri Press, 2006).

23. Henry Cavendish, "Bigotry and Ignorance in Deep South," *Chicago Daily Tribune*, July 22, 1951, 114.

24. Alexander Holmes, "Another Side of Segregation in the South," *Los Angeles Times*, January 9, 1956, A5.

25. Robert E. Baker, "Shame Abating Arkansas Fever: Little Rock Feeling a Nation's Disgust," *Washington Post*, September 15, 1957, E3.

26. Harnett T. Kane, "Change in the Mardi Gras Spirit," *New York Times*, January 29, 1961, SM10; Saunders Redding, "The South and Society," *New York Times*, October 31, 1965, BR88.

27. George Gallup, "How North, South View Each Other," *Los Angeles Times*, May 27, 1957, 30.

28. See John Shelton Reed, *The Enduring South: Subcultural Persistence in Mass Society* (Chapel Hill: University of North Carolina Press, 1972), 25.

29. Disney went so far as to repudiate *The Song of the South*, and the film is still not available for purchase in the United States.

30. The dramatic change in filmic portrayals of the South is discussed in, among other books, Scott Von Doviak, *Hick Flicks: The Rise and Fall of Redneck Cinema* (Jefferson, N.C.: McFarland, 2005), and Andrew B. Leiter, ed., *Southerners on Film: Essays on Hollywood Portrayals since the 1970s* (Jefferson, N.C.: McFarland, 2011).

31. See John Shelton Reed, *Surveying the South: Studies in Regional Sociology* (Columbia: University of Missouri Press, 1993), 51–65.

32. The word *redneck* first appeared in print in the 1830s and was used to denigrate the missionary efforts of the Presbyterian Church, which tried to appeal to working-class whites that other denominations deemed unworthy.

33. For a discussion of the "declension" of the redneck stereotype, see James C. Cobb, *Away Down South: A History of Southern Identity* (New York: Oxford University Press, 2005), and Jim Goad, *The Redneck Manifesto: How Hillbillies, Hicks, and White Trash Became America's Scapegoats* (New York: Simon and Schuster, 1998).

34. "The Various Shady Lives of the Ku Klux Klan," *Time*, April 9, 1965, 24–25.

35. Cobb, *Away Down South*, 1.

36. Elizabeth Young, *Disarming the Nation: Women's Writing and the American Civil War* (Chicago: University of Chicago Press, 1999), 293.

37. Jim Cullen, *The Civil War in Popular Culture: A Reusable Past* (Washington, D.C.: Smithsonian Institution, 1995), 199; Tom Dunning, "Civil War Reenactments: Performance as a Cultural Practice," *Australasian Journal of American Studies*

21, no. 1 (July 2002): 64; *Anti-Neo Confederate Blog*, http://newtknight.blogspot.com/2007/06/confederate-reenacting-gets-ugly.html (accessed December 2, 2012).

38. Lain Hart, "Authentic Recreation: Living History and Leisure," *Museum and Society* 5, no. 2 (July 2007); Brian Britt, "Neo-Confederate Culture," *Z Magazine* 9, no. 12 (December 1996).

39. Laureen Fagan, "Re-enactors Rip TV Flag Documentary; History Drives Them, Not Political Agenda," *South Bend Tribune*, March 15, 2001, A1.

40. Jeffry Scott, "History Channel Film Draws Ire of Reenactors," *Atlanta Journal-Constitution*, March 13, 2001, 2C.

41. David Bauder, "Civil War Re-enactors Push for Boycott; The History Channel: Many Believe that the Network Is Portraying Them as Racists," *Telegraph Herald*, March 17, 2001, A8.

42. Civil War News online, http://www.civilwarnews.com/archive/articles/hist_channel.htm (accessed December 2, 2012).

43. Tony Horwitz, *Confederates in the Attic: Dispatches from the Unfinished Civil War* (New York: Pantheon Books, 1998), 81–86, 282–311, 336–51.

44. Amazon.com customer reviews for *Confederates in the Attic*, http://www.amazon.com/Confederates-Attic-Dispatches-Unfinished-Civil/product-reviews/067975833X (accessed December 2, 2012).

45. Tim Wise, http://www.timwise.org/2010/09/south-carolina-republicans-show-their-racist-asses-again-this-is-a-historical-constant-actually/ (accessed December 2, 2012).

46. Associated Press, February 16, 2003.

47. Episodes "Way to Go," *CSI*; "Cloudy with a Chance of Gettysburg," *Without a Trace*; "Silver War," *NCIS*; "A House Divided," *The District*; "Weekend Warriors," *Psych*; and "The Dentist in the Ditch," *Bones*.

48. Apparently, there was something of a historical misunderstanding among the show's writing staff: narrow waists were desirable for nineteenth-century women, not men.

49. Episodes "To Love and Die in Dixie," *Family Guy*; "When It Rains It Pours," *30 Rock*; "The Red Badge of Gayness," *South Park*; "The Sweetest Apu," *The Simpsons*; "Civil War," *Everybody Loves Raymond*; "Foxworthy Shall Rise Again," *The Jeff Foxworthy Show*; "Civil War Games," *The Jeff Dunham Show*; "The Battle of Bikini Bottom," *SpongeBob SquarePants*; and "Like Chickens . . . Delicious Chickens," *Mr. Show*.

50. "'Living History' on Civil War Battlefields," http://www.cnn.com/2011/LIVING/04/09/civil.war.reenacting/index.html (accessed December 2, 2012). Reader comments are presented unedited.

51. Interview with Robert Lee Hodge, October 25, 2006.

52. Interview with Duke Harless, April 20, 2001.

53. Interview with John Quimby, May 2, 2001.

54. Alan T. Nolan, "The Anatomy of the Myth," in Gallagher and Nolan, *Myth of the Lost Cause*, 11–34.

55. The *Camp Chase Gazette* was first founded as a unit newsletter by William Keitz in 1971. It expanded its circulation dramatically in the 1980s and now sells approximately 8,000 copies a month.

56. The magazine is published ten times per year, so fifteen years equates to 150 issues.

57. The portrayal of the Confederacy in popular magazines, particularly in artwork, is addressed in Gary Gallagher, *Causes Won, Lost, and Forgotten: How Hollywood and Popular Art Shape What We Know about the Civil War* (Chapel Hill: University of North Carolina Press, 2008).

58. Interview with Mark Silber, November 11, 2012.

59. Gary W. Gallagher, "Jubal A. Early, the Lost Cause, and Civil War History: A Persistent Legacy," in Gallagher and Nolan, *Myth of the Lost Cause*, 35–59.

60. To take one example, the Gettysburg reenactment of 1998 drew 30,000 participants, while the Vicksburg reenactment on the same days drew 4,000.

61. These numbers are even more difficult to assess than the overall troop strength of the two armies because many units were transferred into and out of them. Nonetheless, this estimate was affirmed by noted expert Robert Krick.

62. Nolan, "Anatomy of the Myth," 17.

63. Interview with David Upton, January 11, 1999.

64. Quoted in Gordon L. Jones, "Gut History: Civil War Reenacting and the Making of an American Past" (PhD diss., Emory University, 2007), 338.

65. Quoted in Mark L. Shanks, "Who Wears the Blue and Grey? A Survey of Civil War Reenactors" (unpublished paper).

66. Interview with David Pleger, February 12, 1999.

67. Shanks, "Who Wears the Blue and Grey?"

68. E-mail from Don Worth to the author, May 2, 2001.

69. Greg Romaneck, *A Civil War Reenactor's Guidebook: Tips and Suggestions from the Field* (Berwyn Heights, Md.: Heritage Books, 2009), 30.

70. Levi Miller, "Letters to the Editor," *Camp Chase Gazette* 22, no. 10 (December 2005): 4.

71. Jones, "Gut History," 334.

72. Greg M. Romaneck, "Racism: An Issue for Living Historians," *Camp Chase Gazette* 18, no. 7 (October 2001): 50–51.

73. Interview with Gregory Urwin, September 6, 2004.

74. For a thorough narrative of the incident, see "Protesting the Klan at Gettysburg," http://www.bivouacbooks.com/bbv5i3s2.htm (accessed December 2, 2012).

75. Jonah Begone, "Advancing the Southern Cause," *Camp Chase Gazette* 17, no. 7 (October 2000): 56–57.

76. Save the SCV homepage, http://www.savethescv.org/ (accessed December 2, 2012).

77. Quoted in Horwitz, *Confederates in the Attic*, 246. *Farb* is reenactor slang for "phony."

78. W. James Booth, *Communities of Memory: On Witness, Identity, and Justice* (Ithaca, N.Y.: Cornell University Press, 2006), 3.

79. Southern Poverty Law Center, http://www.splcenter.org/get-informed/intelligence-files/ideology/neo-confederate (accessed December 2, 2012).

80. Peter S. Carmichael, "Truth Is Mighty & Will Eventually Prevail: Political Correctness, Neo-Confederates, and Robert E. Lee," *Southern Cultures* 17, no. 3 (Fall 2011): 6–27.

81. "Should We Still Associate Racism with Southern Heritage?" http://www.c-spanvideo.org/clip/4091984 (accessed December 2, 2012).

# Afterword

## *Untangling the Webs of the Civil War and Reconstruction in the Popular Culture Imagination*

## *David Madden*

Pursuing research for my ninth novel, *Sharpshooter* (1996), I gathered around me, over many years, more than 1,500 books, including scholarly and popular nonfiction and both popular and literary fiction. From those books I gathered thousands of facts about every facet of the tangled webs of the Civil War and Reconstruction. The first draft was more than 2,000 pages long; the published novel is less than 160 pages short. During the fifteen years between the first long draft and the final short book, the mere accumulation of facts proved less and less meaningful; but my selection of facts and placement of facts in contexts that ignite the reader's emotions, imagination, and intellect produced a novel that Civil War historian James McPherson called "unique," full of new insights.

Only thirteen years old when he took up his rifle, Willis Carr, the hero of *Sharpshooter*, is still trying to focus the war in his sights at age ninety. "Why," he wonders repeatedly, "since I was in every battle, East and West, with General Longstreet, and since I am the one who shot General Sanders—but I'm not sure—why, why do I feel that I missed the war?" The veteran sharpshooter and I had the same mission—to target the facts. But the more facts we got on target, the more we felt—he as a participant looking back and I as a space-age American citizen bemused and beguiled and bewitched by the facts—that we had missed the war.

The theme of *Sharpshooter* is that all the participants, soldiers and civilians, missed the war as it happened and in memory. The vision out of which

I created and developed the United States Civil War Center at Louisiana State University derives from the same conviction. And today, individually and collectively, no matter how many books we read or write, we miss the war to the extent that we fail to untangle the webs of facts we know and view them in the richest possible contexts and to illuminate them by personal emotional involvement, imaginative conceptualization, and complex intellectual implication. Possession of the facts and the artifacts alone is not enough. It is not only the dull recital of facts that makes history dry and remote for many American children and adults, it is dull imagination.

The events of each decade in American history have provided a fresh perspective on the Civil War. As they did during the centennial of the 1960s, professional historians, amateur historians, and ordinary citizens revisit, rediscover, and redefine this central event of the American experience—"the crossroads of our being," as popular historian Shelby Foote often said. Thus, we reflect on the past, experience the present, and enlighten the future by the fitful light of shifting interpretations.

By understanding every aspect of the war, we can understand ourselves in the world today, both our dark problems and our bright prospects. We Americans have always missed the war by focusing too much and too long on the most popular aspects of it—battles and leaders. That focus distracts us from our deeper purpose: to trace back to Reconstruction, to the war itself, and to the antebellum era the origins of the forces at work in our culture today. Among the dark problems, racism, violence, economic instability, and distrust of government daily stare us in the face. The promising benefits to society of the many technological inventions, medical discoveries, industrial techniques, and business methods that evolved out of the war have been only partially fulfilled or have been postponed, partly because the problems put a drag on the pace of progress.

Context is everything. By context, I mean tangled webs of causes and tangled webs of consequences. Facts alone fail us. Imagination alone fails us. Emotion alone fails us. But emotion, imagination, and intellect, acting together, make the facts stand up and speak. In my novel *Sharpshooter*, Willis Carr has struggled with that process ever since he heard the last shot fired:

> I *know* now most of the available *essential* facts. But that is not enough to let me rest. Most of what I know now about the war that I fought and killed in, I got from eyewitnesses later—and from

books. I hate my ignorance as if it were a disease. I want to get cured. Facts are like medicine. I want to *know*. Or my ignorance is like a human enemy I must slowly conquer, a hostile neighbor. Ignorance is bliss, though—until what you don't know kills you.

I make lists, and count, and compare, and contrast, and parallel, *to see*. Dates anchor. Everything is in a name. Names of places tell where, and suggest what and how and why. But newspaper headlines are snares.

Even though I am obsessed with fact-finding, I cannot swear authenticity for what I have written over the years or may yet write. My imagination leads a life of its own.

You, whoever you prove to be, you who find and read what I have pieced together like fragments found on the field, must collaborate with me in a conspiracy against the tyranny of mere facts. Each man is duty-bound to conjure, call forth, breathe life into, imagine. The unimagined life is not worth living. I see General Longstreet coming. Look. Coming—distance, like a thunderclap, vanishes, and he's standing on a bridge.

It is not the academic historian who has initiated, inspired, and dominated the general public's upsurge of interest in the Civil War that has continued for almost thirty years now, but the popular culture imagination. It is the novelist, such as Michael Shaara, author of *Killer Angels*, and his son Jeff, author of *Gods and Generals*, and Charles Frazer, author of *Cold Mountain*, and the moviemaker, such as Ken Burns with his monumental documentary, and the directors of *Glory* and *Gettysburg*. Most historians attract a limited audience. In the popular imagination, it is novelist Shelby Foote, the author of *Shiloh*, who began his three-volume history *The Civil War: A Narrative* in the 1950s, who is our greatest Civil War historian.

It is the novel as an art form, more than the history book or even the movie, that has the potential for making the greatest contribution to our grand and crucial effort not to miss the Civil War. Here is my choice of five novels that realize that potential most effectively: Mark Twain's *Huckleberry Finn*, as harbinger of the war to come; Evelyn Scott's *The Wave*, the fullest rendering of all the elements of the war; William Faulkner's *Absalom, Absalom!* the most psychologically symbolic work; Joseph Pennell's *Rome Hanks*, a northern version of Faulkner's novel; and Robert Penn Warren's *All the King's*

*Men*, which renders the legacy of the war and Reconstruction, manifested in many facets of popular culture.

In *All the King's Men*, which is on almost every list of the ten or more greatest American novels, Robert Penn Warren clearly demonstrates one of my major criteria for determining the great Civil War novel—that the author imagines innovative ways to show how the war may become and stay a part of both the characters' and the reader's everyday consciousness. In chapter 4 Jack Burden tells us about his research into the tragic, Civil War–era story of his supposed distant kin Cass Mastern, a story the characters and events of which parallel those of the modern-day characters. Jack Burden tries to escape from the present into his research into the history of his family, only to discover that past, present, and future merge in alarm. For this process, Jack's metaphor is the spider web. He tells us that:

> Cass Mastern lived for a few years and in that time he learned that the world is all of one piece. He learned that the world is like an enormous spider web and if you touch it, however lightly, at any point, the vibration ripples to the remotest perimeter and the drowsy spider feels the tingle and is drowsy no more but springs out to fling the gossamer coils about you who have touched the web and then inject the black, numbing poison under your hide. It does not matter whether or not you meant to brush the web of things. Your happy foot or your gay wing may have brushed it ever so lightly, but what happens always happens and there is the spider, bearded black and with his great faceted eyes glittering like mirrors in the sun, or like God's eye, and the fangs dripping.

The charged image of the spider web, located in the middle of the novel, connects and electrifies all other elements and techniques in *All the King's Men*.

Thirty years ago I invented a term for such an image in artistically successful works of literary art: the charged image. The electrical charge the image possesses is generated by the flow of emotion, imagination, and intellect throughout the work, and that charge affects the reader.

The charged image is that image which activates and illuminates all other elements—character, conflict, plot, theme—and techniques—concept, point of view, style—in a work of fiction. The memory of a charged image may last a lifetime. Remember *Don Quixote*, *Huckleberry Finn*, and *The Great Gatsby*.

What do you see? A charged image in each: Don Quixote attacking the wind-mill, Sancho Panza his witness; fugitives Huck and Jim on a raft on the river; Gatsby gazing at the green light at the end of Daisy's dock. For a century or more, few readers have read *Don Quixote*, but the image of Quixote is so pow-erfully charged that millions the world over see it immediately when they hear his name.

The web in *All the King's Men* took shape in the past, continues to be woven in the present, and is a paradigm that presages the future. The narra-tive concept of *All the King's Men* is this: each person, the so-called innocent and the so-called guilty, contributes to the creation of the web. The spider is destruction in one form or another, from psychological trauma to physical actions to death. By taking on the burden, from private and public motiva-tions, of tracing the evolution of the web and all those who contributed to its creation, Jack Burden, the novel's narrator, touches the web in such ways as to contribute to the lethal touching acts of most of the other major characters. The thematic concept of the novel is that no matter who a person is or what course of action or what type of inaction he or she takes, he or she will inevi-tably touch the web and thus stimulate the drowsy spider into motion, and that both innocence and guilt, good and evil, the creative and the destructive impulse, are finally irrelevant to the nature of things, to the way things are among human beings.

The charged image and related elements and techniques enable us to reexperience and interpret the entire novel through a scrutiny of the fourth chapter, which develops the effect on Jack and other characters, past and pres-ent, of the tangled webs of the Civil War and Reconstruction. By depicting the consequences of the war, seen at work in the Depression, Warren's novel is even more expressive of the war and its effects than are most novels set only during the war itself.

Because the Civil War provides the single most provocative perspective on the entire American experience, can only a southerner—even at this late date, standing in the crossroads of our being where the traffic is heaviest—write the great Civil War novel? And, given the major importance of that era in American history, wouldn't it simultaneously be the great American novel? My present choice is *Absalom, Absalom!* the greatest Civil War novel and thus the great American novel.

Ostensibly, the epic antebellum saga of the Sutpen family, spanning the years between 1807 and 1910, is not considered to be a Civil War novel as such, but is a work broader in scope. Even though *Absalom, Absalom!* does not directly depict the war, it is my choice as the greatest Civil War novel because of the provocative ways the war is alluded to and its effects are implied more than dramatized. Faulkner implies myriad ways in which life in the South led up to the war and was profoundly traumatized by it and, more emphatically, by Reconstruction. In not dealing directly with battles, Faulkner evokes, in his pervasive use of the technique of context and implication, what is more important—the war's effect on Americans, especially southerners, right on up to you and me.

By one of my criteria of innovation, *Absalom, Absalom!* illuminates the war in unique ways. Five different characters' meditations on, and retelling of, the story of Colonel Sutpen span the antebellum period, the war, Reconstruction, and the turn of the century. Quentin Compson, his father, his grandfather, a reclusive old lady, and even his Canadian roommate at Harvard ensnare the reader in a process of memory and imagination that spins webs upon webs. Faulkner's own distant voice contrasts with Quentin's meditative and fragmentary narrative as it toils compulsively toward some quality of omniscience.

Permit me to risk pomposity by making several declarations: that all southern literature comes out of the Civil War and Reconstruction, and that all southern novels are about the Civil War and Reconstruction. The lingering effect of the war and Reconstruction has so permeated southern history and consciousness that anything a southerner writes derives from that prolonged effect process, and that process itself is delineated in *Absalom, Absalom!* more deliberately and clearly than in any other southern novel. By contrast, there is no such thing as a northern novel, nor a true Civil War novel by a northerner. *The Red Badge of Courage*, for instance, the one in most popular use in schools, is about war per se. Is there such a thing as a northerner in the same profound sense that Americans know there is definitely such a thing as a southerner? The idea of northerners, or Yankees, exists only in the minds of southerners; southerners, however, are both very real and very surreal to northerners. Popular culture keeps the stereotypes of Yankees and Rebels alive in the popular imagination.

Colonel Thomas Sutpen, man of action in the antebellum, Civil War, and Reconstruction eras, is not, as he is too often held up to be, the protagonist of *Absalom, Absalom!* Rather, it is Quentin Compson, the most passive of Sutpen's vicarious witnesses, who is the protagonist. The most pertinent way to show that Quentin is the protagonist is to examine the techniques of the art of fiction that Faulkner employs in this novel to express Quentin Compson's consciousness as the most trenchant expression of the effect of the legacy of the Civil War at the deepest existential level.

A catalytic experience for civilizations throughout history, war, especially the Civil War, is a catalyst for Faulkner personally and for all his characters, especially Quentin Compson, whose consciousness is at the center of Faulkner's creative consciousness. Obsessive talk of external historical forces ignites forces of emotion, imagination, and intellect in Quentin's consciousness and unconsciousness. Quentin so seldom acts on or interacts with other characters that readers are enabled to respond only to his consciousness as he passively reacts to and reluctantly, but in anguish, meditates upon the actions of others. Quentin is Faulkner's expressionistic embodiment of the process that makes all southern literature about the Civil War.

Exhorted to listen, Quentin is the principal listener to the tangled web of storytelling in the novel. Not Quentin but Faulkner is the primary narrator. That some critics mistakenly identify Quentin as the primary narrator only testifies to the strength of the impression one gets of the pervasiveness of his consciousness, an effect toward which all Faulkner's techniques are deliberately working. Only through an awareness of Faulkner's artistry can the average reader feel the full impact and respond to the myriad implications of Quentin's drama of consciousness.

Paradoxically, Quentin's narrow, single-minded consciousness is at the center of Faulkner's myriad-minded consciousness. And paradoxically, Quentin experiences the war and Reconstruction more intensely than most, but he misses it at last because he fails to untangle the webs and understand how touching them can become a vital, positive element in his consciousness.

To the terminology of the criteria for the ideal Civil War novel, a word Coleridge applied to Shakespeare, and a word also applied to Faulkner, might be profitably added: "myriadmindedness." Perhaps in the new millennium will appear a novelist who not only feels, imagines, and ponders all the facets of the war and its many implications already depicted in novels but also deals with startling new facets and implications, a novelist who can control aesthetically that vast range of possibilities with a technique and a style that are the products of "myriadmindedness." To respond to such a novel, as one way to untangle the webs of the Civil War and Reconstruction, readers also will have to cultivate "myriadmindedness." In fact, the age of the Internet makes that demand upon us.

In 1996, as founding director of the United States Civil War Center, I requested and received a congressional resolution formalizing the center's name and mission, which is to study the war from the perspective of every conceivable academic discipline (including popular culture), profession, occupation, ethnic group, gender, and age and to facilitate the planning and events of the sesquicentennial. The United States Civil War Center proposed legislation in 1998 to create a sesquicentennial commission. Fifteen years later, it languishes in Senate committee.

But let's march backward to the Civil War centennial in the early 1960s. In 1962—the most active and successful of the four years devoted to the centennial—multitudes of American citizens were commemorating the anniversary by attending such popular culture events as pageants, solemn wreath-laying ceremonies at monuments and in cemeteries, battlefield tours and reenactments, roundtable discussions, speeches, exhibitions, lectures, and conferences; by reading pamphlets, history books, poetry, and novels; and by attending plays, movies, and concerts. The centennial celebration lasted as long as the war itself, but battles had to be waged at the national, state, and local levels just to create the centennial and to conduct these commemorative activities.

None of the major forces that troubled the planning and the conduct of the centennial is active today. Those forces were the Cold War and its daily, vividly hovering threat of universal annihilation; the civil rights movement; and the looming Vietnam War. Civil War memory "impinged upon" anticommunism and civil rights battles. Opposing forces within the centennial initiative were nonhistorians, who stressed celebrations as profitable entertainment, and academic historians, who stressed dignified scholarly activity. Forces posing possible problems in the coming years for the sesquicentennial are preoccupation with the Iraqi civil war and possible war with Iran, major economic instability, and, once more, conflicts between those who wish to celebrate the battles and leaders of the past and those who wish to meditate upon the negative and positive aspects of the legacy of the past in the present and the future.

Post–Civil War events such as Reconstruction, which lasted more than twice as long as the war, and its legacy are at work in American lives daily now, as are cultural forces that prepared the way, for good and ill, for the centennial. Shelby Foote has bemoaned the dearth of books and the lack of public memory of and interest in Reconstruction, which he declared is "one of the sins for which America can never atone," and the other sin is "slavery," a guilt shared by North and South.

In the 1960s the civil rights movement was threatening to rip the fabric of the culture straight down the middle. The perilous present mimicked some of the issues and conflicts of the past. Northern attempts to compromise on the depiction of the causes of the Civil War and on the role of blacks in both the Federal and the Confederate military were weak and the opposition of southerners was strong, prompting Walker Percy to declare in 1961 that in both the planning and the activities of the centennial, black Americans were "the ghost at the feast." He could have argued that another "ghost at the feast" was Reconstruction, without which the war would not have hovered to this day over the American experiment but would have ended in that genteel moment when General Lee offered his sword to General Grant. The civil rights movement was a replay for both North and South of the issues of slavery and abolition.

William Faulkner declared that opposition to equality is "like living in Alaska and being against snow," and he claimed that it weakened our war against communism. Looking back to that era, Americans promoting the sesquicentennial can take heart. It is in the nature of American culture today that the Emancipation Proclamation and the role of black soldiers will play a major part in the sesquicentennial, without significant conflict. Opposition from the South, to which progress has come at last and that has attracted great numbers of citizens born in the North and in other countries, will be fainthearted at worst. However, a sufficient number of southerners will insist on activities that honor their ancestors, and how to accommodate them will be one of only a few problems carried forward from the 1960s. With "reconfigured power relations" stimulated by the civil rights movement, and with dramatic progress in racial tolerance in all segments of American society since the mid-twentieth century, black participation in the sesquicentennial in every city will be, one may envision, commensurate with blacks' role in the Civil War. Among the very different kinds of participants at "the crossroads of our being" there will, very likely, be much less contention.

The Cold War is over and the Berlin Wall has fallen, but new foreign dangers have arisen, forming the backdrop to the drama of the sesquicentennial.

The peril facing the nation in the 1960s—civil war in Vietnam—faces the nation fifty years later—civil war in Iraq. We may contemplate some of the differences, and novelists may dramatize them in the coming years. Public sentiment and protest today do not compare with the situation in the 1960s. All indications active now suggest that the plans for and conduct of the sesquicentennial will be far less clear-cut than the centennial was; that it will employ, more likely than not, the expertise of a gamut of disciplines, professions, and occupations; and that it will therefore be so myriad-minded in all respects that no single contentious faction will be able to gain traction.

The popular culture imagination will open many previously closed doors on the Civil War, enabling students to go far beyond the narrow confines of the centennial. The richest study is one that reaches out and brings into play every conceivable strand of the web of the war.

In contrast to the centennial's dramatic first year, fitful middle years, and final year of indifference, twenty years of interest in the Civil War generated and sustained by popular novelists, filmmakers, and some historians bode well for a longer public involvement in the sesquicentennial. Just as we credited novelists, dramatists, poets, and filmmakers for arousing interest in the Civil War among American citizens leading up to the centennial, we can credit the same popular cultural forces for doing an even better job in the past three decades. While Carl Sandburg's multivolume narrative of the life of Lincoln aroused an interest in the Civil War years in the 1930s, one difference between the pre-centennial and pre-sesquicentennial eras is a greater number and better quality of histories generated in the past four decades than in the 1950s.

A major project for the current commemoration may well be the publication of hundreds of studies that continue and expand on the interdisciplinary perspectives on the Civil War and Reconstruction that have been in welcome fashion for the past two decades. These studies draw on anthropology, engineering, medicine, and the roles of ethnic groups, women, and children—all relatively ignored or simply neglected in the 1960s. We may imagine that during the sesquicentennial, feature films and documentaries will not only be different from the great movies of the past—*Birth of a Nation*, *Gone with the Wind*, *The Horse Soldiers*, *Shenandoah*, *Major Dundee*, *Glory*, *Gettysburg*, *Gods and Generals*, and Ken Burns's masterpiece *The Civil War*—but will deal, in greater numbers, with more difficult issues. From William Gillette's *The Secret Service* to McKinley Kantor's *Andersonville*, no great plays about the war were staged before, during, or after the centennial. The challenge in the years to come is clear for playwrights. Since Aaron Copeland's *Lincoln Portrait* premiered in 1942, no great orchestral or operatic works have resounded in the American consciousness. The great Civil War painting has not yet appeared on a museum wall. Of the finest Civil War artists, very few Americans are aware of Winslow Homer. Thus, some popular culture doors remain closed.

As they did during the centennial, celebrants will once again attend pageants, battlefield tours, and wreath-laying ceremonies at monuments, especially in cemeteries. The reenactment movement got a great boost during the centennial, and Civil War movies such as *Gettysburg* gave it another; with the addition of living history involving women and children, many more reenactments will take place during the sesquicentennial. There will be far more roundtable discussions because the increase in roundtable groups also gathered momentum in the 1960s. The public will have access to far more exhibitions, including traveling ones, in different kinds of places. Lectures and conferences will take up a greater number and a wider variety of ideas. No great speeches from the centennial are recited today, but maybe some of the new ones given during the sesquicentennial will resonate in the American consciousness during the bicentennial.

Above all, citizens will be reading many more books written from a wider range of perspectives. Walt Whitman, one of the greatest of Civil War poets, said, "The real war will never get in the books." The bardic voice scarcely murmurs. Stephen Vincent Benét did not get the real war into his popular epic poem "John Brown's Body," a 1929 Pulitzer Prize winner, nor has any other major poet, except perhaps Allen Tate's "Ode to the Confederate Dead," published in 1926, nor thirty years later his student Robert Lowell's "For the Union Dead." African American poet laureate Natasha Trethewey's 2006 Pulitzer Prize–winning poem "Native Guard" may be a harbinger of what is possible for the sesquicentennial years.

A decade ago, in *Phi Kappa Phi Journal*, I posed questions that I hoped writers in every discipline and profession would take up in the twenty-first century—the sooner the better. Along with the popular culture entertainment and the celebratory features, perhaps such questions as the following will be taken up. Here are a few, staring us in the face: What were civilian life and death experiences during the Civil War and Reconstruction? (The fact that 30,000 civilians died is little known.) What was the role of each ethnic group (Jews, African Americans, Native Americans, Asians, etc.) in the war, and how do their experiences compare? In what ways was the Mexican-American War legacy active in the Civil War? How does Reconstruction in the South compare with our reconstruction efforts in enemy countries after World War I and World War II? Why are northerners more fascinated with southern generals than with northern generals? What were the psychological effects of war and Reconstruction on children? How is the influence of religious rhetoric and political oratory manifested in the diaries and letters of soldiers and civilians, North and South? Over the past 150 years, how have books written for children shaped our attitudes about the war's cause and its legacy? Which special circumstances spurred innovations in technology? How have fiction, poetry, theater, and film shaped our vision of the war? What was the role of engineers in the war? What might geographers contribute to our understanding of the war? How does the Chinese Taiping Rebellion and reconstruction compare with the American Civil War and Reconstruction, both of which occurred in the same decade? How can the American Civil War provide a model for constructing a philosophy and a psychology of the phenomenon of civil wars worldwide and throughout history?

These questions may seem to some rather esoteric, but they have the potential to stimulate the popular culture imagination. Consider the *Titanic* and compare it with the sinking of the *Sultana*. How can we, at long last, inspire Americans to commemorate the greatest maritime disaster in the history of the nation—worse than the *Titanic*? The steamboat *Sultana*, carrying homeward about 2,000 Union soldiers who had been released from Cahaba and Andersonville prisons, exploded in the dark and the rain several miles above Memphis. More than 1,500 soldiers and about 200 civilians drowned, as President Lincoln's funeral train was crossing the country. This event is a symbolic expression, embodying every adjective for the sad loss of the Civil War. Missing so far is a national conceptual imagination that places the *Sultana* disaster in a tragic light. Meanwhile, the darkness of that night still hangs, almost 150 years deepening, over the smoke, the screams, and the prayers of the victims and the compassionate cries of the rescuers, some of them Confederate soldiers who were also returning home. Only the light of an extraordinary imagination can unvex and raise this unique and complexly meaningful event from the bottom of the Father of Waters.

The sesquicentennial will be the last opportunity in our lifetime to commemorate and meditate on the epic conflict that produced a unified nation that can still claim uniqueness. Listen once again to the voice of Willis Carr, sharpshooter:

> While connecting one thing to another, especially opposites, I may connect with what is essential to my own emotional, imaginative, and intellectual well-being. In striving to experience through others fully what I missed, I reached the realm of the impersonal. Feeling, imagining, thinking neither as General Sanders nor as myself. Because of General Sanders, whether I shot him or not, and through him, I have achieved over the years, for a while, omniscience, of a sort, and felt the simultaneity of events, actual and imagined, now, I could probably imagine everything in detail if I set about it, and had life left, time.

When Willis Carr tried to gather the facts, he discovered he had missed the war, until he realized at the end that in imagining many facets of the war, with empathy for other people, he had finally, deeply experienced it more fully than anyone he knew—than anyone I know.

# Acknowledgments

This collection of essays originated from papers presented at the national meetings of the Popular Culture Association/American Culture Association. The editors thank the authors for revising and updating their essays and for their cooperative spirit. They accepted the many revisions and met their deadlines with cheer and good humor. At the University Press of Kentucky, we thank Anne Dean Watkins and Bailey Johnson. Anne Dean supported the project from the beginning, and her keen insights into the world of academic publishing and spot-on critiques of the manuscript moved the project to completion. Bailey encouraged us as due dates approached and showed a seemingly inexhaustible supply of patience when answering our questions. We also thank Linda Lotz, whose superb copyediting sharpened the writing in all of the essays.

# Contributors

**Randal Allred** is a professor of English at Brigham Young University–Hawaii. Specializing in nineteenth-century American culture and literature, Allred is the author of the forthcoming *Battles without Bullets: Civil War Re-enactment and American Culture,* as well as articles on battle reenactment and "living history." He is the current area chair for the Civil War and Reconstruction paper sessions at the national meetings of the Popular Culture Association/American Culture Association.

**Christopher Bates** is a lecturer at California Polytechnic University, Pomona. His work focuses on the memory of the Civil War, particularly as expressed through battle reenactments. He is currently at work on a book-length treatment of the subject and edited *The Encyclopedia of the Early Republic and Antebellum America* (2010).

**Daryl Black**, PhD, serves as executive director of the Chattanooga History Center. He also teaches courses in public history and the American Civil War era at the University of Tennessee at Chattanooga. His scholarly work focuses on the intersection of identity, history, and memory between the American Revolution and the late twentieth century.

**Jacqueline Glass Campbell,** PhD, is the author of *When Sherman Marched North from the Sea: Resistance on the Confederate Home Front* (2003). She has served as a consultant for the History Channel and is a member of the Curriculum Reform Committee for the Carnegie Teachers for a New Era Initiative.

**Matthew Eng** serves as deputy educator at the Hampton Roads Naval Museum and as a coordinator for the Civil War Navy Sesquicentennial. He received a BA from James Madison University and an MA from Old Dominion University.

**Susan Chase Hall** recently received her PhD in history from the University of California–Riverside. She is director of the Brea Museum and Heritage Center in Brea, California. Her research focuses on preservation of both the built and the natural environments and their role in remembering the past. She served as webmaster and research associate for the Civil War Preservation Trust from 2002 to 2005.

**Paul Haspel** is a lecturer in English at Penn State University. His articles on regionalism and history in film and literature have been published in a variety of scholarly journals, including *Studies in Popular Culture, Southern Literary Journal, Studies in American Culture,* and *Journal of Popular Film and Television.*

**Lawrence A. Kreiser Jr.** is an associate professor of history at Stillman College. He is the author of *Defeating Lee: A History of the Second Corps, Army of the Potomac* (2011) and the coeditor of *Voices of Civil War America: Contemporary Accounts of Daily Life* (2011). He is currently researching a project on newspaper advertising during the Civil War era.

**David Madden** specializes in creative writing, short stories, drama, and fiction writing and is the founder of the Civil War Center at Louisiana State University. He has penned hundreds of short stories, poems, and critical essays and is the author of many books and collections. Madden is the former president of the Popular Culture Association (1976).

**Brian Craig Miller** is an associate professor and chair of the Department of History at Emporia State University. He serves as the book review editor for *Civil War History* and is the author of *John Bell Hood and the Fight for Civil War Memory* (2010) and *A Punishment on the Nation: An Iowa Soldier Endures the Civil War* (2012).

**Michael W. Schaefer** is a professor of English at the University of Central Arkansas. He is the author of *A Reader's Guide to the Short Stories of Stephen Crane* (1996) and *Just What War Is: The Civil War Writings of De Forest and Bierce* (1997), as well as numerous articles on Civil War subjects. He is also an associate editor of the *Encyclopedia of American War Literature* (2001).

**Daniel W. Stowell** is director of the Papers of Abraham Lincoln. He is the author or editor of five books, including *The Papers of Abraham Lincoln: Legal*

*Documents and Cases* (4 vols., 2008); *Rebuilding Zion: The Religious Reconstruction of the South, 1863–1877* (1998); and *In Tender Consideration: Women, Families, and the Law in Abraham Lincoln's Illinois* (2002).

**Alfred Wallace,** a PhD student at Pennsylvania State University, is writing his dissertation on the Federal military occupation of the Mississippi River Valley. His major research interests are military occupations as social, military, and political phenomena and how wars and history are remembered, particularly in board games.

**Robert E. Weir,** PhD, is a visiting lecturer at the University of Massachusetts at Amherst. He also teaches history at Smith College and is a freelance journalist. Weir is the author or coauthor of six books, the latest of which is *Knights Down Under: The Knights of Labour in New Zealand* (2009).

# Index